LIBERTY STREET

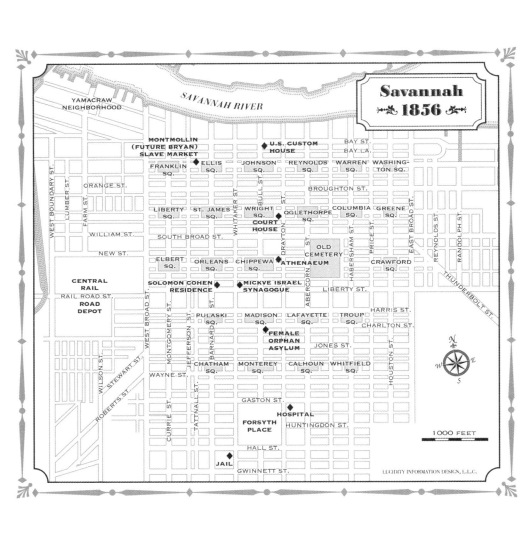

Savannah 1856

SAVANNAH RIVER

YAMACRAW NEIGHBORHOOD

MONTMOLLIN (FUTURE BRYAN) SLAVE MARKET

U.S. CUSTOM HOUSE

BAY ST.
BAY LA.

FRANKLIN SQ.
ELLIS SQ.
JOHNSON SQ.
REYNOLDS SQ.
WARREN SQ.
WASHING-TON SQ.

BROUGHTON ST.

ORANGE ST.

WEST BOUNDARY ST.
LUMBER ST.
FARM ST.

LIBERTY SQ.
ST. JAMES SQ.
WRIGHT SQ.
OGLETHORPE SQ.
COLUMBIA SQ.
GREENE SQ.

COURT HOUSE

WILLIAM ST.

SOUTH BROAD ST.

WHITAKER ST.
BULL ST.
DRAYTON ST.

NEW ST.

OLD CEMETERY

ELBERT SQ.
ORLEANS SQ.
CHIPPEWA SQ.
ATHENAEUM
CRAWFORD SQ.

HABERSHAM ST.
PRICE ST.
REYNOLDS ST.
RANDOLPH ST.
EAST BROAD ST.

CENTRAL RAIL ROAD DEPOT

RAIL ROAD ST.

SOLOMON COHEN RESIDENCE
MICKVE ISRAEL SYNAGOGUE

LIBERTY ST.

ABERCORN ST.

THUNDERBOLT ST.

WEST BROAD ST.

PULASKI SQ.
MADISON SQ.
LAFAYETTE SQ.
TROUP SQ.

HARRIS ST.

MONTGOMERY ST.
JEFFERSON ST.
BARNARD ST.

CHARLTON ST.

FEMALE ORPHAN ASYLUM

JONES ST.

WILSON ST.

CHATHAM SQ.
MONTEREY SQ.
CALHOUN SQ.
WHITFIELD SQ.

HOUSTON ST.

WAYNE ST.

STEWART ST.

CURRIE ST.
TATTNALL ST.

GASTON ST.

ROBERTS ST.

HOSPITAL

FORSYTH PLACE
HUNTINGDON ST.

1000 FEET

HALL ST.

JAIL

GWINNETT ST.

LUCIDITY INFORMATION DESIGN, L.L.C.

N
W E
S

LIBERTY STREET

*A Savannah Family, Its Golden Boy,
and the Civil War*

JASON K. FRIEDMAN

THE UNIVERSITY OF
SOUTH CAROLINA PRESS

© 2024 Jason K. Friedman
Maps and family tree © 2024 Robert Cronan

Published by the University of South Carolina Press
Columbia, South Carolina 29208

uscpress.com

Printed in the United States of America

Library of Congress Cataloging-in-Publication Data can be found
at http://catalog.loc.gov/.

ISBN: 978-1-64336-469-8 (paperback)
ISBN: 978-1-64336-470-4 (ebook)

In memory of my father,
W. LEON FRIEDMAN JR.,
1933–2020

Is that why war endures?

No. It endures because young men love it and old men love it in them. Those that fought, those that did not.

—Cormac McCarthy, *Blood Meridian,
or The Evening Redness in the West*

Omar, 3d Caliph, said four things never returned. The spoken word—the shed arrow—past life—& a neglected opportunity.

—Gratz Cohen, handwritten
on a card in his Bible, 1865

Contents

List of Illustrations

Cohen–Gratz Family Tree

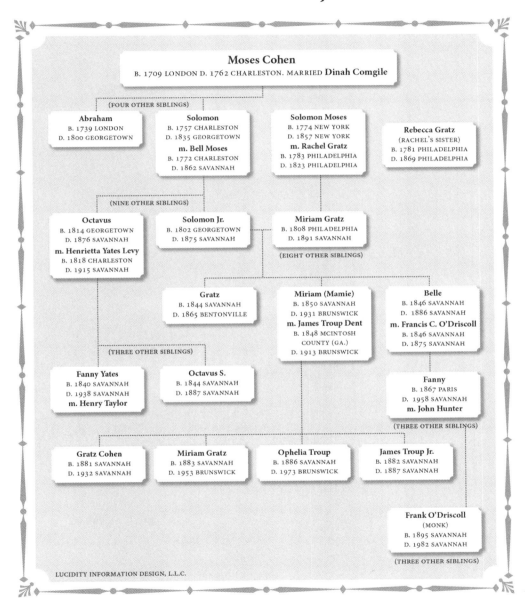

Moses Cohen
B. 1709 LONDON D. 1762 CHARLESTON. MARRIED **Dinah Comgile**

(FOUR OTHER SIBLINGS)

Abraham
B. 1739 LONDON
D. 1800 GEORGETOWN

Solomon
B. 1757 CHARLESTON
D. 1835 GEORGETOWN
m. Bell Moses
B. 1772 CHARLESTON
D. 1862 SAVANNAH

Solomon Moses
B. 1774 NEW YORK
D. 1857 NEW YORK
m. Rachel Gratz
B. 1783 PHILADELPHIA
D. 1823 PHILADELPHIA

Rebecca Gratz
(RACHEL'S SISTER)
B. 1781 PHILADELPHIA
D. 1869 PHILADELPHIA

(NINE OTHER SIBLINGS)

Octavus
B. 1814 GEORGETOWN
D. 1876 SAVANNAH
m. Henrietta Yates Levy
B. 1818 CHARLESTON
D. 1915 SAVANNAH

Solomon Jr.
B. 1802 GEORGETOWN
D. 1875 SAVANNAH

Miriam Gratz
B. 1808 PHILADELPHIA
D. 1891 SAVANNAH

(EIGHT OTHER SIBLINGS)

Gratz
B. 1844 SAVANNAH
D. 1865 BENTONVILLE

Miriam (Mamie)
B. 1850 SAVANNAH
D. 1931 BRUNSWICK
m. James Troup Dent
B. 1848 MCINTOSH
COUNTY (GA.)
D. 1913 BRUNSWICK

Belle
B. 1846 SAVANNAH
D. 1886 SAVANNAH
m. Francis C. O'Driscoll
B. 1846 SAVANNAH
D. 1875 SAVANNAH

(THREE OTHER SIBLINGS)

Fanny Yates
B. 1840 SAVANNAH
D. 1938 SAVANNAH
m. Henry Taylor

Octavus S.
B. 1844 SAVANNAH
D. 1887 SAVANNAH

Fanny
B. 1867 PARIS
D. 1958 SAVANNAH
m. John Hunter

(THREE OTHER SIBLINGS)

Gratz Cohen
B. 1881 SAVANNAH
D. 1932 SAVANNAH

Miriam Gratz
B. 1883 SAVANNAH
D. 1953 BRUNSWICK

Ophelia Troup
B. 1886 SAVANNAH
D. 1973 BRUNSWICK

James Troup Jr.
B. 1882 SAVANNAH
D. 1887 SAVANNAH

Frank O'Driscoll
(MONK)
B. 1895 SAVANNAH
D. 1982 SAVANNAH

(THREE OTHER SIBLINGS)

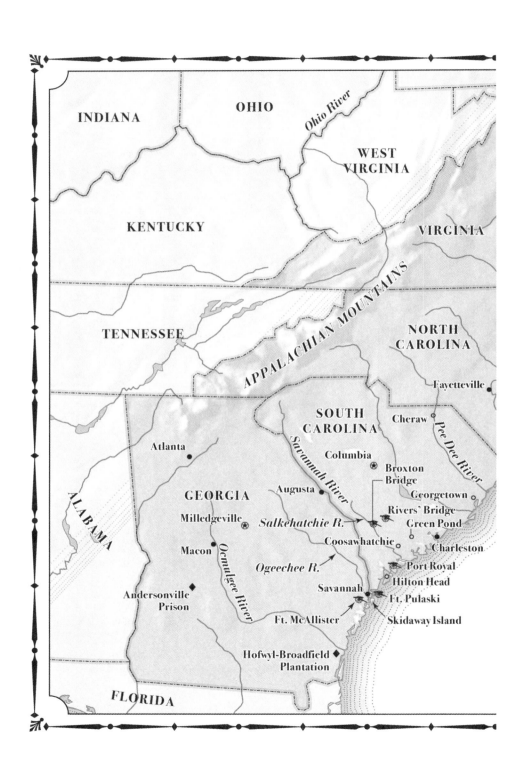

MARYLAND  DE

NJ

Manassas

Washington, DC

Culpeper

Chancellorsville

Fredericksburg

Charlottesville

VA

James River

Richmond
(CAPITAL OF THE CSA)

ATLANTIC OCEAN

Raleigh

Bentonville

Goldsboro

Averasboro

Cape Fear River

Gratz Cohen's
⊰⊱ Civil War ⊰⊱

- ✪ US AND CSA CAPITALS
- ✪ STATE CAPITALS
- ● MAJOR CITIES
- ○ SELECTED TOWNS
- CIVIL WAR BATTLEFIELDS
- ◆ OTHER HISTORIC SITES

0   100 Miles

0   100 Kilometers

LUCIDITY INFORMATION DESIGN, L.L.C.

Prologue

As dusk fell on March 19, 1865, a young man rode onto an open field on Reddick Morris's farm, near the rude market village of Bentonville. Southeast of the prosperous capital Raleigh, due south of the county seat, and west of the railroad hub of Goldsboro, Bentonville was a pinpoint on the map of Eastern North Carolina with no strategic importance at all, a dozen cabins near a creek, surrounded by pinewoods. The young man, Gratz Cohen, was a poet and an intellectual; a year earlier he'd been studying languages and law at the University of Virginia, the first Jewish student there. He was of slight build to begin with, but thin now to the point of emaciation, following a bout of typhoid fever he endured *before* leaving his hometown of Savannah on the path of war. Now, three months later and three hundred miles from home, the skin hung between the fine bones of his face like a sagging tent. He was in constant pain from a chronic problem with his feet, and weak from hunger and exposure to more-or-less ceaseless rains. But that morning on the farm of John Benton the sun had shone on a world in bloom, perfumed by peach blossoms and pine, birdsong in the air, and the bit of hardtack and fat bacon in Gratz's belly was enough to keep him going without detracting from the hunger and light-headedness, and always the pain in his feet, that had put him in a state of ecstasy. "I find that I have brought much suffering on me by this mode of life," he wrote. Suffering had indeed become his mode of life, sharpening his sense that he was playing a role cast by nothing less than Providence. It was in this exalted state that he hurtled toward his end, just three weeks before Robert E. Lee surrendered to Ulysses S. Grant.

Gratz was born on a Sunday and believed, according to German legend, that fairies watched over him; this was what the Christian Sabbath meant to this Jew. Perhaps he felt especially protected today, also a Sunday, though it would prove to be the last day of his life. The end came in the form of a bullet, which tore through his skull. Fate had chosen this place, where nothing had ever happened before, to be the site where two great armies collided in one of the last battles of the Civil War. Gratz was a volunteer aide-de-camp, a scribe and all-around right-hand man, to Confederate general George P. Harrison Jr., a fellow Savannahian who at twenty-three wasn't much older than Gratz himself. On the first day of the fight, as the sun sank behind the trees, one group of Confederate soldiers after another moved across the field at the Morris farm until they were thrown into disarray or "torn to pieces," as a sign at the site today unsparingly notes, by groups of young men from Union states. And then the rebels, what was left of them, crept away. This was the pattern, enacted from late afternoon until after night fell, as a fog came on and the smoke from the firing settled upon the land.

Harrison's brigade went last, advancing a few paces to form a new front line, but relentless gunfire and rapid volleys of canister rounds from Federal cannon caused them almost immediately to drop to their bellies like the soldiers preceding them. The smoke was white and thick all around you, with flashes of gunfire tearing through it like a scrim. It had an odor, the smoke, but you didn't smell it so much as eat it, and what you were tasting was metal and rotten egg. You couldn't see your hand before your face, you couldn't see the enemy at all, though he seemed to be all around you.

Gradually the firing slowed and in the darkness Harrison's men were withdrawn to the earthworks on the other side of the ravine, hidden in the trees, and those who returned to the field did so only at their peril, to gather the wounded and collect the weapons of the dead and, if they dared, the dead themselves.

Introduction

Like every ghost story, this one begins with a house. It's an 1875 Greek Revival townhouse in the historic district of Savannah, the city where I grew up, and while I must have passed it again and again—the Civic Center, on the next block, was where I once participated in a sixteen-piano rendition of "The Star-Spangled Banner"—the first time I really saw the house was in a real estate listing I perused in San Francisco, where I now lived.

Own a piece of history!

So the listing exhorted prospective buyers of a condo in the "Solomon Cohen house." My husband and I bit, but not because we thought it was a building any more historic than anything else in downtown Savannah. My hometown is full of mansions of note, but this wasn't one of them. This was creative realtoring, though I got a kick out of the fact that a house named after a Jew, whoever he was, was considered a selling point—the names ascribed to the city's important houses run along the lines of Davenport, Green-Meldrim, and Owens-Thomas.

On the other hand, considering that everyone who buys property in the historic district seems to come from up north or out west, they could have called it the Abraham Lincoln house and no one would have bat an eye.

The so-called Solomon Cohen house is on one of the historic district's main east-west thoroughfares, its median planted with oaks, their candelabra arms festooned with Spanish moss. In the listing, the townhouse, presided over by magnolia trees, appeared to be composed of perfectly stacked blocks of white stone. An iron gate secured the recessed entrance to the sidewalk-level apartment, and directly above, the big red front door, under a twin-paned transom window, was lighted by what looked like a gas lamp. Tall windows were crowned by pointed neoclassical pediments, and the distance between floors suggested soaring ceilings. The building's facade, though smudged from water running down it, gave the impression of clean simple elegance, and behind it a lot of space.

The pictures of the apartment itself, one flight up from the parlor level, were noticeably few in number and of terrible quality, as if someone had held up a camera here and there and, without looking through the view finder, clicked. But I was intrigued, maybe for the same reason that a friend's future girlfriend answered his ad on match.com: *His picture was so bad, I figured he had to be sincere.*

I asked our real estate agent, Chris, to check it out for us. He sent us a video he made as he walked through the place. *Now I'm in the little front room, which has a lot of light and a fireplace,* he narrated. *This is the living room, which is big. Another fireplace. Broom closet or something. This back bedroom is bigger. Another fireplace. There's a hole down here in the baseboard, might be from termite damage. Or mice. Kitchen's a nice size, needs work.*

I called Chris right away and asked if he liked it.

"Well," he said with typical candor, "it'd be good for a weekend rental but I wouldn't want to spend *too* much time there."

But I knew I would. Chris's tour had captured everything the pictures in the listing tried to hide—the awkward shape of the back bedroom, how little closet space there was, how much work the place needed. He let us know just what was crappy about the apartment and what was acceptable. But he entirely missed the place's potential. How lovely it could be. That was okay—the promise of beauty wasn't his concern, looking out for us was.

So we made an offer sight unseen, and Chris negotiated us a nice discount to pay for all the work the apartment would need.

As savvy as I thought I was about real estate, I wasn't as cool as I appeared. How could I be, when I was buying a place in the hometown I'd fled three decades before? When I was apparently trying to prove you *can* go home again. I could visit my parents without staying with them, and meet them as I did everyone else in my life, as an adult. The apartment would be a financial investment, but also an investment in my past.

Of James Joyce's three writerly weapons—silence, exile, cunning—only number two can I truly be said to have obtained, and then only by accident. At the age of eighteen I hadn't intended to escape the South, but that's what I ended up doing. Fleeing from the good son that I was, and from a small stifling place where everyone knew me better than I knew myself, or thought they did. Now I was back. But the foothold I'd gotten in the past turned out to be from a more remote time than I'd expected.

The day came when, for the first time, I stood before the building on Liberty Street with a key to one of its flats in my pocket, admiring the stacked blocks of white stone picturesquely streaked with historic grime. The townhouse is at the end of the row, a set of three that Solomon Cohen developed at the same time, and I walked over to the side, where a narrow passage between the freestanding house next door and my building revealed that its eastern wall was made of brick. And that therefore the front of my rowhouse was also brick, which I now saw was covered in stucco and scored to look like stone. Congenitally naive, I noticed only after buying the apartment on Liberty Street that the building's facade, like many of its era in the historic district, was an illusion.

Savannah grey brick is famous locally for its rough beauty. The bricks range in color from faded grey to dark brown, and in their lack of uniformity lies their charm to us now. And it isn't just their color that varies; they're porous, prone to crumbling in the region's subtropical rains, held in place by mortar smudged thickly between them. Even when they were new, no two were alike. They were hand-made of clay on the Hermitage Plantation, three miles upriver from Savannah. The hands that made them belonged to enslaved people, and if you look closely you might be able to spot, on some of them, heartbreaking dents made by thumbs.

This look, so popular now, didn't impress in the nineteenth century. If you were going to put your best foot forward with brick, let it be uniform in size and color and shape, machine-made up north, as you see in the Kehoe House on Columbia Square, now a (supposedly haunted) bed-and-breakfast. And nothing could be classier than stone. But you don't find stone in the coastal Lowcountry—for that you have to go to the granite mountains of North Georgia or even farther afield. Well, my building's trompe l'oeil facade fooled me. Scored stucco looks good too, though the pristine elegance for which the builder had aimed was only going to be restored with a power wash and a paint job, and I sort of liked the facade as it was. Stucco doesn't just conceal, it also protects, as some historic district homeowners discovered when they had their stucco removed (a practice since outlawed) to reveal the dissolving brick beneath.

Chris was right about the place—it wasn't in the greatest shape. And I thought I was right too—all it needed was a little TLC, at least to brighten it up and make it a comfortable place to stay. We had the heart-pine wood floors in the living room and bedrooms stripped and polished to a high gloss, and the puke-colored walls painted a creamy beige in the bedrooms and living room. Only a remodel was going to give us a fabulous kitchen, but our budget forced us to be creative with what we had. For the walls we chose a robin's-egg blue, and we diverted the eye from the cheap counter-tops and cabinets, not to mention the rust-colored diamond-pattern lino-leum mat, with cheery art. We filled the rooms with mid-century furniture from local secondhand stores and stuffed the bookcase with old paper-backs donated by a friend.

The apartment came with a white particleboard armoire that Chris was kind enough to dispose of before I had to lay eyes on it. It also came with a big gold-framed mirror angled over the mantelpiece to add a note of glitz to the place's austere elegance, the brass chandelier doing its part too—those were staying. And at some point during my first stay I opened a drawer in a kitchen cabinet and found something else: a sheet of paper printed with information about the house and the man after whom the listing agent had named it.

> Built for Solomon Cohen, alderman and postmaster of Savannah.
> He was the brother of cotton merchant Octavus Cohen. . . . Given his
> extensive real estate holdings, Cohen must have had extensive business
> interests. . . . His son Gratz . . . enlisted in the CSA and was killed in
> the Battle of Bentonville in the closing months of the war. . . . Solomon
> Cohen was a wealthy slave owner by urban standards with a total of
> twenty-three servants, most of which were sent out to work for others.

I'd almost forgotten about him. On the Internet, before we'd even put in an offer, I'd found a few references to the man who'd had my house built, but researching its history had been a single item on my checklist, far below the boring tasks required to buy the place.

Product of an enterprising writing team responsible for a series of essential picture books about Civil War Savannah, the page I'd found in the drawer would turn out to be not wholly accurate. But for now, standing on the linoleum in the odd-shaped kitchen of my 140-year-old flat, I realized that the armoire and the mirror and the chandelier weren't the only things I'd been bequeathed. A legacy of slavery—this I'd also inherited, not just as the owner of this particular piece of property, or as a Savannahian, or even as a Southerner, but as an American. It was an inheritance I'd managed to avoid claiming. Whenever I thought about the education I'd received growing up, both the formal one I got in classrooms and the casual one I got everywhere else, it was with anger, for how blindered I'd been to the cultural upheavals sweeping through the country—it was the '70s—and how little I'd been taught of my hometown's history, certainly of its slaveholding past. I moved away and never looked back, and I remained as ignorant as I'd always been.

But I didn't intend to stay that way. How, in good conscience, could I? This was a house that came with a story, one that was also my own.

2

When my husband and I were looking for a place in the historic district, my father, who owned and managed rental property, regretfully informed me that there were no deals left in Savannah, he himself having gotten the last of them some forty years earlier. And not only would I be a damn fool to pay the prices they were asking downtown, who wanted to go there anyway? The crime! Plus you couldn't find a parking space, and when you did, you had to pay, and not just a couple of quarters either! You couldn't pay *him* to go downtown. Which was exactly where I wanted to own a home.

My father and I couldn't seem to have a conversation without getting into an argument. He complained that I always took the other side of every issue, something I never quite understood, for couldn't he equally be said to always take the other side of every issue from me? But it was true we used to agree more when I lived under his roof. He hadn't always seemed to be such a belligerent conservative, and I certainly hadn't always been a touchy liberal. But now there we were, at an impasse we couldn't get beyond—until I began writing fiction in college. Like all young writers

I wasted no time getting the old-timers in the family to tell all. This was something my father was more than happy to do; he had stories he wanted to tell and a lifetime of grievances to get off his chest. Writing was his preferred way to communicate. He wrote me long letters, then long emails, and I would reply with more questions, and in this way our relationship unfolded and endured.

And so when Solomon Cohen came unexpectedly into my life, my father didn't seem surprised when I expressed my determination to know this man's story. He'd never heard of Solomon either and admitted to knowing little about antebellum Savannah. Clearly! If he did, he wouldn't be so bullish on the Old South, which he often summoned in conversation, drawing out the vowels as if to prolong his stay there. He had a way of making this mythical time and place seem at once present for him and irrevocably lost, nowhere reflected in the old buildings downtown. I figured that Jews couldn't have fared so well in the actual Old South. The lynching of Leo Frank in 1913, that's about as far back as my Georgia Jewish history went; I was as ignorant as he was, but I was falling back on certain prejudices, just as he was.

My father had a couple of books for me to read. I followed him into his "man cave," formerly my brother's bedroom, and we stood before his library, made up mostly of biographies of conservatives like Ronald Reagan and Clarence Thomas, along with a few books on the Holocaust. My father took from a shelf Robert N. Rosen's *The Jewish Confederates*, and sure enough, Solomon Cohen's story was in it, along with that of hundreds of other Jewish partisans. This meticulously researched book portrays a world largely free of anti-Semitism, where Jews thrived and so were willing to sacrifice everything for its preservation. *The Jewish Confederates* celebrates the men who fought for their regional homeland, despite the cause for which they were fighting, and I'm sure my father, a man who never went to war but always felt under attack, identified with this feisty bunch. For my part, the book opened my eyes about how at home Jews felt in the nineteenth-century South.

Next Dad handed me a first edition of F. D. Lee and J. L. Agnew's *Historical Record of the City of Savannah*. A friend of the family had informed him of the value of this little black book, a few years older than my house on Liberty Street, and so he kept it in a freezer bag somewhere safe. My father handed me this rare book the way, when he was dying, he would give me his gold-plated wristwatch and my grandfather's bar mitzvah ring. He was passing along treasures—but the book was something he knew I would use.

3

A town you grew up in is a palimpsest of your past lives—the steakhouse on the river where I went on a tortured prom date, the hotel where the gay bar once stood before it burned down. (I'd thought I'd been going to the city's one queer watering hole in stealth, those summers back home, until my mother called me at college up north to tell me about the fire.) When you walk through a city where your parents grew up, the archaeological layers beneath your feet run even deeper. Here is the former drugstore where my mother sat with friends and had a Coke while eating her bagged lunch when she was in college. The Georgia Historical Society's high-vaulted Hodgson Hall, with its arched windows and wrought-iron railings, was the library of the state college she attended, and as I took my seat before a two-headed lamp, I imagined my mother sitting here, projecting onto her reading the intense focus she brings to everything.

Digging around online, I'd begun to see what a big shot Solomon Cohen was. His résumé was long, with careers as a lawyer, banker, politician, postmaster, and real estate developer, and endless volunteer positions like president of Savannah's Mickve Israel synagogue, one of the oldest congregations in the country, whose sweet one-room museum, to its credit, identifies Solomon foremost as a "defender of slavery." He was also a founder and officer of the Georgia Historical Society, at the corner of Forsyth Park, on the border of the historic district. Solomon Cohen showed up in the Historical Society's online catalog, so I'd slipped out of a hot spring day and into cool, dim Hodgson Hall to see what artifacts of his life I could find.

A reference assistant brought me a folder with the handwritten text of a twenty-four-page eulogy that Solomon delivered there; a speech titled "A Discourse on the formation of the Constitution of the United States delivered as an Introductory to a course of Lectures of the Georgia Historical Society"; and correspondence from the Confederate States of America to Solomon in his capacity as postmaster, with such juicy bits as "In reply to your letter of the 5th inst.—I have to state that you were not allowed the whole amount claimed for postage on dead letters returned to the Department in the 1st quarter 1863, because the bills were not received from the Finance Bureau."

It wasn't the most auspicious start.

Gratz Cohen was mentioned on the fact sheet left in my apartment, and I'd seen references to him in *The Jewish Confederates* and elsewhere. Like me, he grew up Jewish in Savannah, devoured literature and was moved to write it himself, and went far from home to get educated. But at first I was captivated by his pictures. A family portrait showing Gratz as a boy with a huge book on his lap. A studio portrait of him, beardless and handsome, with his right hand tucked into the coat of his uniform. And a painting of Gratz in the same uniform, perhaps even based on the photograph, though looking quite different—with a faint moustache but fairer, prettier.

I asked the reference assistant if she had a folder on Gratz, but I wasn't hopeful. In *The Jewish Confederates* Gratz counts as just one more young man who gave his life for the region where his family, and fellow Jews, had prospered—a cardboard cutout who, I figured, must not have left much of a trace in his twenty years on this earth. And so I was surprised when she came back with a greater haul than for Gratz's father, not a folder but, rather, two old books, blank ones you write in. One was bound in dark brown leather, its spine intact except for the fraying top third. The word "Autographs" is imprinted on the cover in a fancy gold font; the stems of the letters sprout leaves. Most of its gold-edged pages are blank; the ones that aren't contain good wishes from friends, many including bits of verse, the Victorian equivalent of signing a yearbook. These inscriptions tend to express a hope for brighter days, the succinct contribution by one Mary L. Minor—"Your bright smile haunts me still"—summing up not just the mood of the times but the melancholy optimism I would come to hear in Gratz's writing.

The other book was his journal, covering his years at the University of Virginia, 1862 through 1864. Its spine had been mostly eaten away but the book's green marbled cover and thick ruled pages had held up through the years, though the first few pages were surgically cut out. When I turned it over and upside down, the book opened to a catalog of the seven boxes of books Gratz took with him to college.

And two loose pages fell out, each covered with a maddening, faded scrawl that might have had something to do with why his own words have played so small a role in how Gratz Cohen is remembered. This quest was starting to feel like the start of an old novel, where a manuscript is found in a valise or otherwise makes it into the narrator's hands. Stray pages just kept turning up. On one of the pages that fell out of the journal was written a bittersweet poem about a "servant," here a genteel word for "slave," who had gone missing:

> He was my Geni fairy & my elf
> And fate has stolen from me half my self
> Where is he now my spirit yearns to know
> His loss has plunged me into endless woe

It's the first thing I read in Gratz Cohen's hand. Right from the start I felt thrust into an intimacy with him, an uncomfortable one, since this poem wasn't meant for my eyes or anyone else's. I didn't yet know whom he was talking about or what happened to this person, other than that he was no longer in Gratz's life. But what was easy to hear was how young Gratz was when he wrote it. These are the kinds of feelings you commit to your journal because you just have to get them out, work them out—and there's no one you can tell.

I put down the page and opened the journal. The first entry, dated October 14, 1862, the start of Gratz's first year in Virginia, is a similarly moony meditation in prose about a beloved vanished intimate, an enslaved man, whom Gratz heaps with pet names: "Ebony Idol—My Sancho Pansa—Lil Black—My Shadow thou wast indeed—" It's an apparently endless list, along the lines of "Geni fairy & my elf" in the poem. However cringeworthy these endearments are to us now, it's clear this was no ordinary servant, at least not to Gratz.

And unlike in the poem, in the journal Gratz gives this man a name: Louis.

4

You can barely scan a Savannah newspaper from the mid-nineteenth century without finding Solomon Cohen's name, as you'd expect of a man who played so many parts. Gratz Cohen did nothing in his twenty years on earth to merit a mention in the paper until his very last moments, when he got himself killed. Still, in the last century and a half, there have been a few pages written about him.

I find a single account of his life and death, a short sketch including a photogravure of him in uniform, which appears in *The University Memorial*, a collection of contemporaneous portraits of University of Virginia alumni who died in the Civil War. Gratz's anonymous biographer, drawing on letters and interviews with "stern men," came up with such a paean to his subject's youth, beauty, and brilliance that I wonder if mine is the only eyebrow that's been raised. Gratz's death is especially stirring: he dies from a bullet to the head immediately after delivering a report in his commander's tent, the smile remaining on his "beautiful face even in death."

This book came out in 1871. Four years before Solomon Cohen's death. I wonder whether this description of his son's demise comforted him. Whether it eased the pain of Gratz's mother, Miriam, to read that her son smiled as a bullet tore apart his brain.

To say this account is hard to believe is, I'm starting to see, somehow missing the point.

I read sketches and obituaries of other Civil War soldiers, and coverage of the war in the Savannah papers, and these accounts are all written this way, casting their subjects in the most heroic light. At least the editor of the *University Memorial* volume shows his cards right from the start, abandoning all pretense to objectivity or even realism: "No apology, it is believed, will be required for the publication of The University Memorial. The people for whose eye it is intended do not believe that the sword is the arbiter of right, nor have they ceased to cherish the principles which they made so gigantic an effort to maintain. They are not afraid of their kinsmen who fell in the great Confederate struggle, and who, sleeping now by mountain and river, in forest and field, in glen and dale, have bequeathed to them as a proud heritage the glory which their heroism achieved." I am not among those for whose eye this account was intended. But here it is, a perfect expression of the Lost Cause, whereby Southerners turned their loss into a kind of victory, a noble struggle against tyranny, this forgotten book part of a PR blitz whose extraordinary success endures to this day. For romance a Union soldier just can't compete with a rebel. What makes me misty-eyed is that this was a war that ended slavery and saved the Union. The struggles of those who fought for a different outcome— these had never moved me.

And yet it was Gratz Cohen I was stuck with. He was the one who haunted my house, though he'd died ten years before it was built.

I find a column-length obituary of Gratz by Samuel Yates Levy, an in-law of Solomon Cohen's and publisher of the *Savannah Daily Herald*, where the piece appeared a year after Gratz's death. That brief, touching account by someone who knew him has Gratz dying by leading the charge at Bentonville, in North Carolina, a different and even more heroic end than in the *University Memorial* account: "foremost in the front and in the thickest of the contest, animating the men by voice and example, he fell dead, without pain or suffering." The obituary seems more plausible than the *University Memorial* account, though the image of Gratz Cohen leading the charge with a hearty rebel yell seems at odds with the obituary's earlier description of his "natural delicacy of frame and of constitution [that] had been increased by constant and unceasing study."

Death by bookishness, at least as an indirect cause.

The Jewish Confederates, however exhaustive a reference, doesn't get me much closer to understanding who Gratz was. There's an old anti-Semitic canard that Jews are faithful only to Zion. Well, here was a Jew, one among many, who fought for his homeland. The South, that is. Like *The University Memorial*, published more than a century earlier, *The Jewish Confederates* makes no apologies for its boosterish tone. Whoever Gratz really was, whatever reasons he had for going to war, I wasn't going to find answers here.

If anything, the few words that have ever been written about Gratz Cohen, whether or not they were intended to mislead, seem to obscure who he really was. And it seems to me very important to learn who he really was—and how he died. The birthplace I'd fled had drawn me back, and I was a middle-aged man now and saw it with new eyes, beheld it for the beautiful illusion it was. Gratz is like that—beautiful, for sure, but also, I suspect, an illusion. That's what he's become. Let me separate him from the decades of accumulated myth, chip away at the perfect stucco and see what's left. Push past the pretty lies to whatever might lie beneath.

But first I've got to look hard at the facade, the one Gratz grew up behind—not just the one Solomon built to smooth over all those slave-made bricks, but the figurative one he constructed in speeches and letters to pretty up the institution of slavery itself. And the facade the family had built up, one of perfect respectability, of hushed wealth, that remained standing even after the world behind it had crumbled.

PART I
The New World

1

Strange New Land

The New World chapter of the Cohen family saga begins in South Carolina, and that's where I've come, one mild morning in March. Solomon grew up in Georgetown, a patch of high ground hugged by water and marsh between Charleston and Myrtle Beach. The commercial district now comprises a few blocks of faded stucco and brick storefronts, a deli, a home furnishings store, and, when I visit, an old movie theater where a production of Neil Simon's *Odd Couple* is being staged. The strip is open for business, but I have the sidewalk almost all to myself.

I go searching for local history in the Georgetown County Museum, housed in a two-story brick building with the town's ubiquitous black shutters. There's a gift shop, the Rice Trunk, named after a water-control structure used in producing rice, which in the decades preceding the Civil War was exported from Georgetown in greater quantities than from any other port in the world. Upstairs in the museum there's a room with a conference table and books and a jumble of papers and clippings and pictures, a few organized in folders, and it's here that I'm left to find out what I can. It's a far cry from the hushed splendor of the Georgia Historical Society, where it felt that anywhere in the great hall I was being watched by staff waiting to help me—or catch me violating one of that establishment's many rules.

I have better luck at Georgetown's public library, where the wry reference librarian, instantly familiar with me, sits me down in a room and brings me books and folders that in an afternoon illuminate the world of Georgetown Jewry for me. Amazing that there are professionals out there apparently just waiting for me to show up, to briefly share in my quest and join my enthusiasm with their own.

Gratz's great-grandfather was a rabbi, just as my great-grandfather was. In 1749, shortly after his arrival from London to Charles Town (today's

Charleston), Moses Cohen and other Jews of Spanish and Portuguese origin founded Kahal Kadesh Beth Elohim, where Moses led the Orthodox Sephardic service. His title was grand: Haham v'Av Beth Din, spiritual leader and head of the Jewish court. But he also kept a shop. The title was used at Bevis Marks, London's great Sephardic synagogue, which had arranged passage for Savannah's Jewish settlers nearly two decades earlier and where Moses too had prayed—but at Charles Town's Beth Elohim, it was an unsalaried position, like all the jobs in the fledgling congregation.

Unlike his biblical namesake, Moses, this first Cohen father made it to the Promised Land, where he was fruitful and multiplied, naming sons one through three Abraham, Isaac, and Jacob. Then he had two daughters, Esther and Rachel. Gratz's grandfather, Solomon Cohen Sr., was the baby, the child of Moses's old age.

A plaque on Moses's grave identifies him as a COLONIAL MERCHANT AND "LEARNED JEW." The year of their father's death, 1762, coincided with Abraham and Solomon's departure from Charles Town. In tiny Georgetown, where they were likely the first Jews, the brothers were free not just of family and religious ties but also of Charles Town's competitive business world. As the years passed and the memories of that city faded, Solomon Sr. would come to know no home other than Georgetown. Without much in the way of distraction, the brothers were learning about their new world, the commercial center of a vast plantation network. And they were figuring out their place in it.

The waterfront was busy year round with barges and boats loaded with indigo and rice coming downriver to the port to be unloaded and shipped out. Incoming boats passed through a notch in the coast and into Winyah Bay, a silty coastal estuary named after the Native tribe that lived around it until the early eighteenth century. The bay is a feature of the drowned coastline, meaning the land sank or the sea rose, resulting in a flooded river valley, an irregular arrangement of water and land. The waterway narrows and enlarges like a digestive system, supplied by the arteries running through the rich piedmont—the Black, Great Pee Dee, Waccamaw, and Sampit rivers—and emptying into the bay at Georgetown.

Solomon and Abraham learned what the area's planters needed and what they wanted—and maybe even what they didn't yet know they wanted. And the brothers figured out how to get it for their clients. As a vendue master (an auctioneer), Abraham traded in enslaved people, real estate, and other property, as his nephew Octavus would in Savannah. He also owned a blacksmith's shop, whose skilled artisans he held in captivity. Solomon Cohen Sr. followed in his father's footsteps and opened a store, but not so he could freelance as a rabbi. Solomon offered, among other goods, "Oznaburgs and Brandy," as one of his newspaper advertisements was titled. An osnaburg, spelled with an *s* today, is not a cigar; it's a type of coarse cloth that was used in making clothing worn by enslaved workers. The headline alone sheds light on Solomon's clientele, and the range of his offerings—what they needed to produce their crop, and what they could afford to have as a result of it.

In time the brothers took on many other roles on the small stage of the town. Abraham founded the Georgetown Library Society, which raised funds to establish a library, and the Georgetown Fire Company. The brothers served on committees and boards. Their neighbors had been electing them to office long before they themselves could legally vote, in 1790, when South Carolina's constitution gave Jewish men that right. In 1818 Solomon Cohen Sr. was elected intendant, or mayor, of Georgetown. In 1819, at the age of sixty-two, he became a director of the Bank of the State of South Carolina in Georgetown. The Haham's son, orphaned from the age of five, had reached the highest office in town. The shopkeeper's son (and former shopkeeper himself) now directed the flow of capital for a region whose economy was in transition, from one slave-labor-intensive crop to another. Without subsidies from the crown to protect it from growing international competition, the state had stopped producing indigo. The War of 1812 over, the rice-planter class was on its way to becoming even more fabulously wealthy than its predecessor caste in the previous century.

Solomon Cohen Sr. himself seems to have been of this class. He is listed as a planter in city directories and was an owner of Asheton, a rice plantation on an island between the North and South Santee rivers in Georgetown County.

On the wide oak-shaded streets of the original four-by-eight-block grid, sandwiched between the bay and Highway 17, houses of worship appear among gracious homes, some of them dating from before the Civil War. With wraparound verandas and rocking chairs, window shutters a dramatic black against their white wooden sides, these huge houses would make great bed-and-breakfasts, should the secret of Georgetown's existence become less well kept. There's almost no traffic, pedestrian or vehicle.

At Duke and Broad, the street perpendicular to the water dividing the old town in half, is the Jewish cemetery. Surrounded by a spiked iron fence with a locked gate, it's well tended, the grass trimmed around the mausoleums and stones, some old and others new, with plenty of room under the oaks and palmettos to accommodate more Jews, should the need arise. I walk around the fence, hoping to get a glimpse of Abraham's grave. I don't see it but maybe I don't need to. He's all over the historic marker outside the gate.

> This cemetery, established ca. 1772, is the second oldest Jewish cemetery in the state and serves a community which has been significant here since well before the American Revolution. Abraham Cohen and Mordecai Myers, who opened stores in the town in 1762 and 1772, are buried here, as is Heiman Kaminski, who arrived in Georgetown in 1856 and was one of its most prominent businessmen by the turn of the twentieth century.
>
> The Jewish community has emphasized leadership and public service from the beginning: Abraham Cohen, for example, was a member of the committee welcoming President George Washington in 1791. Three of Georgetown's [seven] Jewish mayors are also buried here: Louis S. Ehrich (Mayor 1886–88), Harold Kaminski (1930–35), and Sylvan L. Rosen (1948–61).

Two of the Jewish mayors who aren't buried here are Solomon Cohen Sr. and Jr., the latter having taken the former, after his death, to be reinterred in Savannah, where the family tree had taken new root.

Born in 1802, Solomon Cohen Jr. had lived in Savannah in his twenties for a couple years before moving back to his hometown when his father took ill. What a big fish Solomon Cohen *fils* must have felt in the small pond of Georgetown, South Carolina. Unlike Ashkenazi Jews, Sephardim aren't superstitious about naming newborns after living relatives, and Solomon

Cohen was a name the younger man was proud to bear. But it was small consolation, I suspect, for having returned to the village he'd fled to seek his fortune.

Still, if Solomon, drawn back by duty, knew the narrowness of Georgetown, I try to imagine how his bride, Miriam Moses, must have felt. He was thirty-four, she twenty-eight. Trains and steamers would have taken her away from her large extended family in Philadelphia and down to Charleston, where she would have been greeted by her fiancé. A smaller boat would have carried the pair up the coast and into Winyah Bay. Shivering in the salt air as she passed through the vast marshlands, Miriam must have wondered what she had done.

Neat sausage curls framed the perfect oval of her face; her big light eyes were widely spaced. Solomon was sternly handsome and possessed of a sonorous voice, with a wit and charm he could deploy when necessary. He was a lawyer and judge in the Georgetown District, or county—"the great man of the village," as Miriam's aunt Rebecca Gratz put it. Trained in the domestic arts, Miriam also spoke fluent French, read widely, and as a younger woman had written poetry, some of it gloomy and Byronesque, other poems more fiery and wholly her own. When Solomon first gazed upon her, was it this verse from her collection "Poetic Prophecies," all addressed to an unnamed man, that popped into her head?

The next fair brow you look upon
Will be your own for life,
Then take care how you raise your eyes
If you'd have a lovely wife.

Solomon gulped her down with his eyes, he drank her in. He'd already taken care. For at least two years he'd been corresponding with Rebecca Gratz, who'd raised Miriam since her mother died, when Miriam was just shy of fifteen. In a letter to "My Dear Madam" from January 1834, Solomon thanks Rebecca for the gift of a book on Judaism written by Isaac Leeser, the spiritual leader of her congregation, Philadelphia's Mikveh Israel, and the voice of traditional Judaism in the country. Leeser's book is fine, Solomon writes, but what the Jews of America really need is a volume "examining our doctrine without reference to our ceremonies," one that could be written by none other than Rebecca herself. "I know of no one in America more admirably calculated than you are to perform this sacred task."

He may simply have been buttering her up to ask for her niece's hand, but clearly Solomon knew his correspondent well. The daughter of Central European immigrants who made a fortune in shipping and real estate, Rebecca was a famous beauty whose portrait had been painted three times by Thomas Sully, a fellow Philadelphian and friend. She may also have been memorialized in the sappy but unflinchingly true-to-her-faith Hebrew heroine with the same first name in *Ivanhoe*. Rebecca Gratz had begun founding benevolent institutions at the age of twenty. She'd also been instrumental in encouraging Leeser to give edifying sermons, a Christian tradition that he went on to pioneer in the American synagogue and for which he became nationally known. Rebecca wouldn't write the book that Solomon wanted, but she was quite interested in disseminating Jewish doctrine so as to arm Jews against the tireless Christian evangelizing of the day.

It was Isaac Leeser, that comforting and familiar presence to Miriam, who officiated at her marriage with Solomon, on November 30, 1836. The house into which she was introduced was still in mourning, Solomon Cohen Sr. having died the year before. Miriam must have been a breath of fresh air, this cultured emissary from the North, and she was received with great kindness by all of Solomon's family. She lived with her mother-in-law, Bell, and her sister-in-law Cecilia. Solomon's other brothers and sisters had all married, everyone but his brother Octavus, who'd just decamped for Savannah.

It was a trifling matter, but Miriam, as she would later recall, was unsure how to address the members of her new family. A common situation but one for which she was unprepared. At first she tried not to address them at all, which she feared made her seem distant, if not outright rude, but gradually she began to take her cues from her husband, calling her in-laws as he did. *Sister*, she murmured to her sister-in-law, and kept on saying it, though she already had a sister. *Mother*. And Miriam saw that what felt like a minor concern was in fact of great importance, for soon after she began uttering the familiar but strange words, she became a daughter again, she became a sister.

Miriam couldn't have been happier in the "new & strange circumstances by which she is surrounded," Rebecca reported to her sister-in-law Maria Gist Gratz. Rebecca had trained her niece to place duty above self, to control her emotions, which was the same advice Rebecca gave her sister Rachel, Miriam's mother, as a teenager, though Rebecca was only two years Rachel's elder. Miriam was more successful at suppressing her feelings than Rachel had been. But you don't need to read between the lines of Miriam's reassuring letters to see that despite the welcoming family into which she had married, she was lonely.

She wishes for a magic carpet to transport herself back to Philadelphia to be with Rebecca and the rest of her family, if only for a season, or just the holidays. Letters are far more than a way of transmitting news for Miriam. They're her magic carpet, and Rebecca's as well, ways of visiting with each other when such a terrible distance stretches between them. Miriam passes hours by herself or with her sister-in-law sewing in the silence of the big house, emptied now of almost all the children it has seen born there and made even emptier by a perhaps surprising absence. Solomon himself is often gone, making his legal rounds in the region, traveling to the state capital in Columbia and venturing even farther afield, to Augusta, Columbus, Mobile.

The worst part about having so much time on her hands is that Miriam dwells on the shortcomings she perceives as a wife. She lives in a world of figures—number of days since her last period, count of stitches, minuscule increases to the length of her waist. Ticktock of the grandfather clock marking the long hours of silence in the house and the length of time she's been trying to conceive. Through her constant calculations surely she'll turn up a sign that it's finally happening. Instead she experiences one "disappointment" after another, in the euphemistic way she writes even to her beloved aunt.

Beyond the close world of the house, there's little to distract her from her cares. True, the Jew-less place into which Solomon's father and uncle had wandered is no more. There's still no synagogue, but now there are enough men to make a minyan, gathering in private homes and rooms in the aristocratic Winyah Indigo Society—not that that does Miriam any good. Solomon, despite having no formal Jewish education, is instrumental in keeping up the faith in Georgetown. In her first Passover there, Miriam sees more evidence of her husband's importance: he weighs and distributes matzoth to the community.

There's a community—but not the kind she grew up in. Her home synagogue, Mikveh Israel, was in an Egyptian Revival building, with semicircular galleries for women under a magnificent dome, its renowned leader a close friend of her aunt's and a regular guest in their home. At the time Miriam left, Philadelphia was the country's third largest city and an industrial powerhouse, while Georgetown served a swampy realm that produced half the nation's rice. The port may have been bustling, but how she must have missed her native city, its architecture and squares, its cultural institutions, her family's lively discourse. Well, she could dwell on what she'd lost or she could get used to her new life.

She got on with it, accustomed herself to her "new and strange circumstances," though the presence of enslaved people couldn't have been the oddest. Pennsylvania instituted gradual abolition in 1780, nearly three decades before Miriam was born, but legal slavery persisted in the state until 1847. Still, she now lived in a region whose economic lifeblood was enslaved labor, something her own household relied upon. Black people overwhelmingly outnumbered whites in the Georgetown District, and very few of the former group were free.

The milder Southern climate appeals to Miriam, as do the gnarled old oaks, evergreens, and flowers in bloom even in January. A different world, but maybe in its very strangeness is where its beauty lies.

Finally, it seems, a long year and a half after her wedding, it's happening! Strain of fabric against flesh, her daily needlework, seams let out, the put-on horror that she's getting fat. Secretly she's pleased by the padding her body is taking on. But her face is no fuller than it ever was, her cheeks are no rosier, her skin no clearer—surely the knowledge should show elsewhere than just in her waist. Still, Miriam is hopeful enough to envision a summer pregnancy on North Island, where the ocean breezes will provide relief from the heat. Sea air and bathing have been recommended by her doctor to help her conceive, and Miriam and Solomon plan to return to this favored resort of the Georgetown gentry for her confinement.

With its lighthouse guiding ships around the sandbar and jetties in the bay, North Island is the tip of a string of barrier islands stretching down to Florida. Rebecca Gratz raises an epistolary eyebrow. Will there even be a doctor there, wherever this island is?

In the end it doesn't matter. Miriam is disappointed once again.

Solomon's life has been organized by his responsibilities as a son, returning to Georgetown when his father became ill and marrying, relatively late, only after Solomon Sr. died, in 1835. Three years later, the younger Solomon feels free to move back to Savannah, which has long interested him, maybe because it isn't yet the commercial center that Charleston is and so holds more potential for an ambitious man.

When Miriam announces the move to her aunt, the older woman breathes a loud sigh of relief:

Tho' you were happy in Georgetown, because the home of your Beloved, you will certainly have many advantages in the City which you could not have commanded there. And as intellectual society is one of the most fertile sources of improvement, your capability of enjoyment will advance, as you have opportunities of rising in its circles. I have often regretted that your Husband should be confined to so small a community as Georgetown and I have no doubt he will feel as if his spirit was free to take a wider range among its peers and try its strength among more equal competitors.

2

No One's Paradise

For years Solomon's memory of the place where he'd lived as a younger man must have lain on some back shelf of the mind, purposely set there so that it would be hard to retrieve, so that he wouldn't waste time daydreaming about it when filial obligation had called him back to his provincial birthplace. But the dream city to which he now returned hadn't become the utopia that Georgia's founder, James Oglethorpe, and its trustees set out to create. If it had, Solomon, along with many others, wouldn't have moved there. Georgia's charter declared that "all and every person or persons, who shall at any time hereafter inhabit or reside within our said province, shall be, and are hereby declared to be free" and Oglethorpe himself proclaimed the thirteenth colony "free from that pest and scourge of mankind called lawyers," whereas Solomon Cohen, Esquire, shows up in the 1840 census with twenty-two enslaved people. Savannah's tightly prescribed pattern of squares and the kinds of buildings that could be placed around them had balanced developable land with public space. But as the town's population grew and its limits pushed southward, common space took a backseat and Solomon would have a nice sideline as a landlord and real estate developer.

Still, Savannah in 1839 was no one's idea of paradise. According to *Historical Record of the City of Savannah*, the little black book my father gave me, the weather was terrible and the climate insalubrious: "The year 1839 was one of the sickliest ever known in Savannah. It is remembered as the dryest summer on record, and also a very hot summer. Bilious fevers prevailed in a malignant form, but not yellow fever." The city was no stranger to fevers. There'd been an outbreak of yellow fever in 1827, and despite its absence in the years before Miriam and Solomon's arrival, Savannah, surrounded by marshes and swamps, was notorious enough as a pestilential place that the dangers it posed to Miriam's perfect health was the subject of many exchanges she had with her aunt Rebecca. Miriam tells her not to worry, for Solomon "skreens" her from dangers, literally; he sets up a mosquito net around her bed.

Their relationship is sweet. It shocks me to discover this. "Sweet" is the last word I thought I'd use about Solomon Cohen, whom I first came to know as a hardline lawyer, businessman, and unflinching defender of "states rights," the public image he so carefully cultivated. In Savannah they're no longer young—he's thirty-six, she's thirty—but Miriam and Solomon have a sense of adventure, a pair of explorers in the city, with its charms and its dangers.

Her aunt Rebecca instilled in her the importance of usefulness, and Miriam wants to work with needy children. Although the economy of this town of 11,000 is depressed, its leaders are planning for better times. Two new squares have been laid out on the city's southern end, and on one of them, Madison, named after the recently deceased president, the Female Orphan Asylum is going up. It's a huge neoclassical building with a flat roof and pilasters rising on every facade between big shuttered windows, surrounded by a fence topped with fancy ironwork. The place is elegant and grand, a mansion, and I picture the girls, many of them the children of poor white single mothers, walking for the first time under the fanlight in the wide front doorway and into unimaginable splendor.

Elected the institution's new secretary, Miriam does her best to help. She rises early—in summer at five, when it's still cool—and starts each day reading the Bible and studying Hebrew with Solomon. After breakfast he heads north, to his office in the heart of things, while Miriam goes in the opposite direction, *out* to the asylum. Beautiful Madison Square is today so fully realized that it's hard to imagine it at the edge of the city, the barren square and the empty lots around it just waiting to be filled in.

Every morning at the asylum Miriam mothers the orphan girls; having lost her own mother at a young age, she can identify with her charges. But as secretary, she's doing a different kind of work, filling the same position that her aunt Rebecca always insisted on taking in her own organizations. A secretary transmits the good work done within the walls of an institution to the greater world, recounting the past while looking out to the future, shaping the narrative of the place. As a young woman, Miriam, like her aunt, wrote poetry, which she collected in manuscripts. Miriam may have felt writing poetry wasn't compatible with being a wife, for she didn't appear to write verse after she was married. But as secretary of the Female Orphan Asylum, she claims for herself the power of writing. At least one person finds the product excellent. Solomon, brimming with pride, sends a copy of her first report to Rebecca.

Miriam and Solomon are passionate for each other, and often express their mutual admiration. "If you only knew him as I do," Miriam writes her aunt, "you'd know I've been truly blest." And Solomon is romantic. Fitting his words into a bit of blank space in a letter Miriam has written to Rebecca, Solomon gushes, "Bless you for installing into her infant mind those principles which have ripened into virtues which makes her all that a husband's heart can desire." It sounds like old-fashioned patriarchy, but I think it's love, and a love between equals, based not on their roles in the household but instead on a deepening knowledge of one another. Miriam is domestic, and when she isn't at the asylum, she spends her mornings sewing. But it isn't what she does in the home that makes Miriam all that Solomon desires; it's who she is. Nor does he ever express disappointment at their union's failure to produce the one thing you'd expect a man like Solomon to want: a child.

The disappointment Miriam felt more or less constantly in Georgetown is gone. It's not just that she doesn't speak of it. She's come to accept being childless, another way in which she follows in the footsteps of the woman who raised her. There are so many children in Miriam's life, and not just the orphans. In spring 1840 her sister-in-law Henrietta gives birth to a daughter, and four years later a son. Miriam is especially close to the girl, Fanny, who comes to her for religious instruction. Miriam grew up under her devout aunt's tutelage; she was never a stranger to Judaism. But now, feeling chosen to play a different role in life than as a mother, something she always expected to be, she feels closer to God and experiences more of a spiritual connection to her religion.

Fanny isn't the only child who receives religious instruction from Miriam. Less than a year after Rebecca Gratz dreams up and institutionalizes Hebrew Sunday School in Philadelphia, Miriam opens a local franchise. In letters Rebecca describes the class format: Bell rings, the ten students rise and repeat a short prayer, roll taken, then on to the lessons of the day, which always include reading a portion of the Bible. Class ends with a hymn.

And Miriam has another project: raising money for Savannah's Mickve Israel synagogue to hire a rabbi. Taking charge against the inaction of their husbands, Miriam and Henrietta plan to have a "Community Fair," staffed by women from the congregation, and use the proceeds to establish a fund. Miriam envisions Jews and their Christian neighbors joining forces. The town's non-Jewish religious institutions and benevolent societies regularly call on Mickve Israel to help with their own fundraisers, and Miriam sees no reason why they shouldn't reciprocate.

Rebecca Gratz doesn't see how a fair for Jews could succeed if it relies on Christians not just as volunteers but as customers as well. Rebecca wants to believe Christians are losing their zeal for converting Jews, but she's skeptical that Christians would come to the assistance of the Jewish community. Undeterred, Miriam asks Rebecca to send her some of her fancywork and to ask "all the fair daughters of Israel" in Philadelphia to do the same. Rebecca complies, sending south a box with some cushions and other things, including a pair of bracelets plaited by one of her orphans. Miriam and her female relatives work on a checkerboard quilt. And Miriam sends a letter to Grace Aguilar, one of her favorite writers, asking if she could provide some of her own needlework for them to sell.

A little over a century earlier, forty-two Jews, mostly Sephardim who had fled to England to escape the Portuguese Inquisition, had been on the second boat to arrive in the colony of Georgia, and over the years Savannah's Jewish population rose and fell with the town's fortunes. Although the settlement's Jews founded a congregation within months of their arrival, demand for a permanent building was limited enough that it wasn't until 1820 that one was finally erected, on Perry Lane, less than a minute's walk from the lot where Solomon Cohen would have my townhouse built. The site is now a parking lot, though I'd heard there was a marker somewhere. I must have walked by dozens of times before I realize I've been walking *over* it, a plaque in the sidewalk marking the FIRST SYNAGOGUE IN GEORGIA.

Nine years after it was erected, the synagogue, made of wood, burned to the ground. Another nine years later a new synagogue was finished, this one out of brick. There's a lithograph of it, dated 1871, in the museum in the synagogue's current building, and it's adorable, a neat little structure with four narrow rectangular windows running up one side, the entrance out of

view but apparently on Whitaker, a principal north-south street. The sanctuary was completed at the end of 1838, when Solomon and Miriam moved
to Savannah, though it wasn't consecrated until February 1841.

The building's unconsecrated nature weighed on the congregants; the
sanctuary could be used for services but wasn't quite kosher. Solomon
Cohen finally arranged for the ceremony to be performed by Isaac Leeser,
and greeting him, after all those years away, must have flooded Miriam
with memories and warm feelings for the family and friends she'd left
behind. But as the secretary of the Female Orphan Asylum, Miriam was
following in Rebecca Gratz's footsteps while at the same time becoming
her own woman, someone other than her aunt's niece or, for that matter,
her husband's wife. And so perhaps seeing Leeser brought her, ultimately,
something other than homesickness, the realization of just how far she'd
come, from the home of her youth to what was now her home, period.

At the consecration ceremony Solomon, the congregation's new hero, has
the honor of lighting the Ner Tamid, the eternal light over the altar. It was
rescued, along with the Torah scrolls, from the first sanctuary as it burned.

Grace Aguilar couldn't promise anything for the fair, but she ended up
sending along a few copies of her first book, *The Magic Wreath of Hidden Flowers*, a collection of verse puzzles concealing the names of flowers.
Miriam was free to sell them at her fair. And if she sent over a few more,
might Miriam try to dispose of them for her? So begins a professional
relationship between Aguilar and the Cohens, with Solomon becoming
her Southern agent, publisher, distributor, and publicist. He finds a printer
for her in Charleston. Her new book, *Records of Israel*, is a collection of
historical tales, and she plans to offer by subscription a series on the female
characters in the Bible.

To Aguilar, also a childless woman, Miriam writes that with a niece in
her life now, she feels less of a longing to be a mother. Tells it to her heart,
sets it down on paper. Maybe even comes to accept it, like a humble godly
Jewess in a romance by Grace Aguilar. And the high priestess of Victorian
Jewish literature pronounces Miriam "one of those truly blessed ones, who
receive <u>enough</u> from the hands of their God."

Aguilar praises Solomon for a piece in *The Occident*, encouraging him to
write more. In fact Solomon Cohen is never credited as a contributor to

anything in that monthly Jewish periodical, founded and edited by Leeser, though a piece about Savannah signed A SOUTHERN JEW did come out in August 1843, right before Aguilar wrote him. I might have recognized it as Solomon's work from its windy style: "The end and aim of those who settled Georgia was charity in its widest and most extended sense, and the motto on the seal of the Trustees spoke but the language of truth: *Non sibi sed aliis*—Not for ourselves, but for others. A colony springing into existence under such auspices, with a fertile soil, and a genial climate, soon became an asylum for the oppressed of every land, and every faith." It's a skimpy piece, with obvious inaccuracies. Solomon neglects to mention, for example, that this haven of religious tolerance denied it to Catholics. (And while Georgia's charter was silent on Jews, the trustees weren't too keen on them either.) Moreover, while charity for debtors recently released from prison was one of the stated goals of Oglethorpe and the trustees, and a few debtors were indeed among the "worthy poor" initially supported by the trust, colonists were chosen who could do the hard labor required to hack a European settlement out of pinewoods and marsh and to sustain and defend it.

At any rate, Solomon's piece isn't really intended as a history of the Jews of Savannah, and a few months later a more thorough treatment of Savannah's early Jewish history appears as a corrective by a grandson of one of the original Jewish settlers. Nor is Solomon's essay a job posting, though it does put the word out that the Savannah synagogue is raising money to one day hire a reader and leader of the services, or *hazzan* as it was called in Sephardic congregations. And the piece reports on Miriam and Henrietta's fair, though that account seems more of a response to Rebecca Gratz's initial concern that Christians would have no part in so Jewish an event: "To aid in the object of obtaining a permanent fund from which the Hazan may be supported, the Jewish ladies determined on giving a Fair, and in March last put their plan in execution. They were nobly sustained by *every Christian sect* in this city, and realized more than sixteen hundred dollars, which has already been profitably and safely invested." The fair began on St. Patrick's Day 1843 and lasted several days, and Solomon took the proceeds and, on the synagogue's behalf, bought stock in the railroad.

Rising Fortunes

The Central Rail Road & Canal Company was organized in 1833 to compete with the South Carolina Railroad, which was taking cotton business away from the port of Savannah. The company, soon renamed the Central Rail Road & Banking Company of Georgia, began its first passenger, freight, and mail runs three years later, though it wasn't until 1843 that the route between Savannah and Macon was complete. Its profitability unlocked by the invention of the modern cotton gin, brainchild of a Connecticut Yankee in Savannah some fifty years earlier, short-staple cotton could now easily be transported from the interior of the state to the coast, bypassing river travel. Fast, direct—but the railroad's route wasn't straight, zigzagging instead through plantations to take advantage of the labor supply, which worked out so well that the Central Rail Road eventually became the largest commercial enslaver in Savannah.

But when Miriam and Solomon came to town, the depressed cotton market had sent the railroad's stock tumbling, from $100 to $20 a share, and the people building the railroad, those who got paid in the first place, were now forced to accept three-quarters of their salary in this devalued stock. Torrential rains washed out new bridges, mosquitoes swarmed and killed off the people trying to rebuild the tracks—yet the railroad continued to extend its reach, and in the fall the trains that had mostly been used for mail and passenger trips now roared into Savannah full of cotton.

But there was little demand for it. Exports of cotton through the port fell by half from 1840 to 1841. Meanwhile, the more modest exports of rice remained constant, and ships that had held cotton now transported loads of less-profitable lumber. Savannah was a curious place to move, the port city vibrating like a mirage in the sun's glare, a sleepy backwater where bullfrogs croaked in the swamps around the pretty center and a hot wind off the river stirred up the dusty streets and the railroad was the one thing you could get interested in, though you might have wondered what the point of it was. You could go for a Sunday ride. Or just wander around the new depot, in the working-class west side of town. The city was so broke that it couldn't pay its debts or give raises to its workers. Even the rabbi-less synagogue, though only ten years old, had fallen into disrepair. This was where Solomon chose to move his family.

Still, if Georgetown was too narrow a place for the Cohens, Savannah was wide open. You could get in on the ground floor—and hope that one day there'd be some upper stories. Or build them yourself. The city's earlier hopes—silk, Madeira wine—had faded fast, and now its leaders were betting on it to become a hub for the processing and shipment of the state's agricultural products, as well as a banking center. At least that was the plan. It took a certain type of person to come here, a risk-taker, ambitious, prone to faith. But there were a lot of those people. Over the previous decade, the city's population had grown by half. Solomon and Miriam were part of a great migration to Savannah, including other Jews born in the South and, increasingly, the states of Germany. Everywhere these people saw not what wasn't there but what could be. The rich weren't getting any richer, but they sure acted as if they were about to be.

The railroad stock in which Solomon invested the synagogue's permanent fund was still cheap. For years the proceeds of the synagogue ladies' homey quilts and lace tablecloths helped fuel the Central Rail Road's quest for additional "motive power." Five years after Miriam and Henrietta's first fundraiser, the fund had grown big enough for the congregation to begin looking for a rabbi in earnest, and ads were placed for a *hazzan* versed in the Portuguese service.

The rise in the town's fortunes was figured by Solomon's own. He'd hung out his shingle as soon as he got there, advertising his services, under the heading Law Notice, in the newspaper: "The undersigned (late of South Carolina) will attend to the practice of Law and Equity in this city, and also to any professional business in the adjoining districts of South Carolina. Office over the store of Messrs Price and Veader." For years Solomon travels back and forth across the river, working in the state he's just left while building up a clientele in the one to which he's moved. As a commissioner of South Carolina for Savannah, he's empowered to notarize deeds executed in Savannah for use in South Carolina. President Martin Van Buren appoints him to be United States attorney for the Southern District of Georgia in the fall of 1840, the same year that Solomon joins forces with another lawyer, who jointly advertise that "they will attend the Courts of the United States at Milledgeville [the state capital] and Savannah, and the Superior Courts of the several Counties in the Eastern Circuit."

Every weekday morning Solomon Cohen walks to the Bay, today's Bay Street, the wide avenue at the very top of the bluff, where he's bought an office building. When he's in town he sits in his respectable office and writes and receives letters, a cache of which I find in the Georgia Historical Society. These letters go out to New York, Florida, South Carolina, and Alabama. He even has some business with Rothschild Bros. in Paris. He writes in his capacity as alderman, chairman of boards, administrator of estates, and agent of clients.

Solomon is no slouch in the extracurricular department either. At the Georgia Historical Society he gives a public lecture on the Constitution, sharing with a new audience the states-rights gospel he's long preached to South Carolinians. "States were, and are Sovereign," he says in that address, "except perhaps as far as they have delegated a portion of their Sovereign power to be exercised by the General Government under the Constitution of the United States." Perhaps. Solomon represents his ward—a grouping of blocks around a square—on the board of health, an important position in a city regularly threatened by disease. He's appointed secretary of the Bank of the State of Georgia, and like Miriam is charged with reporting on his institution's performance. His first report encourages shareholders in the groundless optimism that the town's entire business community has willed itself to feel: "Resolved, That the Bank is in a sound, and healthful condition, with ample means to meet its liabilities; and that although the stock is now depressed, in common with every other description of property, yet Stockholders may confidently look forward to an increased value, when better times shall appreciate other property."

Solomon is a member of the city's finance committee and the Committee on Public Sales. He's president of the Union Society, the distinguished old organization that brought Jews and non-Jews together to aid poor children and widows. He's a founder and the first president of the Hebrew

Benevolent Society, which benefited indigent Jews. And he sets himself up as a mortgage lender, as my lawyer grandfather will do a century later. Solomon draws on his cachet as an officer of the town's most prestigious organizations and clubs to attract business, and his connections in the business community in turn make him the ideal board member.

Almost immediately he establishes himself as a spokesman for the Jewish community as well, speaking at a meeting about the so-called Damascus affair of 1840, when thirteen members of the Jewish community of that city were imprisoned and tortured for supposedly murdering a Christian monk to use his blood in rituals. Rebecca Gratz presciently found something in this atrocity to applaud, calling the moment "quite a new era in the history of our people," as it was the first time American Jews organized themselves to persuade the federal government to exert its influence on behalf of international Jewry. Meetings were held in cities across the country, and the one in Savannah, called by the mayor himself, shows how the town supported its Jewish community, even on matters far beyond the city limits. The meetings worked, the outrage bubbling up from towns and cities across the world succeeding at having the nine living prisoners released, though not, of course, quashing violent anti-Semitism in Syria and elsewhere.

At the mayor's meeting Solomon expresses thanks "to the Christians of this community for their generous sympathy." A few years later, in his anonymous piece referencing Miriam's fair for the synagogue in the *Occident*, Solomon will heap praise on Christians simply for being, well, Christian: "That spirit of charity which presided at the birth of our Colony, still reigns and sheds its benign influence over the hearts of our Christian friends; and on this occasion charity was seen in all its loveliness, and felt in all its heavenly force—prejudice and sectarian intolerance stood rebuked and abashed, and the heart of the Jew was gladdened by the tender sympathy and open-handed charity of the Christian." It wasn't just an echo, this mawkish gratitude toward Gentiles; it was one of Solomon's themes.

This brilliant, learned workaholic who was always the most reliable guy in the room, the one you could count on to get any job done, who'd risen to the heights of Savannah's social structure—I think he realized how easily it could have gone another way. How capricious Christian tolerance could be. A man like this might feel he has something to prove. He might not want to rock the boat.

Between riding the circuit in southeastern Georgia and practicing in South Carolina, Solomon is away for weeks at a time. In November 1842 he's elected a Georgia state senator, the first Jewish person in this role, and resigns his post as district attorney. Miriam travels with him to Milledgeville for a legislative session. She enjoys herself there. But usually when Solomon travels, she stays in Savannah. And even when her husband's home, he's often away, working in his study, as he does Sunday mornings. Dutiful, uncomplaining, Miriam reasons that at least they get to spend the Sabbath together, and that all this work he does now means they'll be able to enjoy their old age with each other.

Miriam accustoms herself to being left alone. But it's a different kind of aloneness than she felt in Georgetown. Here she's part of a community of people she finds intelligent and interesting. She visits friends. She goes to synagogue. She teaches Sunday school. She walks out to the orphan asylum. She does needlework to benefit the poor. She tries to repair whatever in the world she thinks needs fixing.

She misses her aunt and her father—a man whose news Rebecca passes on—and the rest of her relations in Philadelphia. But she no longer needs her family the way she once did. Inevitably a gulf develops between Miriam and Rebecca, now that the latter's charge is beyond her control. For years they don't see each other, and Rebecca's image of her niece seems to be fading. Now that she's no longer one of us, Rebecca worries, she must be one of them. Miriam is a Southerner now, which means she's under suspicion as a religious renegade, or at least considered in danger of being blown off course by the new wind fanning the region.

Charleston's Beth Elohim, whose first religious leader was none other than Solomon's by-the-book grandfather, is now, to Rebecca's alarm, "in danger of falling into error through the spirit of innovation." Rebecca's Philadelphia synagogue, Mikveh Israel, follows the traditional Portuguese service, which excludes her from participating or even understanding what's going on, sending her to popular authors for a book of daily prayers, but whose alternative, the more modern service proposed by the Charleston Reformed Society of Israelites and then ensconced in Beth Elohim, she considers a slippery slope toward ruin. Although the Gratzes are from the Prussian realm of Silesia, Rebecca puts the blame squarely on "the German reformers," grousing that "there seems no end to their innovations & enlightenment." After a visit to Savannah, Miriam's sister Sarah assures Rebecca that Miriam keeps a traditional Jewish home.

About another difference between North and South, it's Rebecca who raises the subject with Miriam, again and again. With a raised brow Rebecca writes of crossing paths with the famous abolitionist Lucretia Mott. Next Rebecca tells of a Philadelphia rabbi who "has made his first mistake, or you may say false step by preaching an anti-slavery sermon, though by no means an abolition one." Rebecca Gratz is against slavery, but she's also skeptical of abolitionists, whose efforts she considers counterproductive in improving the conditions of enslaved Blacks. And as a Philadelphia elite, Rebecca opposes any attempt to disrupt the social order. The rabbi's error? *He gave offense.*

Maybe Rebecca is trying to tell Miriam that she's not going to judge her for the way she lives. But Miriam doesn't comment on the rabbi's faux pas. She commits herself to no position on abolitionism, and anyway, she tends not to respond to her aunt's provocations.

When Rebecca begs her to visit, Miriam puts her off, saying she can't leave her husband for so long. Rebecca resorts to the tried-and-true lever of guilt: I hope I'm still alive by the time you decide to come! Finally, in the summer of 1843, the Cohens spend two months on the road, including making a visit up north. Solomon returns to Philadelphia at the start of 1844—he doesn't share Miriam's compunction about leaving one's spouse alone—and Rebecca regrets that he didn't bring her. Solomon's trip was easier than expected. And Solomon himself isn't what Rebecca had expected. The last time she saw him he showed her the poker face he displays to business and political colleagues, looking out from under his strong brow but revealing none of his thoughts or feelings. He was reserved, polite, respectful. A good lawyer, he prepared remarks. But this time he dispenses with set speeches. He's family.

In the first half of 1844, probably June, Miriam and Solomon visit Rebecca again, with their four-year-old niece, Fanny, in tow. Fanny's mother, Henrietta, is very pregnant and remains home, but it's decided, as these things were, that the girl, who's been looking a little pale, could benefit from a change of scenery. Miriam is like a second mother to Fanny anyway.

In her Philadelphia home, Rebecca Gratz reigned. "Queen of the Jews," a congressman acquaintance called the great lady, not unaffectionately. But she was queen of secular society as well. Intellectuals, writers, artists—these were the people who gathered in her parlor. The Savannah relatives got to meet one such luminary that summer: Fanny Kemble, the British actress, playwright, and memoirist under whose spell Rebecca had fallen when she first saw her perform Shakespeare.

Kemble, who's married to the Philadelphian Pierce Mease Butler, has written a memoir whose publication her husband has so far successfully suppressed. Butler owns a rice plantation ninety miles south of Savannah, and he and Fanny spent a winter there. *Journal of a Residence on a Georgian Plantation in 1838–1839*, when it's finally published, in 1863, will find a place on Rebecca Gratz's bookshelf and in the national consciousness as an account of the horrors of slavery, including rampant sexual abuse. When Miriam and her family meet her in Philadelphia, Kemble and her husband are separated, though still living in the same house. Butler's philandering has weakened a marriage already strained by Kemble's disgust with her husband's enslaving, and it's the threat of never seeing her two daughters again that Butler hangs over her head if she publishes her memoir.

Whether Miriam is as fascinated by Kemble as her aunt (or for that matter young Fanny) or whether Miriam sees a cautionary tale in this fellow cultured woman who went down to a strange land, she doesn't record it. Miriam has been an uncomplaining wife and lived as the locals do; Kemble has not and is paying the price. But something has happened, after nearly eight years of marriage, to unsettle Miriam's orderly life and challenge what she's come to believe about herself.

She's pregnant, about four months along.

I know this only because I do the math. It's her attitude that throws me off. What a change since those first couple of years of her marriage, when an unexpected press of fabric at her waist could send Miriam to her calculations about how far along she might be. The false vanity, the giddy plans—none of that now. When she gets home from her trip north she writes Rebecca that the journey back wasn't too tiring and that the *pain in her side* that she felt in Philadelphia is now gone.

And she asks her aunt for help hiring a nurse: "I should like to have Mary Ann Smith, but before you say any thing on the subject to her, I wish you to inquire particularly of Charlotte with regard to her character and capabilities for the situation of nurse & whether she thinks that Mary Ann would be suited for that capacity. . . . I wish her to come the last of October, beginning of November. . . . I should retain her, should I no longer require her as a nurse, as a seamstress. I should like to know about the matter, as soon as you can conveniently ascertain." Miriam goes about this as coolly and methodically as if looking for a new matron for the orphan asylum. She betrays no excitement or anxiety at all, never mentions her pregnancy or plans for her confinement. She speaks in euphemisms: *Should I no longer require her as a nurse.* How skilled she's become, over the years, at keeping her heart safe from harm.

Little Castle

Having learned his story backward, I can accurately predict this baby will grow up amid riches untold even by the town's tireless boosters. Gratz is born just as the recession is nearing its end. Happy days are here again, and they'll continue until the war begins, sixteen and a half years later, and the port is blockaded and the town's newest raison d'être, like the previous ones, is gone. The Bible tells of barren women giving birth, tales as real to Miriam and her family and friends as anything they lived themselves, and Rebecca is quick to compare her niece to Hannah, whose story is read in synagogue every Rosh Hashanah. But unhappy Hannah's frantic praying in temple caused the high priest to accuse her of being drunk, while Miriam calmly accepted her lot as a childless woman; her younger sister Sarah despaired of ever being able to live as calmly in the present moment as Miriam did. No one would ever have accused her of being drunk, certainly not in synagogue, where she'd stopped asking God to grant her something He clearly had chosen to withhold.

And yet here it was, the impossible baby, born into a country where the seams of unity were straining, even within each political party. The previous year, Solomon was a member of a state committee to recommend the Democratic presidential candidate, and the resulting report, adopted at the 1844 Georgia Democratic State Convention, instructed delegates to the national convention to nominate John C. Calhoun. Solomon, his reputation in the party rising, was appointed a delegate to that convention.

Calhoun, a former US vice president, was from South Carolina and fought for everything that Solomon too believed in—low tariffs, slavery, and states rights, including that of nullifying federal law deemed inimical to state interests. Solomon became an adherent of these causes as a lawyer and Nullification Party representative in South Carolina, and they found great support among slaveholding Democrats in Georgia's Black Belt, which ran diagonally through the center of the state. In these counties Black people outnumbered whites, the soil was rich, and cotton production was soaring. But Calhoun was anathema to many North Georgians. And the last thing the national Democratic Party wanted was to nominate a man like John Calhoun, in no small part because of his enmity toward the party itself, and at their national convention he was quickly dispatched. The front-runner was former president Van Buren, whom the Southerners opposed because he was against the annexation of Texas, a potential new slave state. If the pro-annexation Calhoun wasn't going to advance, then they certainly weren't going to let the anti-annexation Van Buren become the party's candidate.

Delegates from Georgia and other slave states blocked Van Buren in favor of Tennessee governor James K. Polk, who'd initially hoped only to be on the ticket as Van Buren's vice president. But Polk was an enslaver and in favor of annexation, and so he was acceptable as a candidate to the Southern delegates and went on to win the nomination, the first dark-horse candidate to obtain the nomination of a major political party in this country. The Democratic Party held together and so did the Union, but the intraparty conflict, for both Democrats and Whigs, between Northern and Southern states was a sign of greater discord to come.

This was the other big thing that happened to Solomon Cohen in November 1844—his man, albeit a compromise candidate, won the presidency.

The Austrian university city of Graz dates to the twelfth century, which is when the German name Graz first appears, but its derivation from a Slavic word meaning "little castle" suited Gratz Cohen. Little castles are what we all are, fortifications against the threats beyond our skin, but for Gratz, the enemy lay within the walls, and he couldn't get out. From his "earliest youth" he watched the other children frolic but couldn't play as they did. They seemed light-hearted, natural as animals, whereas Gratz thought ceaselessly, which made him unhappy, because his thoughts revealed the distance between him and them. He was trapped within himself.

But he willed himself to appear like something he wasn't, and in Gratz's case it worked, convincing his father at least—or maybe Solomon just wanted to believe he had a cheerful boy. Gratz would write of this period of his childhood as the time when the *blues,* or *blue devils,* first latched on to him. It's the same language that Abraham Lincoln used to describe his own depression.

It might even have made Gratz sadder, or more frustrated, that he felt this way in such a happy home. His father's political career is taking off and he's frequently away, but Gratz is surrounded by adoring women—a nurse, a doting grandmother, a loving aunt, in addition to a mother who may have felt at peace without a child but now is thrilled to have one. To Rebecca Miriam feels compelled to acknowledge his perfection: "My little darling is the picture of health. I wish I could just imprint his little form on this sheet for you, as I flatter myself you would admire him." Busy Solomon may only show up from time to time to play with the boy, but he too is smitten. Miriam wonders what her husband is going to do without his "doating piece" when they travel north to visit her family. In the spring of 1847, Miriam writes Rebecca that Gratz talks about what he intends to do in "'Philadelphia & at the North' as familiarly as if he had been there already."

In August of that year, three months shy of Gratz's third birthday, Miriam takes the steamer to New York with him and his year-old baby sister, miracle child number two, who's been experimenting with verticality, supporting herself on furniture as she goes. Solomon is too busy to leave town. Miriam shows Gratz and Belle the sights, including taking them for a walk around the naval yard in Brooklyn. Rebecca meets them and the family goes down to Philadelphia together.

After one look at her great-nephew, Rebecca falls, hard. In her home Gratz charms servants and relatives alike, and he's the subject of conversation for months afterward. Rebecca longs for him when he's gone, cherishes his "innocent prattle," begs Miriam for cute anecdotes. Gratz sends kisses, pressing his lips to the edges of his mother's letters. Miriam circles the spot and identifies it as "Gratz's kiss for Aunt Becky." In letters it's delightful to watch Rebecca, who so often takes a pedagogical tone, be reduced to simple adoration. Solomon sends her a package of grits, for which Rebecca thanks him and remarks: "I'll think of little Gratz who enjoys it so much. Tell Gratz his kiss came very safely and was very sweet."

From the start he's the focus of everyone's affection and hopes. He's brilliant and beautiful, precociously verbal, sweet as pie. One of those kids who are more comfortable around adults than other children, a perfect little companion. Miriam and Solomon are proud of their golden boy—as long as he acts like a boy.

Shortly after returning from that visit north, Miriam takes Gratz out of his dress. Boys and girls of the era were kept in similar dresses until the age of five or six. But Gratz still hasn't turned three. Rebecca has only seen him in a dress, which she found too becoming to change. Besides, dresses are far more comfortable than pants, she informs her niece, providing for ease of movement and freedom for the limbs. And Rebecca believes the change of costume makes boys grow up too soon. Once he puts on his first pair of trousers, a boy feels he's become a man, a delusion that seems to be just what Solomon and Miriam are hoping for.

Poor Gratz—his folks try to butch him up at the age of three. But it doesn't seem to have worked. Gratz in short pants is as sensitive as he was in a dress. Victorian men, especially unmarried ones, had much more license than guys today to be emotional; they could read or even write poetry without having their masculinity questioned. You'd think a little boy could catch a break. But Gratz's sensitivity alarms his parents. Well, I imagine it upset Solomon and by extension his wife, who later wrote Rebecca seeking advice about an incident that demonstrated the gender trouble they'd been sensing. Rebecca's reply to Miriam sought to put into perspective her niece's genuine concern that her four-and-a-half-year-old son . . . cried at the death of a bird.

Maybe he didn't just cry. Maybe he was inconsolable. He must have seemed too old to be crying in the first place. By this point the family had moved into their new home on Liberty Street, and I imagine Gratz going out into the garden one morning and seeing the dead bird lying on the brick paving.

By the time Solomon returns from work the bird has been disposed of and his son's tears dried. But Miriam gives him an accounting. His home is the one place in the world where Solomon feels he doesn't have to perform, and he allows his stern closed face to relax and register concern. Miriam turns to the mentor who raised her and guided the instruction for countless other children, and Rebecca replies, once again, as the voice of reason: "We must try to regulate dear Gratz's sensibility without hurting those feelings so promising of future good. When rightly directed & under proper control, the child who weeps at the death of a bird will be kinder of animals and benevolent from natural impulses, which you will know how to cultivate." Benevolence and kindness—these were among the qualities that made Rebecca fall in love with her great-nephew. She wasn't about to discourage them.

5

Braving the Boomtown

The house that Gratz grew up in is a few doors down from mine, on the corner of Liberty and Barnard. It's now a gorgeously restored bed-and-breakfast called the Stephen Williams House, with a hair salon on the ground floor. The working-class bar on the ground floor that my grandpa frequented is long gone, along with every other trace of the working class in downtown Savannah. I've passed the inn now dozens of times. I've even walked up to the front door but, finding it locked, gone away. There is no buzzer or bell, and knocking gets no response.

Solomon Cohen bought the place from Williams in 1840, for $5,000. It's a big Federal-era house, with a square of porch and a Doric-columned overhang on the parlor floor and two pedimented dormer windows peeking out of the gabled roof, the building's western side shaded by a great live oak. The top two floors are made of clapboard painted grey, while the bottom is brick stuccoed over and scored to look like stone, like my townhouse. The entire yard behind the house, where a brick carriage house (possibly including slave quarters) once stood in its northwest corner, is now a lovely garden paved in limestone, with a lion's head spouting water into a tiny pool afloat with lily pads and enclosed in grey brick. Various plants, including some topiary, rise from pots and raised beds, but there's no trace of the huge camellia bush, with its dozens of crimson-hearted blooms, that thrived when the Solomon Cohen family lived here. There's a bit of garden statuary, a table and chairs, a bench in a little bower off to the side. The yard is walled but it's an inviting wall, covered in vines and crowned by lanterns, and the gates are open during the day.

I've wandered in a couple of times admiring it all, remembering that *paradise* comes from the Persian for "walled garden." Today I walk through the open gate, but instead of milling around I cross the garden and take the steps up to the porch, a recent addition stretching the width

43

of the building on the parlor floor. There's comfy furniture, fans turning lazily overhead. I go to the back door—and open it.

The first thing I notice is that the back parlor of Gratz's house, now a music room, does not contain mismatched furniture and a wild assortment of art, as our parlor down the block does. Everything I see is an antique, a period piece, though Gratz never laid eyes on any of it. The furnishings aren't original, but this is the house decorated in the exotic Empire style that was still popular when Solomon and Miriam Cohen first lived here. I move deeper into the house, passing under an arched opening that leads from the back parlor to its mirror image in the front, also full of antiques. There's a portrait of some aristocrat over the mantel, which is decorated with a pair of Chinese blue-and-white porcelain statues bracketing a pair of gilded Greek-style urns, and an assortment of luxuriously upholstered chairs on an Oriental rug, and a bench covered in a leopard-skin pattern, and amid this colorful jumble, on the far side of the fireplace, is a small gentleman who says, "Hello. May I help you?"

This is Dr. Albert Wall, the proprietor of the inn, whom I've luckily caught between cooking breakfasts from historic recipes for his guests and piloting his boat. I tell him I bought an apartment in the Solomon Cohen townhouse down the street, and that seems enough to identify the place for him. I want to see the room where Gratz grew up but he tells me the guest rooms upstairs are currently occupied. We move into the front hall and talk a bit about the house. When you use Google Earth to view it from above, the house appears to be conjoined twins, its gabled roof doubled at the front and back of the house. The tax records show that in 1851 Solomon made improvements that nearly tripled his home's value, and I speculate that this was when he doubled its size to accommodate the three children he must have thought he'd never have. Dr. Wall and I are standing in front of a stairway like none I've ever seen. The stairs begin at the back of the parlor floor, and every railed landing, as the staircase turns, is visible from below and above. The stairs seem to rise into light. Dr. Wall points out that the risers are twinned, like the front and back rooms of the house, though one set of risers is slightly higher than the other. "Well, we've beat this dead horse long enough," he suddenly announces when I inquire about the steepness of the steps, and it occurs to me that I'm standing exactly where Gratz must have stood as a six-year-old as he prepared to go for a walk that

Solomon mentions in a letter, and I start to feel as the boy must have, a little desolate, already gone.

By the time I step inside the Stephen Williams House, I've been research-ing the Solomon Cohen family for months. Miriam has an archive in the Southern Historical Collection at the University of North Carolina, Chapel Hill, and I spent a chilly fall weekend there, in a poorly heated cottage near campus with a door that didn't lock. The reference librarian told me that the collection had been digitized, and so I could have scanned it from the comfort of my home. A novice's mistake that left me feeling foolish, but only for a moment. A cache of Gratz's letters is stored there, and though I would later study them online, I was glad to be able to hold the brittle pages in my hands, observe the variety of paper stock, and feel a direct connec-tion to their author. Most of these letters were written during the war, on whatever paper Gratz had at hand.

Rebecca Gratz's archive is in Philadelphia, but from home I sift through digitized versions of those letters for any nugget about Gratz. I find letters from Miriam and different sorts of writing for Solomon than the busi-ness correspondence in the Georgia Historical Society. The occasional letter—or few words scribbled in the margins of Miriam's writing paper— that Solomon wrote Rebecca shows a face other than the one he displayed to the world, a more sensitive side, though one he reveals only grudgingly, even to his own family.

It's in one of these letters that I learn Solomon has a policy not to talk about his own children. A strange sort of rule, and one he breaks to kvell a bit about six-year-old Gratz, and what stokes the father's pride is his son's courage in venturing out on his own through the rough-and-tumble city. It's a little anecdote I can't shake, for it seems to hold the key to their rela-tionship, and one I might be able to use to unlock the mystery of Gratz's life and death.

And so I put together what pieces I have and imagine what that day would have looked like for Gratz Cohen.

Saturday, spring 1851. A six-year-old boy stands on the wide heart-pine boards in the foyer of his house, preparing to leave. He's small for his age and looks even smaller against the tall, broad door, its arched fanlight stretching to cover the six-pane sidelights as well. Light presses in, illuminating the books in glass-doored cases under the stairs, just a few of the hundreds of volumes the house is stuffed with. Gratz's home is full of people—sisters, parents, cousins, aunt, grandmother, Irish servants and Black ones—but you'd never know it. At that hour, midafternoon on a warm weekend, the house itself seems to be asleep, just as baby Mamie, his new sister, must be, and he can hear over the silence the tick of the clock, the click of his mother's knitting needles, and the flap of his father's newspaper turning. His parents are in the parlor to his left, seated on either side of the fireplace, each engrossed in their respective activity.

Solomon and Miriam *idolize* the boy, Samuel Yates Levy will write fifteen years later. Certainly each parent creates him in his or her own image, the way the ancients imagined their gods, as divine versions of themselves. For Miriam, Gratz is the epitome of kindness, tenderness, love. For Solomon, he's courageous, manly. Each sees evidence in the boy to support his or her version of him. But Solomon can imagine what Miriam cannot: a version of the boy that isn't perfect. This is because of the word that nearly everyone uses to describe him: *gentle.* The bird: two years later Solomon can still picture the scene—the dead creature he himself never saw, the disconsolate boy he unfortunately did. And this *gentle* Gratz, when Solomon allows himself disgustedly to think it, is so intolerable that it scarcely takes form in his head before he wants to throw it to the ground, destroy it as Moses did the golden calf, that false god.

To Rebecca, Solomon will explain why he lets his six-year-old child explore the boomtown's roughest neighborhoods on his own. Such adventures confirm to him that his oversensitive boy has toughened up. "I do not check him," Solomon breezily writes, because he would "rather love his memory" than that the boy have "one drop of coward blood in his veins."

Gratz is always setting out, leaving home again and again, trying to prove exactly what his father feels he must already possess: courage. But first, a little show in the front hall of the great house. An obedient boy, he won't simply sneak out. He's seeking his parents' permission, though perhaps he secretly he hopes they won't give it.

I am leaving, Gratz announces, his voice loud against the muffled sounds of the house.

Oh? asks his father, looking over his newspaper. *And where to, may I ask?*

To the river.

But you are too young, says Solomon, *and that is too far away.*

I am not a baby now, Gratz insists. *I have already shed my teeth.*

His parents laugh and Miriam sets down her knitting and stands. *Why must you go so far, darling?* she asks.

Because I must, he answers his mother plainly.

This is the season when the thriving city is bursting with dock workers, and public drunkenness and rowdiness, even in broad daylight, is a scourge Miriam reads about in the papers and has seen her share of herself, reaching even into her own respectable neighborhood. But before she can say anything more, her husband has said, *Then go you must.* And so now it is too late for Miriam to speak, and Gratz comes over and kisses her goodbye.

Thirty years earlier, when Solomon still lived in Georgetown and Miriam in Philadelphia, Liberty Street was Savannah's southernmost limit. Beyond it was the city commons, which corresponded to the farm district that Georgia founder James Oglethorpe envisioned in his regional plan, of which the town of Savannah was but a single, small piece. Oglethorpe imagined a New World colony, rooted in English agrarian values, that was free of the urban ills, real and imagined, of London at the time. In elementary school I was taught that Savannah was the only city in the country that stuck to its original plan, and the evidence on the ground seemed to confirm it, though never having traveled, I had to take it on faith that my hometown was unique in this regard. Once a portion of pine forest was cleared from the bluff—in the famous engraving *A View of Savannah as It Stood the 29th of March 1734*, the woods around the year-old settlement stretch toward infinity—Oglethorpe stamped his obsessive grid onto the flat land, and by the time Gratz opens his front door 117 years later, the pattern has been extended east, west, and south, and what he sees is simply the other side of his residential street.

With all the improvements to their home, the year 1851 was a significant one for the Cohen family. It was also a big year for Savannah. The ward pattern was extended for the final time, with Troup Square, today one of the loveliest, laid out just below Liberty though well to the east of Solomon's house. But Oglethorpe never intended the squares to multiply beyond the original six, however irresistible it is to imagine the founder's modular ward system extended ad infinitum, as far south of the river as the eye can see. Oglethorpe's original plan for Savannah comprised six wards around six squares, with "trust lots" on the east and west sides of each square and "tything lots" of identical size to the north and south. The tything lots were intended for a house and a garden in back, while trust lots were meant for public uses like churches and markets. The city plan largely endured, but the ideals it reflected were abandoned within a couple decades of the colony's founding. Private houses went up on the trust lots, prime real estate with a larger footprint than the residential lots, and as the town expanded into land designated for villages and farms, Oglethorpe's mix of residential, commercial, and civic structures gave way to purely residential wards populated by wealthy families seeking to insulate themselves from the sounds and smells of commerce.

The lots to the east and west of the town were designated in the original plan as "garden," but in the last decades of the eighteenth century, free men of color lived in hastily built wooden houses in the garden lots to the east. I learn from Thomas D. Wilson's wonderful monograph *The Oglethorpe Plan* that in the 1840s, two wards were laid out in this area in a conventional grid "to accommodate African American railroad worker housing." The cheap worker housing that sprang up on the swampy west side of town similarly dispensed with such niceties as squares. These neighborhoods clearly violated Oglethorpe's plan, but even those wards laid out more or less as he intended no longer worked the way he'd hoped, with, as Wilson puts it, "spatial equality as a foundation for social and economic equality."

However intended they were for markets and military encampments, the squares were always symbols of the rural nature of the colony as a whole. The wards they anchored were the materialization of an ideal, of equal ownership and common purpose, the town's physical layout forcing you into contact with your neighbors, each ward not just a neighborhood but a collective, with shared responsibilities and duties. The interlocking wards formed a place where no one would get rich but nor would anyone be poor, and all men were free. But that was a long time ago. The profit-driven Savannah of 1851 has its own imperative, to house the wharf workers and railroad workers and merchants and professional men that the city requires in increasing numbers. When six-year-old Gratz steps out into the hot bright world, the town designed for communion and cooperation among neighbors has become a city of strangers. And most everything is for sale.

And so he sets off—*cheerfully*, his father will later observe. But Gratz isn't cheerful. He doesn't have the words for it yet, but he feels people shouldn't burden others with their problems. It's a matter of duty, a human obligation. Sorrows are secrets you confide to your journal, as Gratz will come to do, and to your horse as you're galloping so fast that no one could possibly overhear you. There is nothing he loves more than home and the people in it, especially the women—and yet he is always leaving it and will continue to do so his entire life. For now, six-year-old Gratz smiles and his father finds him cheerful.

He told his parents his destination but not his route. They didn't ask, perhaps assuming he'd take the most direct way to the river and, despite leaving by the south-facing front door, head due north, passing what's now called the Harper Fowlkes House, with its four great columns and lotus-leaf capitals, a temple of a house that makes his own home look modest, then through one square after another, each with mansions around it. But instead Gratz heads west down Liberty Street, toward the railyard.

Truthfully, it doesn't matter where he goes. Simply moving through the world by himself makes him feel better, if only because it distracts him from his cares. But he's found that the busier the neighborhood, the better he feels. When he reaches West Broad, the railyard that begins across the street fills his head, the screen to which his thoughts stubbornly cling is covered, for a while, by the sights and sounds of the world, allowing him, blissfully, not to think at all.

Here is the terminus of the Central Rail Road, its other end in Macon, with connections to Atlanta and beyond. Savannah is the final continental stop for the fruits of the interior. The cotton and lumber that will be processed and stored in the warehouses along the river before being loaded onto waiting ships, the brokers and merchants who trade in these commodities, and increasingly pleasure-seekers lured by the city's leafy charms and ocean air, all of these the trains bring.

A great labor has begun here, on the other side of the street, where the bones of the men who fought the Revolutionary Battle of Savannah are being exhumed, and the marsh, unquiet with frogs and source of the bad air that seasonally sickens the Forest City and contributes to its dangerous reputation, is being drained. The railroad company is building a freight yard and two new terminals, and a repair shop with a great brick smokestack and a turntable where a locomotive on its track can be redirected into any of forty bays in a wondrous roundhouse, all of it starting to rise before Gratz's eyes.

He steps out onto West Broad, which seems huge to him, waiting for a break in the steady rattly traffic of carts and carriages and wagons and groups of men on foot to make his way across the wide plank road, the only non–dirt road in town, connecting the railroad station with the wharves and warehouses and processing plants a few blocks north. Nobody seems to cross this road but him, everyone is going toward the river or coming back from it. And yet nobody so much as looks at him as he reaches the other side, walks into the brick building with the pointy pediments and arched windows facing West Broad, and moves on to the long chains of cars behind locomotives hissing steam, bearing the big dirty oblong things you wouldn't recognize as bales of cotton save for the few flashing puffs of white trying to pull free.

This little delicate-featured white boy isn't where he's supposed to be and has no role in any of the human transactions around him. No one knows he's the son of the cashier of the Central Rail Road and Banking Company of Georgia. Solomon oversees investment in the railroad, in all the activity that Gratz finds himself in the middle of, and pays out its accelerating profits, in addition to serving as a director of the board in a time of physical expansion.

Gratz heads north on West Broad, sticking to the western edge of the street, passing the railroad's huge brick freight department, getting now into the working-class neighborhoods. The sun raises sweat on Gratz's forehead. Railroad and foundry workers and longshoremen and draymen and artisans, white and Black, free and enslaved—here to the west of the city center the working class of the city live in low-slung unpainted wooden rows and boarding houses, balconies drooping overhead as if about to tip into the street.

As Gratz approaches Yamacraw, site of the Native settlement on the bluff when Oglethorpe arrived and now a mix of mansions and worker housing, the streets seem to fill with people. He's almost at the edge of the bluff, with its warehouses and rice mills and tanneries, its steam-powered cotton presses to compress the ragged bales into tight blocks, as well as the brothels of Indian Street. Gratz's perennial sadness is chased away by the world rushing around him, everything, he marvels, about to collide though nothing ever does. People, carts, carriages, and now, descending the cobblestone ramp to the river, he sees the boats jostling one another where they're tied up at the wharf, their masts a forest stripped of leaves. A hot breeze blows across the water from the South Carolina marsh, bleached by the afternoon sun, and the blankness of the background brings into relief the activity in the foreground, just as the sound of the wind over the slow-flowing river creates a sort of vacuum into which the human sounds rush. Clatter of hooves and wheels on cobblestone, song of men loading bales of cotton and casks of rice, shouts from no apparent direction, thud and crack and sough and creak of maritime trade, and suddenly the shriek of gulls descending en masse out of nowhere to alight onto a spill of grain, the birds clearing a place for themselves in a scene where Gratz himself can see no path forward.

The narrow street stretching out before him is so thick with drays as to completely obscure the cobblestones. And yet the conveyances manage to pass each other, their drivers possessed of an aggressiveness and fearlessness which Gratz himself must summon simply to move forward. It occurs to him that if he were heedless and simply plunged in without looking, he would be struck almost instantly—and the offending cart would keep going, the river of commerce closing in around him. For everything is in motion around him, as if this were the real fear, to stop. And so he takes a deep breath, brave swallow of pine and dung, and forces himself to smile, so as not to be seen as a helpless child, an object of pity, and he walks, sticking to the shadows of the ground floors of the buildings rising above the Bay, where his father and uncle Octavus work. The stone and brick sides of the dark forbidding buildings are rough against his jacket and under his palms as he brushes up against them.

On the wharf Black and white men work side by side, powerful and beautiful as gods in myths, loading cotton, rice, and lumber as well as sundries such as tallow, beeswax, and copper ore onto the boats. The crates they're unloading contain the goodies demanded by Gratz's family and the rest of the town's upper class—cherry brandy, port wine, lemon syrup, walnut oil, claret, champagne, Cuban cigars, Malaga figs, embroidered Swiss robes, silk hose, pianofortes, and books of poetry and chivalric tales—as well as mundane food staples and building and farm supplies. And people too—the boats have brought passengers, who must make their way through the commotion as Gratz does, though always when they disembark they stop and look around, trying not to appear lost. People of all shades, from deepest black to pale white, move with determination around him. The differences in legal status among Black people are unknown to him, the various badges they're forced to wear signifiers from a language Gratz doesn't yet speak, though it's one he lives and breathes at home as out in the world.

As the sun falls somewhere behind him, Gratz turns off River Street and walks up the steep ramp, the dark lanes on either side stacked with cotton, and heads toward home and his family—suddenly he misses them so! It saddens him to think he might have caused them even a moment's worry, and he picks up his pace, though his legs and feet ache.

He passes through Reynolds Square, then crosses Broughton, the town's main commercial street, before reaching Oglethorpe Square, where the smell of chinaberry sweetens the air. Just as the squares and the grid of streets organize the city, there is an order to the world and everyone has a place in it. This is what he has seen today. Despite the apparent chaos of the railyards and the wharf and the roads connecting them, there is a method to it all, though one naturally he cannot yet know. But that it exists he is sure. Rich or poor, Black or white, everyone has a part to play in the great machinery of the city. Everyone, that is, but Gratz himself, who is in the way, superfluous to the workings of the world, a passive observer and nothing more, though he takes comfort in the belief that one day he too will have some part to play, whatever it may be.

Ebony Idol

Gratz comes home to a boy around the same age, his best friend, who also lives in the Cohen household. But the 1850 census doesn't name the other boy, because he is enslaved. I don't know whose child Louis was or where his people came from or much beyond the fact that the two boys grew up together. These kinds of arrangements weren't all that uncommon in wealthy families in the pre–Civil War South: two children play together and at a certain point one exercises his authority over the other. Some of these relationships continued into adulthood, even outlasting the war.

"The servants"—this is how Gratz's letters home, a decade later, refer to the people who worked in his parents' home. He usually closes by sending "the servants" greetings. But Louis, by then no longer a playmate, he refers to either by name or as "my valet." Louis would likely have slept in Gratz's room, on a pallet kept during the day under the bed, a high one so that its occupant could catch a river breeze in the warmer months. Louis's duties would have included lighting the morning fire, drawing Gratz's bath, setting out his clothes, getting him into them, and whatever else he was ordered to do. The two photographs I find of an adolescent Gratz portray him as a well-groomed dandy, suggesting that Louis had his work cut out for him.

When Gratz was writing for himself, in the journal he would keep in Virginia, he drew on an astoundingly varied set of pet names for Louis: *Ebony Idol, my Sancho Pansa, Lil Black, Geni fairy, my elf* . . . Was Louis shorter than Gratz? Younger? Solomon's 1850 United States Federal Census slave schedule includes a four-year-old and a six-year-old enslaved male, both of whose color is denoted as "B," for "black." A decade later, Solomon's enslaved workers include a "black" fourteen-year-old and sixteen-year-old. Either of these could be the Louis who appears in Gratz's most intimate poetry and prose. A Louis a bit younger than Gratz, who turned sixteen in November 1860, might explain, beyond racism, why Gratz appeared to infantilize his valet.

But another series of pet names shows that Gratz thought of Louis as something more essential, the other half of a whole: *Shadow, second self, half my self*... I wonder what Gratz called Louis to his face when no one else was around and how Louis felt about it. This was a relationship that took a certain denial and led Gratz to flights of fancy. But for him, at least, it was undeniably real.

The intensity of Gratz's feelings for Louis was something Miriam either didn't notice or didn't find necessary to comment on. As far as she was concerned, her son's soulmate was his sister Belle, a look-alike of Gratz's but with dark hair that hung in sausage curls alongside her face. Miriam describes the pair as constant companions and confidants, accounting for their intimacy by their closeness in age, just a year and a half apart. They were still sleeping together when Gratz was twelve, and I imagine them as loving twins, curled in each other's arms, though judging by the visual record, Belle matures faster than Gratz and looks much older.

The siblings grow up in the squares, playing in them nearly year round, supplied with picnics of apples and cakes. Orleans Square, named for the 1815 Battle of New Orleans, is on Barnard Street just north of the house. Pulaski Square, to the south, was named after the Revolutionary War hero Casimir Pulaski. More centrally located, to the northeast, is Chippewa Square, commemorating the Battle of Chippewa in the War of 1812.

It surprises me to realize that the busy utilitarian squares would have been more welcoming places to kids than the manicured plazas they are today. It was only in the early 1850s, when Savannah's budget was finally recovering from years of recession, that the City Council began reconsidering how to beautify the squares. From their start as community gathering places and military training grounds, the squares had been more about common purpose than leisure. In 1850 they were pretty enough, carpeted in emerald lawns, but picturesqueness was not their point, as it is today. The squares contained water pumps and cisterns and engine houses, and most were free of monuments (however they commemorated some battle or great man) and open to the sky. Gratz and Belle would have found ample space to picnic and run and play.

Gratz would have been around seven when the transformations began, one square at a time. The sandy walks were paved with gravel, elegant benches put in, the squares themselves graded and fenced in by iron railings, their entrances enlarged to accommodate the passage of the newly popular hoopskirt. Water coursed through underground pipes and spouted from the mouths of cast iron nymphs. The strange ugly engine houses, in appearance the dwelling of a witch, relocated. The chinaberry trees, judged unsatisfactory, removed and new varieties of trees added: oak, magnolia, crepe myrtle. The city was falling in love with the squares, and with itself. For this was what a city that could afford it did—make pleasurable spaces for its citizens. But for Gratz and Belle, the squares had always been enchanted places.

An idyll—this is how Miriam portrays Gratz's childhood. In the spring of 1856, when Gratz was eleven and Belle almost ten, the Sunday school pre-Passover examination was such a success that the parents put on a picnic for the children and their teachers. Miriam describes it in a letter to Rebecca: "We made out early in the day to a beautiful shady retreat about a mile from the city. There was music & the children danced & gathered wild flowers & sang, and exercise gave them fine appetites to due [sic] justice to a well spread table under the shade of some fine old oaks hung in festoons with the heavy moss which forms a peculiar feature of our woods. . . . I wish you could have heard Belle recite her piece of German Poetry, & Gratz sing a German song."

The picnic had been organized by a "German" and was attended by more "Germans" than "Portuguese" Jews, reflecting demographic changes to Savannah's Jewish population. The fundraising work that Miriam began more than a decade earlier finally paid off—Mickve Israel had its first full-time *hazzan*, a Prussian immigrant named Jacob Rosenfeld, as well as a newly refurbished sanctuary. The Sunday school had grown; it was no longer in Miriam's home and she was now the president.

Sentimental details such as the ones Miriam reported weren't to Solomon's taste, though he was a teacher at the school and could easily have observed them for himself. What he reports, on the rare occasions when he writes about his family, adds up to another version of Gratz's childhood: a boy growing into a brave young man.

Today Savannah is known for its St. Patrick's Day festivities, but in the mid-nineteenth century there were far more excuses for parades, the Battle of New Orleans and May Day among them, and they had a more openly martial bent. Georgia was originally of strategic importance as a buffer between the Spanish in Florida and the older English colonies to the north, and a bloody Revolutionary War battle, a victory for the British, had been fought here. The need to defend itself was built into the isolated city's psyche, though by the time Gratz was a kid, the town's dozen volunteer militias, with colorful names such as the Phoenix Riflemen, the Irish Jasper Greens, the German Volunteers, and the Savannah Grays, spent more time parading along the Bay and up and down Bull Street than defending the city. They were handsomely uniformed, these men, and they marched to the patriotic tunes played by enslaved musicians.

Gratz became smitten by these spectacles. He and his friends outfitted themselves in whatever clothes their mothers and servants could provide and in these motley uniforms marched through the streets. Little legs trudging through sand, heads under mismatched caps as the sun bore down through the double rows of water oak and chinaberry trees. What did all this mean to Gratz Cohen? Costumes? Play? A way to connect with other boys? In a letter to Rebecca, Solomon described his son's ragtag infantry with amusement, but he also sounded proud of his son the boy soldier.

The solitary walks, the marches with the neighborhood boys, the traipsing to picnic spots beyond the city limits—it was a childhood spent in motion. And then it came to an end. Whether abruptly or gradually is unknown, but it's when Gratz is thirteen that we first start hearing of the troubles with his feet. I don't have Miriam's letters in which she first talks about these problems, but Rebecca is relieved to hear the family has found a solution. "I was rejoiced to receive your letter as I felt some anxiety about your son Gratz's feet, of which I heard something, without knowing whether he was suffering from accident or disease."

Walking becomes painful for Gratz, so too standing for long periods of time, and he begins to wear a pair of orthopedic boots. Lord Byron, whose writing Miriam loved and Gratz would adapt in his own poetry, was born with a deformed right foot and wore a shoe with a metal leg brace and a strap tied around his shin. Pictures of these sorts of boots are frightening, the way they caged the leg in leather and metal. That iron rod running up his leg must have prevented Gratz from bending his legs normally, causing him to move, and feel, like an automaton. No wonder he finds them "inconvenient," these hideous things. However the distance between himself and the other children has narrowed over the years, it gapes now once again. The blues seize and hold him more tightly than before. But to the world he shows a brave face.

A podiatrist friend of mine, when asked for a diagnosis, suggests club foot. But with this condition Gratz wouldn't even have gotten as far as he did, figuratively and literally, in the army. And it would have been evident at birth, with attempts to correct it much sooner than adolescence. There would have been no question of whether the source of his foot troubles was "accident or disease." My friend's thoughts run to congenital pes planovalgus—flat feet—or tibialis posterior dysfunction, the same condition acquired from physical activity and usually affecting a single foot. But as a former Marine doctor, my friend discharged people for the condition and doesn't see how Gratz could ever have had a military career.

Well, he shouldn't have.

A diagnosis of flat feet is also consistent with the claim, in the *University Memorial* sketch, that Gratz had "'deep-seated inflammation in the ligatures of both feet,'" especially if you replace the word "ligatures" with "ligaments." The ligaments and tendons of the feet stretch so tightly that the arch drops. An orthopedic boot could have been a treatment for flat feet caused by some trauma. But in Gratz's case, the condition seems to have gotten progressively worse, and soon the only solution was to be off his feet entirely, in bed, say, or on a horse. The torturing pains that Gratz experienced from standing for too long or even from moderate walks were certainly possible symptoms of flat feet.

I don't know if this diagnosis helps me understand Gratz any better, but I think I'm a little closer to feeling what he felt.

Soon after these letters about Gratz's foot problems comes the first word of his writing. This can't be a coincidence. He gets used to the boots but his mobility is limited. With long walks no longer possible, Gratz, always a big reader, now finds the freedom to go wherever he wants with his pen. He surprises Miriam on her forty-ninth birthday with a "sweet Tale," which cheers her up, for she woke that morning "with an appropriate feeling of sadness!"

The literary theme that Gratz would pursue in his college years—the ravages of time—worries him even as a child. Here's Rebecca's assessment of a poem that Miriam sends her: "Your Dear Gratz's easy, smooth versification is beautiful he shows a decided literary taste and excellent feeling, in defending the much abused state 'of single blessedness.' Old maids are generally in young folk's way & are rarely reminded of the charms that have passed away. Perhaps Gratz meant to warn some favorite belle of the danger involved by young beauties, if they permit the 'Roses fade upon their cheeks.'" What a wonderful teacher Rebecca Gratz must have been, to take this boy's poem so seriously. But you don't need to imagine a girlfriend for Gratz, as Rebecca does, to understand why he'd choose this subject. Gratz lives in a houseful of mature women, including his mother, who's much older than his friends' moms. Gratz might be writing, as Rebecca suggests, to warn some pretty girl not to let herself go, for fear of inviting competition from other women. But having read his later poems on the subject, I imagine the same feeling motivated this one: the fear of losing to time the beloved mother figures in his life.

And Gratz has found another way to fly: on his horse, named, naturally, Belle. He tries to dismiss his sorrows as petty but still feels the need to unburden himself of them, and Belle proves the ideal confidante.

Gratz reveals this years later, in a letter from Virginia urging his father not to sell his horse. He doesn't specify his sorrows to Solomon, though he'd later write, "I remember bright summer days in my earliest youth, when the sense of existence was so oppressing & there was no comfort, for I could not seek relief from what I knew not how to explain." Gratz's existential woes, though he partially discloses them to an aunt, remain private, perhaps even to himself, for he has no words to describe them.

I picture this young man riding through the pinewoods around Savannah, or along the river bluff, the path sloping down from the city center, trees giving way to marsh as the salt air streams across his fine features and tosses his wavy hair about, riding so fast as he approaches the edge of the continent you'd think he's preparing to spring off the packed sand

and astride his Pegasus leap across the ocean to the Old World, whose languages and manners he already knows but upon whose soil he has never set foot.

No, Belle is less Pegasus than the equine half of a centaur, whose story Gratz has learned as myth but knows now as truth.

As their little center of civilization recedes behind them, Gratz speaks, his voice a whisper as Belle picks her way across swampy spots, Gratz feeling her haunches relax with each word. And now hear him roar against the wind as she finds firm ground and gallops, his voice the medium through which his being flows into hers, and together this fused creature moves majestically through the world, conferring meaning on the landscape simply by passing through it. The horse hears only the voice, the shapes of the words, the emotion with which they are expressed, but still the rider feels understood, consoled. Sympathized with. And he knows his confidences will be kept.

PART II
The Center Cannot Hold

7

A Man of Many Hats

I lose Gratz's trace in the 1850s, the years when he's growing up and becoming himself. The little boy braving the boomtown on his own will reemerge from his quiet years of study as an adolescent, but on a political stage to some extent set by his father. And Solomon, during this decade, is all over the place. For health reasons that remain unclear—neuralgia comes up in letters, weeks at a sulfur springs resort help—he retires from practicing law and turns his energy toward other pursuits. As cashier of the Central Rail Road and Banking Company of Georgia, he's working bankers hours, which allow him a walk or ride with Miriam every afternoon, much to her relief, having spent so much of their marriage alone. Solomon continues to buy land, paying taxes on $21,500 worth of real estate in 1852, $22,400 in 1853, and $29,300 the following year. With rental property occupancy rates approaching 100 percent, real estate is a good business. Solomon also owns a lot of railroad stock, which climbs during the 1850s.

The built environment of the town is soaring too. Tens of thousands of bricks go into the new railroad complex as well as an office building for the railroad bank. Elegant stores with stone and iron fronts go in on Broughton, the main shopping street. There's a big new hotel. The US Custom House, a granite temple with carved lotus leaves curling from the capitals of its columns, rises on the Bay. Solomon's Liberty Street house, once at the town's southern border, becomes more centrally located by the day, as Savannah pushes inexorably away from the river. Massive private homes with fanciful wrought iron screens and railings and gates, such as cotton merchant Charles Green's Gothic Revival mansion (now the Green-Meldrim house), go up on lots facing the squares, the ones that were designated for public buildings in the original city plan.

The most populous city in Georgia, a top port—but Savannah seems like a set of unresolved contradictions. The planned city ne plus ultra is growing so fast that it's bursting out of its seams. Oglethorpe's interplay of streets and squares is still stamped upon the center. But just to the east and west, urban planning drops away entirely, in a warren of dark alleys and firetrap wooden buildings. These are neighborhoods where public decency laws are enforced only in intermittent periods of reform, for the Irish laborers and saloonkeepers are kept with carrots in the Democratic fold and Black people are sometimes allowed their small measure of resistance, like smoking in public and breaking curfew, to forestall any greater show of it. The good life of the city center couldn't exist without the slums to the east and west and the city leaders know it, so a tenuous balance takes hold and remains throughout the 1850s. No matter the neighborhood, Savannah is a rowdy place—and menacing by night.

And the city of possibilities that Solomon and Miriam first knew is full of people too dull to seize them. Although he's known today as the father of American landscape architecture, Frederick Law Olmsted was also a well-known journalist and travel writer, and he found the biggest threat to the Forest City's continued viability as a commercial center to be "the dead weight of a numerous unproductive class of exceedingly ignorant, unambitious indolent people." No-account whites were a constant in travelers' disparate observations. Visiting during wartime, some ten years after Olmsted, Sir William Howard Russell, then a *Times* of London reporter, wrote, in *My Diary North and South*:

> It had the deepest sand in the streets I had ever seen; and next, the streets were composed of the most odd, quaint, green-windowed, many-colored little houses I ever beheld, with an odd population of lean, sallow, ill-dressed unwholesome-looking whites, lounging about the exchanges and corners, and a busy, well-clad, gayly-attired race of negroes, working their way through piles of children, under the shade of the trees which bordered all the streets. The fringe of green, and the height attained by the live-oak, Pride of India, and magnolia, give a delicious freshness and novelty to the streets of Savannah . . . It is difficult to believe you are in the midst of a city.

An urban center that felt rural, elegant homes on dirt streets—as with the blind men and the elephant, it was hard to grasp just what kind of place this was.

So too Solomon Cohen. He did such a variety of things that you could forgive the twentieth-century academic who identified him as a book publisher. It's true he was responsible for getting Grace Aguilar's work published in the South. But this was just freelancing. He was more typically a lawyer, politician, banker, board member, synagogue president, real estate developer, landlord, businessman. . . . He wore so many hats that he himself, in letter after letter, feels the need to clarify to his correspondent in just which capacity he happens to be, in that moment, writing. For example, in a letter to the rabbi of Charleston's Beth Elohim about indigent Jews, he explains that he writes not as a synagogue president but rather as a concerned citizen.

Concerned citizen—I think that's the capacity in which Solomon is usually writing, whether or not he expresses it, like a yarmulke beneath whatever hat he happens to put on. The 1850s was Savannah's catch-up decade of institution building, and Solomon had a hand in most of them. These were the years when Savannah instituted such newfangled Yankee ideas as public education to deal with the indolent-whites problem; Solomon raised money for the establishment of the Massie School, the city's first free public school, for poor white children. (Black residents opened their own, secret schools.) The streets and squares were now bathed in that Victorian gaslamp glow that's so eerie to us now but was just considered beautiful back then, gilding the world with silvery light, and Miriam and Solomon introduced gas into eight rooms and the entry of their home. The neighborhoods to the east and west would remain dark until the next decade; nor would they benefit at first from the new waterworks that brought river water, though of dubious quality and taste, into the homes and establishments in the center. Drainage of the swamps abutting the town was improved, sewers made the streets more sanitary. All the new infrastructure was inadequate for a town growing so quickly, but by the end of the decade, Savannah had come a long way toward becoming a real city. A citizen leader of this settlement built on sand, this flowering of civilization based on slave labor, Solomon, no fool, knew how easily it could all go away.

It makes sense, then, that the 1850s is when, with steady jobs that keep him close to home, Solomon reenters the world of national politics. He was a delegate to the Democratic National Convention for the election of 1844, the year Gratz was born, and now, eight years later, he's been chosen as a delegate to the 1852 convention.

Solomon approaches politics like everything else—he does whatever it takes to win and seal the deal. And he reenters politics at a moment when it's going to take a consummate statesman to keep it all—the political parties, the Union itself—from falling apart. Solomon isn't that man. But he goes to great lengths to keep his own world together, the region where his immigrant grandfather was able to open a shop and found a synagogue, where his father became a mayor and bank director, the place where the men of his family finally claimed their rights to live as they saw fit. It's the South, not the Union, to which he feels allegiance.

The year 1850 wasn't just the start of the most consequential decade in Savannah's history. It was the date of the deal over slavery that drew the battle lines in national, state, and local politics for the decade. The Compromise of 1850, supported and signed by Whig president Millard Fillmore, had five provisions, including admitting California to the Union as a free state and what would become known as the Fugitive Slave Act, which was key to getting Southern support for the Compromise. The act made all federal officials, wherever they served, slavecatchers. Average people too could be pressed into duty by local officials; at the very least, every citizen of the United States was now bound by a sort of anti–Good Samaritan law. Legally civilians didn't have to capture a fugitive slave they happened to come upon, but if they aided him in any way, they were violating the law. Many Northerners of both parties, Whig and Democrat, were troubled by the Fugitive Slave Act, and many white Southerners were worried, from the moment it passed, that it would be repealed. Though it was an unequivocal victory for the region's business interests, it seemed to make white Southerners more defensive than ever.

The established political parties were falling apart, with new alliances around slavery superseding old ones around tariffs and everything else. In Georgia, the Democratic Party splintered into the Unionists, the name taken by Southerners who supported the Compromise as a way of preserving the Union, and the States Rights Democrats, led by none other than Solomon Cohen. There was no daylight between these two branches on the fugitive slave law, which is the part of the Compromise with which Solomon is most concerned. He isn't even especially pro-secession. But he doesn't trust the Unionists because they've allied themselves with disaffected Whigs. Solomon finds Whigs unreliable on "the slavery question" and fears their influence on his own, sounder Democratic Party.

At the Baltimore Democratic National Convention in the steamy month of June 1852, Solomon tries to persuade the rival Union delegates to cede their rights to his States Rights men as the true Georgia delegation. But as members of the dominant branch of the state's Democratic Party, the Union men rebuff him, naturally feeling they should represent the state at the convention. And so, as Solomon puts it, having "exhausted every effort at conciliation, my opponents had driven me to the only tribunal that could settle the matter and there I claimed all my rights." This was the convention's Committee on Credentials, which issued a report that was largely in Solomon's favor and that the Union delegation found insulting.

Solomon's behavior in Baltimore soon gets back to his home state. In a letter to Georgia governor Howell Cobb, a Union man, Solomon complained, "Ever since my return from Baltimore I've been hearing about my violent opposition to admission of Union delegates. I have heard them with silent contempt because it's my right to oppose them violently or moderately as I please." But in fact, Solomon insists, he wasn't opposed to the Union delegates at all. He was happy that they be admitted "once our rights were recognised." But the Unionists treated the States Rights delegation as "inferiors," and this was why Solomon finally had to appeal to the Committee on Credentials.

If Solomon, in the years after his arrival in Savannah, felt he owed something to the Christian establishment, at the very least gratitude for their "tender sympathy," he has by now become an insider, secure enough, as the leader of a political minority, to vocally assert his long-held principle of states rights. Comfortable enough to let his guard down—and be met with what he sees as hostility by his fellow Democrats. Solomon Cohen's paranoid style is prescient; it will soon dominate the South. But his feeling of being treated like an inferior, which must have been confirmed when his very name was slandered back home, is very much his own. On the questions of importance to his homeland, the South, he is finding that he still has to prove himself sound.

At the convention Solomon pushes for planks in the platform to "unite the South," something more emphatic and rousing than an expression of support for the Compromise, and judging from the final set of resolutions, articles of faith to him one and all, he appears to have succeeded. The ninth, and final, "declaration of principle" is about states rights, though the only one it specifies is the right to own slaves.

> That Congress has no power under the constitution to interfere with or control the domestic institutions of the several States, and that such States are the sole and proper judges of everything appertaining to their own affairs, not prohibited by the constitution; that all efforts of the abolitionists or others made to induce Congress to interfere with questions of slavery, or to take incipient steps in relation thereto, are calculated to lead to the most alarming and dangerous consequences; and that all such efforts have an inevitable tendency to diminish the happiness of the people and endanger the stability and permanency of the Union, and ought not to be countenanced by any friend of our political institutions.

And just in case that declaration isn't clear enough, two other resolutions follow that affirm the Constitutional soundness of the fugitive slave law and condemn any "agitation of the slavery question." The Democratic Party truly had become the party of slavery, and would dominate Southern politics for more than a century, until it became the party of civil rights.

After the denial of a request from a New York delegate for a separate vote on the Fugitive Slave Act, so that his delegation could vote their consciences without torpedoing the whole party platform, the entire bundle of resolutions is voted on and passes overwhelmingly, with only half a dozen voices dissenting. Applause fills the hall and the great body of distinguished men moves on to the next order of business, nominating a candidate for president and vice president of the United States.

James Buchanan was Solomon's man, but Franklin Pierce, the former senator from New Hampshire nominated on the forty-ninth ballot, will do. This dark-horse candidate might represent Northern interests but fully supports Southern ones (though his running mate, William King of Alabama, is a Unionist and moderate on slavery). And Pierce considers abolitionism, not slavery, the existential threat to the nation. When Solomon announces Georgia's vote, he indicates, again and again, that he speaks for the entire delegation of the state: "Georgia, sir, prompted by the same feeling which has animated all her sisters of the South . . . now sends unanimous greeting to the Granite State of the North. She sends her entire and unanimous voice there, and she trusts with confidence that it will reverberate from those hills, which are firm as the eternal hills themselves, the glad tidings of unanimity throughout the length and breadth of our common country. She unanimously gives her ten votes for Franklin Pierce, of New Hampshire." For this speech Solomon Cohen has put on his team player hat, shouting his song of unity from the convention hall and the hills of the land like Walt Whitman himself.

Pierce goes on to win the election and appoints Solomon Savannah's US postmaster, a position his father and uncle held in Georgetown; Solomon's office is in the brand-new Custom House. Pierce proves himself quite sound on the slavery question. He enforces the Fugitive Slave Act. And he supports and signs the Kansas-Nebraska Act, two years later, which annuls previous compromises by allowing the introduction of slavery into the land obtained with the Louisiana Purchase north of the 36°30' line, subject to "popular sovereignty," the will of the people in each territory.

But in 1856, with national fallout from the bloody aftermath of the Kansas-Nebraska Act—armed conflicts arose between advocates of slavery and antislavery activists in the territory of Kansas—Democrats replace the incumbent Pierce with Buchanan, who will support the *Dred Scott* decision, which annuls all compromises on slavery in the territories, guaranteeing the legal status of your slave as your property wherever in the country you go.

8

Bolters and Seceders

Eight years after Solomon was slandered for aggressive behavior toward his fellow members of the Georgia delegation at the 1852 Democratic National Convention, he is again put on the defensive. On the eve of the Civil War, at the Democratic National Convention in Charleston, Solomon does something that will define the rest of his political life and be remembered long after his death. He goes to the convention—and remains there.

While the decade of the 1850s, with its political and judicial victories for the South, appeared to be hurtling the country toward a slave-holding future, Southern political leaders saw it as a decade of increasing humiliation for the region. Each compromise and court case expanded slaveholding rights, but these men considered them the medicine they high-mindedly swallowed to preserve the Union, tasting only a spoonful of sugar here and there. What the North said was good for the Union, the South was now sick of taking. And it could escape no one's notice that over the course of the decade, for every victory that pro-slavery forces racked up, outrage on the other side mounted. The publication, in 1852, of *Uncle Tom's Cabin* helped build abolitionist sentiment. Patchwork compromises and radical Supreme Court decisions were alienating a growing share of the electorate. The Whigs, Solomon Cohen's old nemeses, fell apart, and the Republican Party, a far greater threat to slaveholding interests, was born.

Secession from the Union was looking more and more appealing, and at the Charleston convention, a mini-version of it was acted out.

The party that represented enslavers, the Democrats, now had a front-runner presidential candidate who threatened to undo their political gains. Stephen A. Douglas, who'd recently fended off a challenge to his Illinois Senate seat by Abraham Lincoln, endorsed letting each new state in the Union decide on slavery even though *Dred Scott* had already protected enslavers' property rights in the territories. (It also stated that people of African descent couldn't be US citizens.) In the South the needle of what was acceptable politically had moved well to the right. Why should Southern politicians countenance the concept of popular sovereignty that was enshrined in the now void Compromise of 1850? Popular sovereignty, however, represented the majority will not just of the country but of the assembled delegates at the convention; the Democrats weren't a regional party, they were trying to win a national election.

Northern and Southern Democratic platforms emerged, with four of the latter's six resolutions being about slavery. The Northern platform, by contrast, acknowledged the split in the Democratic Party and resolved to abide by the decision of the Supreme Court on matters relating to slavery in the territories. After a vote was held and the Northern platform adopted, dozens of Southerners walked out, including the entire delegations of several Southern states.

Solomon Cohen and nine of his fellow delegates, a quarter of the original Georgia delegation, remained. The *Official Proceedings of the Democratic National Convention* notes Solomon's claim that the remaining Georgia delegates were entitled to vote for the state. The delegates who withdrew did so *out* of the convention rather than *in* it, Solomon argues, and so those who stayed were entitled to vote *in* the convention.

This highly legalistic argument doesn't work. Caleb Cushing, the president of the Democratic National Convention and former attorney general of the United States, responds to Solomon's address by ruling that the minority delegation has no right to represent the state.

And this is when a Mr. Holden, a member of the Georgia delegation, makes a wonderfully flamboyant appeal of this decision and a defense of Solomon's wish to vote. "Whom the Gods would destroy they first make mad," he begins. "The decision of the Chair is most suicidal and destructive. It destroyed the rights of the State. [Cohen] came here to represent the Democracy of his District. He held that the bolters and seceders did not represent the Democracy of the State; that they did not follow their duty to their State. They came here with instructions to vote, not to bolt."

The Chair says his decision is final, pointing out that he allowed this last speech only as an act of courtesy.

Solomon's obituary in the *Savannah Morning News* of August 16, 1875, will include an unattributed quotation about the 1860 convention that brings his remarks to life:

> He was a State rights man of the Calhoun school, but he felt it to be his duty to remain here. He was actuated by a patriotic purpose to remain here and endeavor to produce conciliation. He implored the North to pause. There was a wide and widening gulf between the North and South. He begged the convention not to increase it. Georgia was a unit. Let them not argue from his presence here any division in her sentiment on the great question. He went into a history of the growth of the anti-slavery sentiment of the North, predicting how the arch fiend, [William H.] Seward, would ride on the waves of faction into the Presidency. In view of these facts, he asked them if the South was not entitled to the guarantee she has been asking for the last three days. He intended to stay here till the last remedy was exhausted.

The guarantee sought by the South was the protection of slavery in the territories, something to which Northern Democrats wouldn't agree.

Solomon Cohen made his professional reputation as a dogged deal-maker, but his attempt to negotiate with the North must have gone over better a decade after war's end than it did on its eve. Back in Savannah after the Charleston convention, gunpowder was fired one night in honor of Cushing, for supposedly having kicked Solomon out of the convention, and now Solomon was being forced to explain why he hadn't been among the bolters and seceders.

The trial—for it was a trial of sorts—took place in the Masonic Hall, on the northeast corner of Broughton and Bull, the busy commercial intersection near the river. The Masons met in what my father's little black book calls an "elegant brick structure," and on May 8, 1860, the Democratic Executive Committee of Chatham County went into session there to conduct a sort of postmortem on the just-concluded Charleston convention and agree on a declaration "of the sentiments of the Democratic party of Chatham county, upon the important questions now agitating the country."

From the *Savannah Daily Morning News* account two days later, I imagine the scene. A hot night, the great hall packed, and through the smoky gas-lit air the names Jackson, Cohen, and Hartridge rise. These are the Chatham County members of the Georgia delegation at the Charleston Democratic National Convention, and they each took a different position on withdrawing from it. Judge Henry R. Jackson's name is shouted loudest, perhaps because he was among the first group of men calling for retiring from the convention when they saw which way it was heading. Julian Hartridge was one of four Georgia delegates who'd been against leaving but, feeling "the vote of the majority should control our action," ended up withdrawing as well.

Henry Jackson, a native of Athens, Georgia, was a local celebrity, a war hero and former diplomat who'd recently prosecuted the owners and crew of the *Wanderer*, a yacht retrofitted as a slave ship by Savannahian Charles Augustus Lafayette Lamar, who kidnapped and smuggled four hundred Africans into the country through the misty marshes and creeks some ninety miles south of Savannah. The Atlantic slave trade had been banned since 1808 but Lamar hoped to test and overturn the federal law, enriching himself in the process. Although the evidence against him was overwhelming, he ended up being acquitted by a jury of his peers, including Octavus Cohen, Solomon's cotton-broker brother, who as chairman of the Democratic Executive Committee of Chatham County has just called tonight's meeting to order.

Judge Jackson takes the stand. His oratorical skills are on full display as he explains why the Southern state delegations walked out of the convention. To applause and cheers he gives the assembled a history lesson, taking them through the insults hurled over the years at the South, every wrong heaped upon wrong, each of them an attempt to limit slavery in the new territories. Popular sovereignty, what Jackson and other critics call "squatter sovereignty," might mean the end of the institution of slavery, or at least ensure its perpetual embattlement. At the Charleston convention delegates from the new, free state of California supported Southern property rights. Texas is a slave state. Why not connect the dots and just chop the country in two, with a glorious Confederacy, a great slaveocracy, stretching from sea to shining sea across the bottom half?

And though Jackson doesn't mention it, what surely feeds his bluster is how rich this new union would be. Slave trading was big business, more profitable than the railroads, and moreover, in the spring of 1860, the South had a dizzying cotton high. Over the previous decade, the number of enslaved workers had increased by a quarter as the amount of cotton the region produced nearly doubled, with its price remaining high. Southern cotton supplied mills in New England and accounted for the majority of US exports. "Cotton is king," the boast coined two years earlier by South Carolina senator James Hammond, signaled Southerners' confidence that no one would dare make war on the cotton states. If they did, Henry Jackson tonight declared, he for one "was ready to go forth on the battle field."

Now the Honorable Solomon Cohen takes the stand to respond to accusations of being a submissionist, of supporting the treacherous Douglas—but for what in return? It was rumored he'd been promised a foreign mission in a Douglas administration. Could Solomon Cohen, a man everyone thought he knew, be, at heart, the kind of man who would sacrifice the Constitution on the altar of the spoils of office?

If there ever was a time when Solomon felt the tenuous nature of his position in the town's social and political structure, of being an insider on the verge of being cast out, it was now. This was a time and place where outsiders rumored to be spies or abolitionist sympathizers could find themselves threatened by mobs, tarred and feathered, or worse. Northern transplants, travelers, crews of ships in port—these were people you'd expect to have other ideas. But paranoia could also turn neighbor against neighbor, shatter longstanding alliances in an instant, and the slightest wrong move—or in Solomon's case, a failure to move, out of the convention hall—could exile you from the community, leaving you to die a kind of death.

Solomon's gaze sweeps the crowd, people he knows, fellow elites. This is what he says to them, that he knows them, and they know him. Know he's been loyal to the South for his entire political life. That he'd never betray the region to which he owed so much. And to set the record straight, no one booted him from the convention, at least not before he himself said he was leaving. He'd remained there as long as he did in "a last attempt at a reconciliation."

As for the bolters and seceders, in spirit, he concludes, he was always among them.

If anyone applauded, the *Daily Morning News* doesn't mention it. Nor does the record show Octavus, Solomon's brother, saying a word. The verdict could still go either way, especially when a committee proposes resolutions to express the will of the Chatham County Democratic Party and the second of them appears to indict Solomon Cohen himself: "*Resolved*, That we recommend and heartily approve of the conduct of our delegates who protested against the action of—and withdrew from—the Charleston Convention." I picture Solomon literally leaping to his own defense as he asks that the second resolution be read again, explaining that he can't vote for such an implicit condemnation of his actions at the convention. But the leading member of the resolutions committee somehow persuades him that the statement means no such thing, and the resolutions all pass unanimously.

When this business is done and another committee is called to announce, in the morning's paper, delegates to the following month's Democratic convention in Baltimore, Judge Jackson rises and asks to say a few words. A hush settles over the hall. The aristocratic Jackson wants to say a few words about his friend and colleague Solomon Cohen. Jackson affirms that Solomon has always sympathized with the course pursued by the men who'd walked out. And that Solomon's "patriotic services in behalf of the South" are too well known to require a "panegyric" by him.

The crowd applauds and Solomon gets up. A survivor, that's what he is, though this time it was such a close call that feelings greater than relief move through him. He expresses gratitude to his friend for vouching for him. Such an endorsement, it goes beyond professional courtesy, it's a true expression of friendship, and, well, Solomon feels that this—*this*—is "the proudest and happiest moment of his life."

9

The Best Bed in the Fort

Fort Pulaski: two words that summon the memory of the hot still summers of my youth, the air so heavy with humidity that even a river breeze—Cockspur Island, where the fort is located, divides the north and south channels of the Savannah River at its mouth—couldn't lighten it up. The turnoff to Cockspur, a fifteen-mile drive from Savannah, is just before the bridge to Tybee Island, where my family had a place two blocks from the beach, a plain little cinderblock cottage without A/C. At night an orange light would sweep across the room I shared with my brother and sister, and I'd wake from a shallow sweaty sleep in time to see a truck crawling down the oyster-shell road, leaving a chemical fog in its wake. An afternoon at Fort Pulaski fit right into these weekends. The fort was a national monument, its mission now educational, but after the first few visits its big guns and restored officers' quarters and other settings no longer spoke to me, the boredom I felt as weighty as the saturated air, though I couldn't say I'd really absorbed what happened there a century before. I was more interested in bicycling down the marshside trails and enjoying the hot dogs my father would grill in the picnic area on the western side the island, well away from the fort.

But now that I see it as an adult and try to view it as Gratz Cohen did, the fort takes on new meaning for me. It's as well preserved now as it was thirty years ago—it looks almost exactly the same, except that I don't recognize the first thing I see when I step off the parking lot. The sign showing wild-eyed enslaved people racing toward the fort in a little rowboat, their path through the marsh lighted providentially by the moon, definitely wasn't there when I was a kid. Until I started this project I didn't know that Fort Pulaski, once it was captured by Union forces, had been a sanctuary for formerly enslaved people. The picture of the fugitives' escape borders on kitsch, but the connection of enslavement to the fort and indeed the war is more soberly told in the round redbrick visitor center.

I continue down the little path alongside the moat. The front of the fort is protected by a triangular demilune, whose great grass-covered mounds are so green and luscious looking on this sunny late-February day that they practically beg me, against park rules, to frolic on them. It wasn't until after the Civil War that the mounds, within the moat but outside the fort walls, were built up and through them a maze of tunnels burrowed that led to powder magazines, tabby-walled rooms that stay cool and dark even in summer. As a kid I liked walking through the tunnels, my only disappointment that they weren't extensive enough to get lost in. But during the war the demilune was flat and grassless, unbeautiful, enclosed in a waist-high wall behind which were gun platforms, kitchens, mess rooms, storage areas, and a guardhouse. The whole island, now so woodsy, was, according to Gratz, completely barren of trees.

It's at Fort Pulaski where Gratz gets his first taste of soldiering. At sixteen he's too young to join the Chatham Artillery, formed in 1776 to protect Savannah against the British, and has to ask his parents' permission, as he did on that day a decade earlier. On that occasion, Solomon let Gratz wander the boomtown streets on his own to encourage his son's bravery. But in the spring of 1861 the action is still very far away.

In response to Miriam's letter informing Rebecca of Gratz's intention to volunteer, here is her aunt's panicked response: "My Dear Miriam, you speak of the probability of your Gratz enrolling which has given me great concern, as he suffers so much with his feet, when taking moderate exercise, that it would be cruel to expose him in a march, indeed you know Dr. Van Buren told you, he could not be received in a regular army on account of it . . . But ♥, do not send your precious boy to certain peril, even if he escaped the other dangers of war." Miriam would have taken seriously the advice of the universally respected woman who raised her and whom she loved and missed so. Still, the peril that Rebecca predicted Gratz would face seems not yet so certain. It's an ebullient time in Savannah, its citizens living in the streets and squares more than usual, and Gratz is caught up in it. In January, after South Carolina volunteers occupied Charleston's Fort Moultrie and United States Army forces had massed at Fort Sumter, white

Savannahians, still heady from South Carolina's secession, wanted to take Fort Pulaski before the federal government could do so and block access to the port. Savannah had fourteen militias and they assembled in the street, with torches raised. Governor Joseph E. Brown stepped in and sent state troops, cheered on as they made their way from their temporary quarters in town to the wharf, then onto the sidewheel steamer *Ida* for the trip downriver to the fort.

They found it barely occupied. The marsh covering most of the island was swallowing up the fort, the moat was clogged with mud and Spartina grass, and when the soldiers crossed the final drawbridge they saw that the naval guns had rusted, the living quarters were inhabitable only by critters, and the parade grounds had been overtaken by weeds. An ordnance officer lived here like Miss Havisham in her mansion, and he immediately surrendered. The Georgia secession flag, with its single red star, was raised over the ramparts. It was the only action the fort had ever seen, and no shot was even fired.

Fort Pulaski was designed by Robert E. Lee himself, when he was a United States Army engineer. Part of a loose string of forts along the Eastern Seaboard planned after the War of 1812, Pulaski wasn't completed until 1847. Its five sides and seven-and-a-half-foot-thick walls were built by enslaved people using twenty-five million bricks, also the product of enslaved labor. Fourteen years later enslaved workers were again loaned out, from nearby rice plantations, to work with hundreds of volunteer soldiers to clear the moat, restore the living quarters and parade grounds, and hoist guns onto the fort's upper level.

The previous fall Gratz had gone to Philadelphia to visit Rebecca Gratz, his aunt Becky. They gathered in Rebecca's home, the Northern relatives who fell in love with him as a child, some literally racing across the parquet floors and Turkey rugs to wrap Gratz in their embrace. He was overwhelmed with dinner invitations, several for each night he was in town.

He'd traveled on his own before, most recently having escaped the pestilential Savannah summer to take the cure in North Georgia and across the border in Tennessee, where the hot springs and pure mountain air were good for the illnesses he suffered even as a fifteen-year-old, alarming-sounding conditions with antique names such as neuralgia and cholera morbus. His letters from Philadelphia were as charming and open-hearted as ever. He never failed to add a "how dye" to his valet, Louis, and the other, unnamed servants—but he sounded political in a way he hadn't before. On November 13, having just turned sixteen, he argued for secession in a letter to Miriam:

> I think it is the duty of every southern state to leave a union, which is a union but in name; it is impossible for a people dwelling from the icy shores of the St. Laurence to the groves, where the mild winds of the Pacific are ever blowing, to have one commonwealth, without which they can not exist under one government. Secession at some day or other is inevitable. Why not let it come now? . . . Let the motto of the South be Justice, Moderation and our rights. . . . The North has shown a total disregard for our feelings and portions of it even taunt and ridicule us.

Lincoln had just been elected, an event that inflamed the South, though the president, however personally opposed to slavery, made it clear that his primary goal was keeping the Union together. But the South had been a powder keg of resentment for a decade; the election was simply the fuse. Solomon Cohen was an ardent states rights man from way back, and no pleasure trip up north could convince his son that the North had the South's best interests at heart.

At the start of June, just days before Gratz arrives at Fort Pulaski, the first federal blockade ship, the USS *Union*, appears at the mouth of the Savannah River. Maritime traffic in and out of the city is its lifeblood—and now the port is closed. In time other federal vessels will join, until a line of ships stretches across the river. But even with just the one ship, Gratz finds at Fort Pulaski a state of dynamic tension in which each side keeps the other in check. Nothing, in other words, is going on.

"We get up, the sun rises, we eat, we sleep, we drill, the sun sets, we go to bed, thus passes our life." Such is Gratz's daily routine. He does his first sentry duty with his first cousin Octavus S. Cohen, who's the same age—and also too young to be there. Octy looks like a less pretty version of Gratz, with a narrower face and a dark moustache. Gratz prefers sentry duty to police duty, which he finds "disagreeable because it involves cleaning up the yard and casemates." Later he discovers an even more unpleasant assignment, fatigue duty, which is "one of the hardest in the garrison" and unlike police duty, not soon over. Whereas police duty might have involved cleaning the troops' living quarters, fatigue duty probably involved the kind of work that had reclaimed the fort from nature, the digging and hauling and lifting that made the place habitable again but that, in the subtropical climate, were jobs never done.

Physical labor of any sort is new to Gratz. It comes as a shock, the soldier's life, which, he reports to his parents, "is indeed a hard one." But in fact Gratz's duties are minimal; there isn't really all that much to endure at Fort Pulaski in the summer of 1861. When he isn't on some kind of duty, his routine gives him plenty of free time. Between 9 and 10, after breakfast, his company drills at the columbiads, the big cannons on the rampart. Between 10 and 2, down time in the casemates, sleeping quarters with views of the inner courtyard on one side and the moat on the other. Two to three: dinner. Then they relax until the mail arrives, at 4, the event that sets everyone on the *qui vive*, as Gratz puts it. Then drill until 6:30, the start of the dress parade and review, complete with music from a "very fine colored band." Supper at 7, then sports on the parade ground or, Gratz's preference, sunsetwatching with friends down at the wharf. Roll call at 9, bedtime by 10.

"I love the soldier's life," Gratz writes his sister Belle, "so full of glory and excitement."

Once he realizes he has the freedom to be himself, soldiering begins to agree with him. He makes the most of the situation—the chores, the longueurs—by seeing himself with ironic detachment, as an antihero. "[M]osquitoes and flies, our terrible foes, rule every thing." His weapon? "What services of mine merited the distinguished honor, which I received to day I can not tell, but I was dubbed this morning knight of the broom, and performed for the garrison of Fort Pulaski the same service that Epaminondas did for the citizens of Thebes."

In his third week at Fort Pulaski he goes to do sentry duty—and two people offer to do it for him. Gratz doesn't find this surprising. The other soldiers' reasoning, that he is "too young to endure the fatigue," makes sense to him. But Gratz decides to give it a try—and pulls it off! "I feel as good as if I slept all night," he reports to his folks the next morning. Perhaps he remembers the special boots he had to wear that set him apart as an adolescent; maybe he's still wearing them. He comes to see soldiering less as a fight against an external enemy than as a test of whether he's manly enough to perform his duty.

"Octy and I are almost as much petted as 'la fille du regiment' was described to have been," Gratz reports a month into his stint, comparing himself and his cousin to the tomboy heroine of Donizetti's opera, the orphan girl who becomes the mascot of the French regiment that adopts her. It makes perfect sense to Gratz that other people constantly want to do things for him.

Octy, despite being a fellow pet, looks out for him. Other soldiers make doing any sort of work largely optional for him, allowing him to enjoy the drills and parades, the music of the military band, the pomp of war that he adores. But it's a Mr. Knapp who truly goes out of his way for Gratz.

We first hear of this person in a July 11 letter that Gratz writes to Belle. The day before, Gratz was sick with a "very severe cold" and "a violent head ache and weeping eyes" that kept him in bed all day. Octy prepared him a footbath and a glass of warm lemonade. Mr. Knapp, not to be outdone, brought him a *bed*. "It is Mr. Knapp's bed," Gratz matter-of-factly explains, "the best in the fort which he brought himself from his casemate, a great distance from mine, this morning for my accommodation."

Noah Barnum Knapp was fifty years old when he volunteered and might have taken a fatherly attitude toward Gratz. Knapp was a trader in leather goods—AT THE SIGN OF THE GOLDEN SADDLE, noted an advertisement for his shop—and a future bank director and judge. He was already one of the richest men in town, much wealthier than Solomon, who might have arranged for him to take Gratz under his wing.

It makes sense that Knapp had the best bed in the fort. But why he should schlep it across the fort for Gratz, and what he ended up sleeping on himself, is what I really want to know. Gratz's own conjecture about this special treatment is fantastic, though he seems to believe it: "I was certainly born under a lucky star, and have good reason to believe in the german legend of a child being born on Sunday being watched by fairies."

Whether or not he was born under a lucky star, Gratz was born soon after photography was. Four pictures of him remain—as a little boy, a boy, an adolescent, and as a twenty-year-old in uniform. I'm looking at the third photograph of him to see what the other soldiers at Fort Pulaski saw when they looked at him. The picture shows his foppish long-tailed tie and the top of his jacket, but mostly it's a headshot, its subject staring seriously into the middle distance but looking inward. This is a psychological portrait: Gratz seems to be thinking, but of what we do not know. The external signs mark him as upper class, but as an individual he betrays nothing. A picture can't ever really get at its subject's soul, but some images, like this one, seem to make a point of this impossibility. At any rate, you don't need to know anything about Gratz Cohen to respond to what's most obvious in this picture: his beauty.

It's one of those faces that arrest you, the features so finely etched and composed that you can't turn away from them. The contrast between the strong chin and Cupid's bow lips inevitably seems a play between masculine and feminine. The wispy moustache contributes to this sense of in-betweenness: it's a face in the process of becoming. Gratz's eyes are dark and soulful, his hair so thick and wavy that it defies its cut, curling against his forehead, clumping around the top of each ear. You can practically see it falling over his eyes and cascading down his shoulders in a style more suited to the Romantic poets that inspired the poetry he'd go on to write. A soldier isn't something you imagine the young man in this picture becoming. It was something he himself didn't foresee.

Gratz isn't cut out for the soldier's life, and so he makes it suit his own. He has Miriam send him his books: math, Greek, Latin, German, French. His fellow soldiers are happy to be enlisted in his studies: "There is a young man here, who has studied German, and he and I are going to study it together." French is his best language, and he finds people to practice with. "Had a petite conversation francaise with Mr. Lama," he reports. John Lama was Noah Knapp's neighbor on Jones, Savannah's prettiest street, and dealt in "Champagne, Brandies, Wines, Whiskies, Segars and Groceries." The leather-goods dealer who gave Gratz his own bed now comes bearing another gift. "Mr. Knapp is devoted to me and today presented me with a pocket French dictionary, prettily bound in morocco." So maybe it isn't just as a father that Noah Knapp relates to Gratz; perhaps it's as one aesthete to another.

From time to time that summer the war intrudes, but as a minor nuisance. "Do excuse this writing for every one is talking around me of a vessel, which we have just fired into, and to which a boat has been sent. Please send me some towels, and a lead pencil."

Going to war at Fort Pulaski was like Walden for Thoreau—far enough to be away from civilization but near enough to enjoy its benefits. Except unlike Thoreau Gratz doesn't sneak home for cookies; instead the little prince has his mom send care packages. "Do send a sponge cake. We all get hungry around noon because of exercise in the columbiads, and the salt air, tho' instead of a hard biscuit, a dainty bit of sponge cake would be the most acceptable thing in the world." Also acceptable: gumdrops, crackers, sweet oil, newspapers, notepaper, a pair of pants. Even a piece of lamb makes its way downriver, for Gratz to enjoy and share with his mates. In exchange he thinks about sending Miriam a fish, but figures it won't keep. He does manage to send her a "champaign basket with soiled clothes."

What a fun way to do the army, like summer camp but with your family close enough to send you food and booze—and do your laundry. It's also a great way to get away from your dad, while enjoying the benefits of a more enjoyable father figure. Like the Lehman brothers, Octavus Sr. made a living as a cotton broker, finding Northern buyers for Southern cotton; he also worked as a steamship agent. But now the port is closed, throwing a wrench into these business models. Still, in his career as a commission merchant Octavus has dealt in pretty much anything you can imagine: enslaved people, real estate, Indian fabric, pork products, sugar and flour, cotton balances, brandy, lead, gunpowder, sterling, guano, peach trees, yarn. And even in wartime he seems able to deliver. In a letter written early in his stay at the fort, Gratz asks Miriam to send him a camp bed, but in the postscript he says never mind, Uncle Octy is sending two, for Octy S. and him.

The high point of the summer, midway through Gratz's stint at the fort, is the Fourth of July feast. Miriam, being female, isn't invited. He expects his mother to provide contributions to the meal, but tells her he hopes his father and Uncle Octavus come down to enjoy it with him.

On July 2, getting a headstart on the festivities, Gratz and his company have "a ball and a grand frolic." In the company of other men he feels free, for the first time in his life, to be a bit of a bad boy. "Our company is the most independent one here, and enjoys itself the most, as the frowns of our captain are not as much dreaded as those of Captains Anderson, Gordon, and Foley. We are a jolly set and have fun in spite of all opposition." At Fort Pulaski that summer, Gratz gets a break from the blues that have haunted him since childhood. The hottest part of the day is R and R time in the cool thick-walled casemates, where "we amuse ourselves in various ways, some lie down upon the light camp beds scattered picturesquely about, some read while others play cards or chess."

On July 3 Octavus arrives like a "regular Santa Claus, laden with good things." Solomon brings provisions from Miriam, and sherry and bitters. The celebration the next day is in "grand style," the artillery fires an eleven-gun salute, and there's a "general rejoicing." An incongruous note of luxury is struck.

Gratz thrives in this all-male world, though he doesn't find it quite male enough. One day a Mrs. Richard Cuyler appears, and Gratz reports to Miriam that he doesn't think the island a "proper place for a lady—even for a day." For her part, the lady in question "seems to like it very much." Well, Gratz breezily remarks, "Chacun a son gout." To each his own.

Sometime during the week after his Fourth of July visit, Solomon sends Gratz a gift for Noah Knapp, a token of gratitude for this older man who's come to serve as his son's protector. While his "charming friend" is out fishing, Gratz writes Belle excitedly of his plan to present him with the gift when he returns. Whatever it is, Gratz wants his father to know "how much he has gratified me in sending it, for no one can be more attentive, than Mr. Knapp is to me."

On July 21, 1861, the First Battle of Bull Run—what Southerners call the Battle of First Manassas—is fought, six hundred miles north of Savannah. It's the first major battle of the war. The Georgia regiment commanded by Colonel Frances S. Bartow, who months earlier had led troops to retake Fort Pulaski, includes friends of Gratz's who are among Savannah's first casualties of the war.

The summer-camp spirit of the fort turns into something darker. Gratz is rarely very revealing with his father; it's his mother and especially Belle with whom he shares his personal life. Even his tone is more formal with his father. But the letter Gratz writes Solomon on July 22 seems to be penned in an entirely different register: "With the most fearful odds against us, Dear

Papa, we have gained a most glorious victory, and the fields of Manassas have not been crimsoned in vain, with the noblest blood in the South." And of Frances Bartow's blood specifically: "his death has consecrated his life, and his crimson life blood as it oozed over that glorious field, washed out his many faults." Bartow was a neighbor of Gratz's on Pulaski Square, just south of the Liberty Street house. The colonel was a lawyer and former politician who surely knew Solomon Cohen and probably had been a guest in his home. Bartow's "many faults" could have included defying Governor Brown, who ordered him to remain at his post defending Savannah, then very publicly denounced him for stealing arms and disobeying orders—Bartow went over his head to the Confederacy's president Jefferson Davis—the governor even going so far as to taunt Bartow by speculating he'd gone to Virginia to enjoy "a more pleasant summer climate."

Some of the Georgia men who, on July 23, are still unaccounted for have come from Fort Pulaski. They're regulars and Gratz is a volunteer; he stayed to hold down the fort. What does he feel? Shame, guilt, relief? All he confesses to is eagerness to join the fight, though it's one he can't really imagine, it's still so unreal. He aestheticizes war, the battlefield touched up with crimson everywhere. He ennobles war, with death the ultimate purifier of sins.

He's good at this. The products of his imagination are truer than the world around him. The earliest photograph I can find of him, around the age of ten, shows him in a family portrait holding a book so massive on his lap that you wonder whether he could even have picked it up. Giving life to the term *voracious reader*, Gratz, at least in his first weeks at the fort, skips the most unappetizing meals and instead reads a book called "Dora's Table Traits, the delicacies of which it treats very often serve me as a barmecidal meal." *Barmecidal*, I learn from the dictionary, means "providing the illusion of abundance" and comes from the name of the prince in *One Thousand and One Nights* who taunts a beggar with an imaginary meal. Except in Gratz's case, the book satisfies in a way the meal never could.

"I am ready to sacrifice my life," Gratz writes, "and you, my dear mother, will willingly see me fall a martyr . . . for the right of men to choose their own form of government. Oh that I were older and better able to share the dangers and glory of this struggle." It's a cruel, or at least clueless, thing to say to your mom. Does Miriam simply chalk it up to her son's youth? Solomon has made his own ill-considered statements in the idiom of sacrifice, but I doubt that Miriam, a transplant from Philadelphia, is all that eager to martyr her only son for the fledgling Confederacy. Still, the war is very far away and the South is in no need of sixteen-year-olds on its front lines, not yet. We don't have the other side of the correspondence, but there's no evidence in Gratz's subsequent letters that Miriam took him or the war seriously enough to try to talk him out of getting himself killed.

In the penultimate letter he writes from Fort Pulaski, with the gloomy news of casualties from First Manassas still echoing in his ears, Gratz goes for a walk. The day's stormy weather has stopped to make way for a magnificent sunset, there's beauty everywhere: "the waters of the moat, swollen by the rain as they dash against the stone cappings round the margin of the moat, make a kind of music, and the only sound that breaks the general stillness." On my visit to the fort I stand at the edge of the same moat that he did, outside the fort and across from the demilune. It's an overwarm winter day, and one after another cars soar over the last bridge before the beach, spanning Lazaretto Creek, where the original pesthouse—*lazaretto* in Italian—was built after slavery was legalized in Georgia. Well before Gratz's day the buildings had fallen into disrepair and a newer quarantine station was built on the same island as the fort, though it was no longer in use, the importation of captives against federal law since 1808 and Georgia law since 1798.

I stand there and listen to the cars and when I turn my head away from the bridge, the roar of the wind fills my ears. The water glistens in the sun, flowing clockwise around the moat—but makes no sound at all. It's early afternoon, whereas Gratz stood here in twilight; instead of a fully manned fort, a national park with a few tourists strolling; and always the sound of the damn cars. Nor is the moat swollen with rain. Still, shouldn't the water make some sound?

I walk a bit, balancing on the narrow brick rim of the moat. Then I stop and stare into the water, and suddenly there it is, the kind of plop you'd expect to hear from water falling on stone, *plop plop plop*, the sounds separated by silence as the water rounds a curve on its slow circuit between masonry walls round the fort, the water not clear but not brackish either, thanks to the system of dikes and canals that a young Robert E. Lee worked out to regulate the tidal water and keep the fort on dry ground.

You had to pay attention to the water to hear it, and it occurs to me that this was when Gratz Cohen learned to listen to things that don't speak.

10

A Little Romance of Excitement

When his Fort Pulaski idyll ends, Gratz takes a backwoods version of the grand tour, passing through Talbotton before a week in Warm Springs, the village southwest of Atlanta where Franklin Roosevelt would take the waters, then LaGrange, Marietta, Spring Hill, and Lookout Mountain, the tourist site with the scenic viewpoint where you can See Seven States: Tennessee, Kentucky, Virginia, North Carolina, South Carolina, Georgia, and Alabama. For three months Gratz travels, sometimes with his sister Belle, and enjoys society life with relatives, as well as various "compagnons de voyage" and friends of his father's whom he meets along the way.

This trip, beginning in early August, is more than a sightseeing expedition. Gratz's Fort Pulaski service, such as it was, has taken a toll on his health. And while Savannah hasn't had an outbreak of yellow or typhoid fever since the devastating epidemic of 1854, Solomon and Miriam aren't taking any chances this summer with Gratz or Belle. But after a month of traveling, Gratz wants to go home, reassuring Miriam that it's "perfectly healthy in Savannah and I actually suffer away from it. . . . Do, dear Papa and Mama, let me come home now." He uses the excuse of having run out of money to forgo plans to see the Blue Ridge, but Solomon ends up financing a week there, to keep him in the cool salubrious mountain air until the danger of disease has passed back home.

It isn't just homesickness that has Gratz feeling stranded. As he moves northwest from the lowlands of Savannah, across the piedmont, and up into the mountains, he finds himself in scenes of misery he never saw when he was volunteering at the fort. He witnesses weather-beaten soldiers returning from fighting in Virginia and, at the LaGrange, Georgia, train station, fresh youths heading off to war amid the "piteous lamentations" of their family members. Many of these soldiers are in the same rail car as Gratz and Belle, who are en route to their uncle Myers' home in Spring

Hill, Tennessee. But however affecting these scenes are, the war intrudes on Gratz's life primarily as a nuisance, shaking up his plans, causing him to spend a "despicable" night at the train station in Chattanooga, where the hotels are all booked and the trains full up with a thousand men in uniform heading north.

Gratz isn't intent on joining them. The farther he gets from Savannah, the more he feels drawn back home. In September 1861 the war was still far away from southeast Georgia, taking place mostly in Kentucky and Missouri, but Gratz has heard from "several military men . . . that the winter's campaign will open in our midst." Word has reached him of an attack on the North Carolina coast that in fact signals a new Union strategy to blockade the Southern coastline and disrupt direct Confederate trade with other countries. Robert E. Lee, now a Confederate general, has gone to Savannah to organize the defense of the Georgia and northern Florida coasts, and Gratz has heard that the Chatham Artillery, the volunteer unit in which he served at Fort Pulaski, has called a meeting, presumably to plan to go into service once again.

Gratz conveys this news in a letter to his parents on September 7, and as the days pass, he becomes more and more desperate to get home, though not explicitly to join up with his old unit, which he never mentions again in his increasingly agitated letters from the hill country. He's a scared sixteen-year-old kid and wants more than anything else to be with his family. So does Belle. By the end of the month, anxious for himself and on behalf of the entire region, he tells his parents he's had enough of his cure tour: "I am in such a state, that I can not stay still, or in one place hardly for five minutes. Our troubles seem every day to increase, and danger to approach nearer, and when I think how little prepared we are to meet the overwhelming force, which has already sailed against our coast, I long to be home again, so that we have resolved to leave here Wednesday." And he longs to be reunited with Louis, of whom he writes, "I hope he's behaving himself."

Holes in his story yawn whenever Gratz is in Savannah and his letters home stop—but apparently the wartime scenes that moved him in upstate Georgia propelled him back into service, for he writes next from a military camp.

Camp Harrison was near the town of Guyton, about thirty-five miles from Savannah. Governor Brown has appointed George P. Harrison Sr. a brigadier general, charging him with starting a camp to train new troops and organizing them into regiments. Harrison owns Monteith, a rice plantation just upriver from Savannah. He has also represented Chatham County in the Georgia House of Representatives and served, like Solomon Cohen, as a delegate to the Georgia Democratic State Convention in 1860. And Solomon has business connections with Harrison, having loaned him money. Gratz's father arranges for him to be the general's aide-de-camp.

Even as Gratz was desperate to flee the miseries of war, he romanticized it as something out of the chivalrous literature so popular at the time. At Warm Springs he wondered "how many a Southern heart must bleed, how many a noble youth must be sacrificed at the altar of our country, still reeking with noble, priceless blood? I have dreamt of the battle two nights in succession, almost the same dream, which I hope will be but a dream." An aide-de-camp is the perfect job, Solomon must think, to indulge his son's quest for military adventure while keeping him in one piece. It was a position of relative safety, normally given to a general's family member, with duties including writing and conveying orders, a task right up Gratz's alley. And Harrison is a man Solomon can trust to take personal responsibility for keeping his son safe.

Gratz isn't quite seventeen when he arrives at Camp Harrison, the general's aide with a rank of captain. Uncle Octy is there, along with his son, Octavus S., newly installed as an adjutant to a regiment. In addition to setting up his son and nephew, Octavus Sr. might have come to do some business; whatever a brand-new training camp needs, Octavus Cohen can surely supply. Gratz gets started right away, "writing some general orders." Harrison's headquarters are in a small log cabin in a pine barren and Gratz's bed is in the general's room. In the morning the winter wind comes rushing with a vengeance through the chinks in the walls. This is Gratz's new life.

Miriam and Solomon come a few days later. The wind whistling through the rude cabin—Miriam must have been unimpressed, because shortly after this visit, Gratz takes up his pen to try to make his mother, and himself, feel better: "Your visit here, dear Mama, I will not say was like a ray of light, thrown over a scene of darkness but it certainly made a bright scene much brighter to me. Do not think of me as absent for my thoughts are ever with you. . . . I am perfectly happy, and contented with the life I have chosen, and the situation which you, my beloved parents have procured for me." He assures her he'll stand up straight.

And he takes down orders for the first regiments of General Harrison's brigade to prepare themselves to march. A Union blockading squadron has begun capturing points along Georgia's short coast, from Savannah to the Florida border. This news brings on "a perfect fever of excitement, and every man in the camp is anxious to go and meet them." Gratz seems to get caught up in all this, announcing to Miriam two days later that he expects to be moved to the coast soon. And he asks her to make him some drawers.

He also asks for a horse, and Louis as a groom, echoing his earlier request of his parents to bring him "a horse, boy and equipments" so that he could appear at the camp's military presentation. He manages to procure another horse, his own being still in Savannah: "Though I am anxious to have my horse here I hope you will keep it in town a few days in order that it may recover from its voyage under James' good care. Tell him I expect him to do his best for it, and to give Louis a lesson or two in the art of keeping horses." And then the letters from Camp Harrison end.

From his correspondence I can piece together Gratz's Fort Pulaski idyll, his trip to the mountains, camp life. But there are no letters from the period during which the *University Memorial* says he was defending the coast as Harrison's aide. Later a researcher I've hired will find, in the Georgia Archives in suburban Atlanta, a pass dated January 25, 1862, which Gratz, as Harrison's scribe, appears to have written for himself.

> The Sentinel will pass the bearer
> Capt. Cohen of Genl Harrison's Staff
> > By order of
> > Brig. Genl Harrison
> > Gratz Cohen
> > Aide de Camp

At first, though, the only clues I have that Gratz really did spend the winter of 1861–62 serving Harrison on the coast are that undated poem that fell from his journal when I first picked it up, as well as his gloomy reminiscences in the Virginia mountains his first autumn in Charlottesville. But the true subject of both of these texts is Louis.

During this period Confederate forces were stretched too thin to do much good, and one by one forts and other key points on the coast fell into Union hands. Fort Pulaski, where Gratz had first volunteered, was among them. In a letter home that first war summer, he wrote that William Howard Russell, the Irish reporter whose letters from the South at the start of the war appeared in the *Times* of London, "thinks our Fort very strong." Russell, whose correspondence was widely read on both sides of the Atlantic, did point out the fort's strengths but also predicted that Fort Pulaski would be "reduced" by modern armament, which is exactly what happened, on April 11, 1862. The callow Gratz of the previous summer, faced with the capture of Fort Pulaski and the closure of the port of Savannah, not to mention the total blockade of the coast, must have grown up pretty fast.

He had a companion to grow up with. I assume Gratz got his horse, but I know he got the "boy" he'd asked for as his groom. (Louis seems to be starting from zero in the art of keeping horses, but this doesn't disqualify him for Gratz.) The conditions were so perfect for escape that Gratz's eagerness to bring Louis to war shows how little he could have imagined that his beloved valet might have had other plans than a life as a slave, despite having sought reassurances, whenever they were parted over the years, that Louis was behaving himself. Port Royal, South Carolina, between Hilton Head and Beaufort, was captured by the Union navy in November, surprising planters and preventing them from fleeing with their enslaved workers to rebel-controlled territory inland, a practice known as refugeeing. Skidaway Island, just south of Savannah, is today full of gated communities but it was where sea island cotton, the kind that didn't require the cotton gin to unlock its profitability, had first been cultivated. In April 1862 the *New York Times* portrayed the island as having been deserted in such haste that dinner was still on the tables of the great houses when Federal soldiers arrived, though in fact Port Royal had been a heads-up for planters in the region.

Into this chaos rode Gratz and Louis, whose affection for Gratz may have been real but couldn't compete with his yearning to escape, an aim he seems to have achieved, according to the first diary entry Gratz will write in Virginia, in which he laments his valet's disappearance. Confederate military units had as their mission less the defense of the coast against the mighty Union navy than the containment of fugitives from slavery. There were no Black soldiers in the Confederate army, but Gratz wasn't alone in bringing a servant to war, and it's easy to imagine this particular duty as the one that made Louis snap.

I can see how an enslaved man attached to an outward-focused Confederate slave patrol, especially one who'd more or less learned to play his part, might have avoided scrutiny. The Union navy had created refuges for the enslaved on some of the islands that planters had deserted. Louis grew up with Gratz in the city, and now, having made his escape, finds himself alone in plantation land on the islands amid the chaos of war. Did he end up finding sanctuary right under the noses of the Confederate forces?

I go to Savannah's gold-domed City Hall, on the bluff overlooking the river, to try to find out. Here in the research library and municipal archives, I pore over the jail registers for Solomon's name. On August 8, 1861, he committed James, likely the same man who cared for Gratz's horse. Reason for incarceration: "Safe keeping." You could imprison an untrustworthy slave if, say, you were going on a short trip; James was confined for four days, at an expense of $2.40. As for Louis, I find an entry from the spring of 1862 confirming that he freed himself—and was subsequently captured.

On April 13, 1862, a "Lewis" belonging to Solomon Cohen is committed to the county jail by one Lieutenant McGree. Reason for incarceration: "Runaway." Louis was gone for up to three months—but he must not have found freedom after all.

The jail, a castle of a building with turrets and a crenelated parapet wall, no longer exists but was located just southwest of Forsyth Place, today's Forsyth Park. The building was made of brick covered with stucco and scored to look like stone. This was where you could have your enslaved worker confined for safekeeping, or whipped the legally allowable number of lashes—thirty-nine per day—if you couldn't bring yourself to do it. And of course the enslaved, like free people of color and whites, could be locked up for criminal reasons.

Louis stayed in jail for thirty days, at a cost to Solomon of $10.20. It's a much longer term than enslaved workers typically served for running away, reflecting the increasingly harsh punishments that enslavers were meting out as the nearby islands fell into Union hands. The jail was a grim place to spend a month, and not just because of the poor quality of the food. By 1860, fewer and fewer enslavers were willing to lock up their human chattel in the county jail, which had come under increasing criticism over the course of the previous decade for its poor ventilation and sanitation and its generally dangerous conditions. In 1857 a jailer had been found using prisoners to work in his own home. A sketch of the jail's whipping room made after the city was captured by Federal forces shows Union soldiers pointing into a cistern identified as a cold brine bath, where slaves would have been dunked after being whipped, to reduce their chance of infection from their wounds and, not incidentally, prolong the punishment.

I don't know what happened to Louis after his jail stay ended. But Vaughnette Goode-Walker, a cowriter of the book about Savannah slavery excerpted in the fact sheet left in my apartment and executive director of the Ralph Mark Gilbert Civil Rights Museum, helps me imagine it. Louis was jailed on the same day that Union major general David Hunter issued General Order No. 7, which freed the enslaved at Fort Pulaski, where Gratz's military service began, and on the island where it stood, now in Union hands. Morally opposed to slavery, Hunter would go on to enlist in the Union army freedmen from occupied parts of South Carolina. Louis would have been released from prison and returned to Solomon Cohen's custody on May 12, 1862, three days after Hunter's General Order No. 11, which declared enslaved people in Georgia, South Carolina, and Florida "forever free"—an unauthorized emancipation order that Lincoln rescinded a week later, just months before making his own Emancipation Proclamation. White Southerners would have thought even less of Hunter's emancipation proclamation than Lincoln did. But now there was a path to freedom for enslaved Savannahians, if only they could get to the safety of Fort Pulaski, and to do this they had to get aboard what Goode-Walker calls the "maritime railroad."

The Savannah River runs down to the fort, but to escape furtively, you have to take the creeks winding through the marsh. When I was a kid my father used to take us on his outboard motor boat through this marsh, its grasses fluorescent green or beige or bleached of color altogether, depending on the season and time of day. Dad took a class to learn how to navigate these creeks, using a set of beautiful charts. At low tide the serpentine creeks are nothing but muddy bottoms studded with oyster shells; if you want to get anywhere, you have to know what you're doing.

Fortunately, the maritime railroad had an experienced captain. March Haynes, a boat pilot and carpenter, may have been enslaved by John C. Rowland and accompanied him to Fort Pulaski after Rowland enlisted in the Confederate army, though Haynes seems to have taken orders directly from Confederate colonel Charles H. Olmstead, commanding officer of the fort, which was increasingly isolated by Federal forces. Olmstead, who admiringly considered Haynes "a black ray of sunshine," sent him on runs to the city to get mail and gather supplies and information. After the fort's fall and Hunter's General Order No. 7, Rowland became a prisoner and Haynes offered his services as a scout to the Union army, and conducted perilous missions through the marsh to bring hundreds of enslaved people to Fort Pulaski. A man as determined to be free as Louis could have been one of them, despite the risks of escape and the harsh punishment with which he was freshly familiar. The census doesn't name Louis or any other enslaved individual; nor do Solomon Cohen's tax records. But the clue to Louis's identity was there all along in the letters a young Gratz wrote home from hill country: *I hope he's behaving himself.* Long before he relinquished his responsibilities as Gratz's groom and ran away, Louis was signaling his unwillingness to fully accept his role as valet.

Those who found sanctuary on Cockspur Island lived in the old construction village, originally used by enslaved and free Black and white workers. Some of the men who found refuge at the fort went on to join the newly organized First South Carolina Volunteer Infantry, a Union regiment composed of escaped enslaved people. Louis might have been one of them. But I can't find a likely candidate in the troop rosters. As for Fort Pulaski records, the census that Union authorities took after occupying the fort ends on April 30, 1862, when Louis was still in jail. In his journal John G. Abbott, a Union soldier stationed at Fort Pulaski at the time, reports on "contrabands" who make their way to safety, but doesn't name any of them. I've lost Louis's trail. Gratz doesn't try to find it, as far as I know, and though he writes "Where is he now my spirit yearns to know,"

Gratz in fact basks in not-knowing, lamenting, in poetry and prose, that he will never see Louis again, at least not in life.

Gratz lasts eight months as Harrison's aide. That's according to the *University Memorial* account, and it checks out. It's eight months from when Harrison issued his General Order #8 appointing Gratz aide with the rank of captain, in mid-October 1861, until he begins writing home from the Georgia Military Institute, in northwest Georgia, in June 1862. His military adventure, according to the *University Memorial*, was cut short when he was incapacitated by his feet. That winter on the coast a cold sharp wind blowing in from the ocean would have stung Gratz's cheeks as he rode on high ground through the marsh. But this was nothing to bear. Being upright on the earth was the real trial, and in the end Gratz's feet did him in once again.

"I hope Gratz won't become a soldier," Rebecca wrote Miriam at the end of May. "He is too young and delicate for a soldier's life."

Did Miriam simply ignore her aunt's advice? Or was Solomon's the only voice that counted? Although at seventeen he no longer needs it, Gratz never does anything without his parents' permission, though he certainly would have done whatever it took to get it—appealed to reason, exercised his considerable charm—determined as he is to give the soldier's life another try. Apparently doing what he does best—serving, in fact, the only way that someone with his physical limitations can—isn't good enough for him. He's a gifted writer and may want to be a poet, but as a soldier he doesn't want to sit around taking down orders.

"My chief ambition and my most ardent prayer is to strike at least one blow in this glorious cause," the seventeen-year-old writes Belle from the Georgia Military Institute on June 6, 1862. "I shall never forgive myself if the strife ends without my doing so." Gratz wants to kill a Yankee, and just one will suffice to avoid any future self-reproach. Maybe this is why this young man so obviously unsuited to soldiering keeps joining up: it's his own war he's trying to win, and what's really at stake is his masculinity. Later in the month he repeats his desire to "at least strike one blow in defence of my birthplace," and he isn't above pulling strings. "Dear Papa— please see General Mercer about securing a position on his staff in case of a fight." (He also asks Solomon to send him some cologne and razors, "as

I am going to become my own Figaro.") But Gratz's romantic dream isn't meant to be realized, at least not yet.

School superintendent Francis W. Capers suggests Gratz's schoolwork is too easy for him and moves him up a class. It's only once he has finished his exams and begun his encampment that the challenges begin. Just a day after arriving at military camp, on July 22, 1862, he takes a hard look at himself. "I stood guard yesterday and last night and suffered terribly, (I am sorry to say), with my feet," he writes his parents. "This morning I can hardly walk." He wants a furlough home to consult his doctor. "It is with great reluctance that I am compelled to propose this, I had hoped to make myself a good soldier the few months that I remained here but I fear that will be impossible." He asks Solomon's forgiveness.

General Capers pushes Gratz once again, making him his secretary, a similar role to the one he held with General Harrison. Gratz is enthusiastic about his promotion. But he doesn't consider his new position soldier's work: "My lameness prevents my performing the least military duty." And his new role is apparently intended to last just until Solomon can arrange to get him home. "To go back to Savannah, with the exception of seeing you all, is perfectly hateful to me," he writes. But he's resigned to leaving. "We all have our crosses in life and of course I must submit."

Little Taste of Liberty

The center isn't holding, the Union is falling apart, and it's taking its toll on Gratz's extended family. The women try to keep it together. Miriam writes Rebecca:

> The South considers herself the aggrieved, not for the last year but for a series of years & it cost her as bitter a pang to dissolve her union with the States as it can the North, now, but she considered it the only remedy & wished to do so peaceably. The North denies her that right & says that Union must be preserved. How can that which is severed be made whole again? God knows how dearly I love both North & South & how many tears this warring of my country men has caused me & how fervently do I pray that bloodshed may be averted for the "voice of a brother's blood will cry from the ground" in either case.

Miriam is sympathetic to the South but presents herself, at least to her aunt, as less the gung-ho rebel than a body caught between opposing forces. Solomon, on the other hand, must suspect Rebecca isn't sound on the issue of slavery, and so he takes it upon himself to set her straight.

Rebecca, like Miriam and other women of the time, usually limited herself to domestic matters in letters to relatives, her overriding concern maintaining family harmony. Whatever she wrote, then, couldn't possibly have justified Solomon's rant. In a letter that has been widely misattributed to Miriam, Solomon accuses the North of a "sickly sentimentality," perhaps an allusion to *Uncle Tom's Cabin*, which came out a decade earlier but remained hugely influential in turning public opinion against slavery. But he reveals his own knack for the sentimental scene: "I do not say that there are no wrongs in the institution of slavery, but I do say that those wrongs are the exceptions. If my slave, nay if our slaves are sick, on their comfortable beds, in their comfortable chambers, they are attended by the same physician, and nursed by the same hands that tend & nurse our wives and children. . . . If our slaves become old and helpless, or broken down by disease, interest, habit, feeling, <u>law</u> compels us to sustain and support them." Solomon's boast can be corroborated, sort of. To escape a yellow fever epidemic that would wipe out 6 percent of the city's population, Solomon and Miriam and the children spent part of 1854 in New York, leaving their enslaved workers behind, including Deas, whom the *Savannah Daily Morning News* called "an intelligent black" in a light news item that spring about the "several African productions, such as coffee, rice and arrow root," that he'd received from a friend in Liberia. How Deas fared that summer I don't know, but another of Solomon's slaves, a married woman named Diana, contracted typhoid fever. (Most of the dying were white; West Africans were largely resistant to mosquito-borne diseases, though not, as widely believed at the time, immune to them.) She was treated by none other than the mayor of Savannah, Richard D. Arnold, a doctor who didn't flee the city with the rest of its upper crust. In a letter he recounts his treatment of Diana and complains of the interference of her church sisters, who prescribed a traditional remedy over the doctor's medicine. But neither treatment could keep her alive.

It's precisely the paternalistic aspect of slavery that Solomon feels makes it superior to a system of paid unskilled labor. Continuing to outdo the day's bleeding-heart fictionalists, he goes on to conjure a "poor consumptive sewing girl, who has been brought to death's door, by the war which Capital ever wages against <u>hired labor</u>," then asks, "can the North say that none of these sustain life by going begging from door to door?" In the eternal war between capital and labor, slavery emerges as the more just alternative to hired labor.

This argument, shocking as it sounds, would have been familiar at the time, as I discover. In 1848 the *Savannah Georgian*, already on the defensive, had declared the institution of slavery a "blessing to both races. We proclaim that our slaves are better treated, better clothed, better fed, more intelligent, more happy than the laboring classes of any part of the world, and defy contradiction."

I do *say* those wrongs are the exceptions.

We *proclaim* that our slaves are better treated.

But the slaves themselves were never encouraged to speak.

In the same letter to Rebecca, Solomon relates a little anecdote in which a woman from Portland, Maine, comes to Savannah with all sorts of preconceived notions about slavery, only to find that enslaved workers are treated well and moreover have "comparatively little to do." This she observed while staying with a local family. "The family," Solomon writes, "had five servants—I beg pardon, slaves." Gratz never uses the word *slave* in letters, it's always the servants to whom he sends greetings. In Solomon's letter to a woman to whom he'd once shown such deference, he sarcastically preempts objections by skeptics, perhaps including his correspondent, to prettying up the situation by not calling a slave a slave.

Solomon Cohen understood how central enslavement was to his world, the one whose civic and business institutions his family had done more than their share to build. As he vividly put it to Rebecca, the South was a body, with slavery flowing through its veins: "Our slaves are counted by millions, & their value by hundreds of millions, and the system is interwoven into the nerves, and sinews, and arteries, and life blood of our social and political organization." Solomon had seen rice-plantation slavery up close in South Carolina, but here in Savannah the lash was administered behind closed doors—public whippings weren't the image of Savannah the city fathers wanted to convey to the world—and no one was standing in infested waters all day. What did the institution of slavery look like to Solomon as he moved through the city?

Vaughnette Goode-Walker leads a tour called Footprints of Savannah and suggested I join the group, then we could talk afterward. We met in Wright Square, where many of the tour guides like to begin. There are architecture tours and general history tours and ghost tours you can take on foot or in a tricked-out hearse or with a ghost-o-meter in hand to register psychic disturbances in the basement of a house—but this was one of the only tours about slavery. Consciously, that is, for isn't that why the dead come back to haunt us, because we've tried and failed to stop thinking about them? Tall and colorfully robed, a walking stick in hand, Goode-Walker began by calling the ancestors. All half-dozen of us stood around her in a solemn and somewhat stunned silence.

She had a binder full of photographs and facts and began by troubling the idea that there were no enslaved people in Georgia when it was founded. It's true that the colony's charter guaranteed its inhabitants freedom. But enslaved workers from South Carolina were used to clear the bluff of its trees and build the original settlement. And while the colonists were banned from owning people, Georgia was no sanctuary for fugitives. Its status as a so-called buffer colony was meant to protect the established English colonies to the north from Spanish Florida below—but the logic for banning Catholics from Georgia, that they would ally themselves with the Spanish, extended to enslaved people as well. With a new English colony in the way, runaway slaves en route to Florida, where the Spanish had promised them freedom, would find no easy way.

Buffer colony—yes, I remembered that from grade school. But apparently I hadn't learned just what it meant.

As Goode-Walker talked I began to feel that the generic-sounding Footprints of Savannah slavery tour was in fact well named, for it seemed the invisible imprints of the enslaved workers and everyone complicit in the slave trade are all that remain of that chapter of history, and I said as much.

"But it's not true," she says. "The buildings are still there."

You just had to know where to look.

The building housing the Bryan Slave Mart, which freed people turned into a school, is still there, albeit repurposed as Woof Gang Bakery for pets. You can walk down unremarkable-looking Bay Lane, once the center of Savannah's slave trade, though the broker's offices and yards and platforms are gone. A few steps from Bay Lane is Johnson Square, the largest of Savannah's squares, and nearly all of Savannah's banks and most of the brokerages that dealt in slaves were tightly clustered in this area. Bay Lane is just south of Bay Street, the wide thoroughfare at the top of the bluff where Solomon's offices were located. Bull Street runs through the city's most elegant squares, and each weekday morning Solomon would likely have taken this route to work, heading east on Liberty Street and then left on Bull, toward the river.

The first square he would have come to is Chippewa, where today wide-eyed tourists gather on benches, from morning till late at night, to hear guides tell them lurid and often fantastical tales of old Savannah, and people of all ages look for the bench Forrest Gump sat on, which was made of fiberglass and since removed to the visitor center. The curbs, pavement, and landscaping were different in Solomon's day, and the statue of James Oglethorpe, the colony's founder, didn't arrive until 1910. But somewhere behind the featureless stucco facade of the Savannah Theatre, on the east side of the square, are the bones of the Athenaeum, with its pointed pediment and porch covering the ground-floor entranceway that I know from photographs. This was where Vice President of the Confederate States of America Alexander H. Stephens gave his famous "cornerstone" speech, arguing that slavery and Black inferiority were foundational to Southern society. Did Solomon attend? Two of the churches and one mansion that I pass on my way to the office I work out of when I'm in town were there in Solomon's time, and I imagine that on a beautiful sunny day, in the relative cool of the morning, he would have strode down the light-dappled path and felt the *constructedness* of the scene, the press of civilization from all sides onto this man-made plot of nature, and he would have looked around the way the Lord Almighty might have on creation, and thought that it was good.

I cross Oglethorpe Street, which was called South Broad in Solomon's day, and walk the two short blocks to Wright Square. Here is the granite boulder memorializing Tomochichi, the pragmatic Yamacraw leader with whom Oglethorpe negotiated a treaty to occupy the top of the bluff and whose actual grave, in the center of the square, was desecrated, in 1882, with a massive cenotaph to William Washington Gordon, the founder of the Central Rail Road and Banking Company and grandfather of the founder of the Girl Scouts. (To the question "Who is buried in Gordon's tomb?" the answer might be "Tomochichi.") Today a group of people are listening to a guide talking about the way three buildings on the square—a church and two courthouses—used and obscured brick in three different ways. Before the war there was a different courthouse on this lot, a textbook neoclassical temple with four Doric columns under a pointed pediment, clean lined and free of architectural flourishes, and it's this courthouse I'm suddenly picturing, as Solomon himself would have glimpsed it from the corner of his right eye.

If it was the first Tuesday of the month, he would have had to press his way through a crush of men, carriages, wagons, and animals, the square transformed into a marketplace of old. In Savannah his brother Octavus had begun his business career by working as an auctioneer in Wright Square. In the *Daily Georgian* on December 5, 1838, the year Solomon arrived in Savannah, Octavus advertised an upcoming estate sale in the square on the first Tuesday of February 1839:

1 tract land on the Altamaha river 500 acres.

. . .

2–3 interest in 1000 acres land in Camden county, on the Satilla River.

1 tract land in Carrol county, No. 113, 11 district, 202 ½ acres.

1 tract land in Early county, No. 256, 21 district, 223 ½ acres.

1 tract land 600 acres, on Brae Island, in Savannah river.

An individual half 50 acres, lot of land in White Bluff district.

6 lots in new lands, Nos. 8, 9, 10, 11, 20, 21.

11 do on and near the Canal, Nos. 26, 27, 38, 30, 31, 46, 47, 48, 49, 50, 51.

"Also, 12 Negroes," the listing closes, like an afterthought.

Slave brokers' wooden stands were fixtures in front of the courthouse, where they stood mutely every day but first Tuesdays, when real estate and all manner of chattel were auctioned off.

This was what Solomon would have heard. I imagine he would have found the raucous scene, with its human noises and barnyard smells, disagreeable. But even if he didn't turn to look, if he kept heading north, he would have come face-to-face with enslaved people coming from the opposite direction. From Bay Lane the shackled slaves, having been fed and exercised and groomed to look their best, were led down elegant Bull Street to the temple of justice, where they'd be inspected and sold.

In her spare, moving memoir, *Reminiscences of My Life in Camp with the 33d United States Colored Troops, Late 1st S.C. Volunteers,* Goode-Walker's "shero" Susie King Taylor, a nurse and educator who was born into slavery, recalls:

I paused and thought back a few years of the heart rending scenes I have witnessed; I have seen many times, when I was a mere girl, thirty or forty men, handcuffed, and as many women and children, come every first Tuesday of each month from Mr. Wiley's trade office to the auction blocks, one of them being situated on Drayton Street and Court Land, the other on Bryant Street, near the Pulaski House. The route was down our principal street, Bull Street, to the courthouse, which was only a block from where I resided.

All people in those days got all their water from the city pumps, which stood about a block apart throughout the city. The one we used to get water from was opposite the courthouse, on Bull Street. I remember, as if it were yesterday, seeing droves of negroes going to be sold, and I often went to look at them, and I could hear the auctioneer very plainly from my house, auctioning these poor people off.

Even in the refined metropolis, where behind the doors of the great houses uniformed servants stood against faux bois walls, ready to serve from silver tureens and pour from crystal decanters, the fundamental horror of slavery, that the enslaved person's body was not his own, was out in the open. Solomon couldn't have avoided it if he'd wanted to.

For a city dweller, Solomon Cohen owned many enslaved people, though far fewer than the area's largest enslavers. With eight enslaved workers living on his property to attend to his family's needs—a small number, he writes Rebecca, considering his social position—Solomon owned more than a dozen other enslaved people that he hired out.

These contracts could be made for limited periods of time to private individuals or companies, or to the city or county, while enslaved workers with trades might have gone into business for themselves. Such "nominal" slaves might have seen their enslavers only when they gave them a cut of their earnings. Skilled artisans living on their own had more freedom than enslaved workers who lived under their enslavers' roofs, but laws governed the work they were allowed to do, as well as circumscribing their movement around the city and their ability to fraternize with one another and stay out late. In public, the enslaved were obliged to wear identification badges, for which their enslavers paid between $2.50 and $10, depending on their skill level and sex.

Packed into a dense city where disease from poor sanitation was easily transmitted, Savannah slaves didn't live as long as their rural counterparts, but the lives they did lead were richer and freer. Even enslaved workers who lived on their enslavers' premises found ways to escape their surveillance. The layout of the city itself helped. The lanes were ways for enslaved workers to slip out the back and connect with others, as well as with free people of color and fugitives from the countryside. If you read the twenty-two-part city ordinance on slavery, you'd think there was no way an enslaved person could take a single step beyond his enslaver's property without violating the law. But as I learn from Whittington B. Johnson's *Black Savannah, 1788–1864*, these laws were flouted regularly. Johnson explains just how peculiar the peculiar institution could be. By allowing, at whim, the laws to be broken, enslavers seized the same sovereignty over their personal property as they expected the federal government to grant the states. The white establishment selectively enforced the rules because the arbitrary granting of personal privileges was a way of preventing revolts—and it worked. In Savannah, Blacks and whites lived in an uneasy détente, within which Black people got to move around the city for reasons other than work despite complaints from white people of such "uppity" behavior as dressing up and taking joyrides in carriages, smoking cigars, and not ceding room on sidewalks. In this way Black people could claim for themselves some measure of the humanity to which they were officially denied.

But what if they escape? a friend of mine asks.

By 1850 enslaved people were held captive by a set of local and federal laws that made a jail out of the entire country. You couldn't be freed by your enslaver or buy your way out of enslavement. If you happened to be free and wanted to come to Savannah to board a ship for Liberia, you had to pay a $200 fee. With the Compromise of 1850 it was illegal not to return an enslaved person to his enslaver. Unless they managed to get aboard the Underground Railroad and flee the country, where exactly were enslaved people going to escape to?

Still, my friend's question was very much on the minds of white Savannahians in the run-up to war. Slave residences weren't meant to be prisons. There was a real jail for this. Enslaved Savannahians, even the ones who lived under their masters' roofs, moved through the city to do their work—go to market, transport goods from the train station to the riverfront, load and unload ships at the wharves—and contemporaneous letters from fretting enslavers suggest that enslaved people did in fact disappear, sometimes for days, down the narrow lanes in the city's crowded working-class neighborhoods. There were far more bars and liquor stores in mid-nineteenth century Savannah than today, which is saying something, in addition to large and small houses of prostitution. The neighborhoods on the east and west sides of the city were packed with Irish laborers, free men of color, country slaves on the lam, urban slaves, and sailors, and most arrests of enslaved people came from these parts of town.

I imagine that all the hand-wringing that enslavers did when they thought their enslaved workers might be out drinking stood for a larger anxiety, that this little taste of liberty, rather than satisfying them, might lead to a greater thirst.

In the *Savannah Daily Morning News* of March 19, 1863, midway through the war, there's a drawing of two round matzoth and underneath them the injunction to bring your boxes right away because this is the last day for baking "Passover bread." This ad butts right up against one headed Negroes for Sale, one of many such ads on the page. The enslaved people in question were not being sold by Jews, and in fact the role of Jews in the slave trade has been notoriously exaggerated. In Savannah Jews owned humans proportionately to their wealth, just as non-Jews did. Most Jews lived in cities, and so most Jewish enslavers had enslaved workers as house servants and far fewer of them than plantation owners did. Still, it was depressing news to me that Jews enslaved other people. Depressing for the obvious reason. News because the liberation story recounted on Passover is central to the Jewish religion! *Because we were slaves in Egypt.*

Solomon Cohen, Savannah's largest Jewish enslaver, would have scoffed at my naivete. I have come to learn that when he defends human enslavement on religious grounds, he's echoing the arguments that were hurled like lightning bolts from the podiums of assembly halls and the pulpits of houses of worship across the land. For a taste of the biblical argument in favor of slavery, I get it straight from the horse's mouth, a famed New York rabbi named Morris J. Raphall, who delivered it as an address in January 1861 and published it later as a pamphlet, *The Bible View of Slavery.* The year before, the English-born Raphall became the first rabbi to give the prayer opening a session of Congress, and he'd long been a leader of New York's

Jewish community and a well-known lecturer; Rebecca Gratz had heard him speak. But the pamphlet propelled Raphall to national notoriety.

It's not just the points of the argument that remind me of Solomon; it's the venomous way in which it's delivered, as if opposition to slavery is defiance of God, not to mention the forefathers of Judaism.

> How dare you, in the face of the sanction and protection afforded to slave property in the Ten Commandments—how dare you denounce slaveholding as a sin? When you remember that Abraham, Isaac, Jacob, Job—the men with whom the Almighty conversed, with whose names he emphatically connects his own most holy name, and to whom He vouchsafed to give the character of "perfect, upright, fearing G-d and eschewing evil" (Job i. 8)—that all these men were slaveholders, does it not strike you that you are guilty of something very little short of blasphemy? And if you answer me, "Oh, in their time slaveholding was lawful, but now it has become a sin," I in my turn ask you, "When and by what authority do you draw the line?"

Raphall claims simply to be providing the religious view, as he's been requested to do, but he reveals his own prejudices with a loopy argument in favor of Black enslavement specifically. Raphall sees evidence of biblical prophecy everywhere he looks. Noah's curse, for example, is realized in the enslavement and persecution of Black people.

But the Canaanites in the Bible aren't Africans. And to seek biblical justification for modern-day slavery, you have to find current prohibitions against incest, concubinage, polygamy, and bigamy as blasphemous as you do abolitionism, a point made by contemporaneous Jewish scholars, including Rabbi David Einhorn of Baltimore. In his rebuttal of Raphall's pamphlet, Einhorn, who ended up being forced to flee the city, sounds flabbergasted that a Jew would try to justify slavery as a "God-sanctioned institution."

But despite his defense of it on religious grounds, Raphall finds slavery as practiced in the American South repugnant, for in objectifying Black people it resembles the heathen, Roman institution rather than the one prescribed in the Bible, in which, Raphall claims, the "slave is a *person* in whom the dignity of human nature is to be respected." (The remedy, then, is for the South simply to adopt the Bible view of slavery.) Solomon too sees "wrongs" in the South's slavery system. But in his business correspondence I find, if not a different side, then at least enough traces of the man's conscience to help explain how he could live in a system he knew was brutal but so unequivocally upheld.

In 1850 Solomon is simplifying his legal affairs to make way for new ventures. The lingering conflict he's trying to resolve concerns an enslaved woman named Sally, who appears to have been held by his late father and now, through inheritance, by his mother. Solomon seems to have some special feeling for Sally, the matriarch of her family—likely the seventy-nine-year-old female "mulatto" listed in Solomon's 1850 United States Federal Census slave schedule. Perhaps she raised him and his siblings back in Georgetown. Now she lives with the Cohen family on Liberty Street.

Sally is old and so is Solomon's mother. When Bell dies, Solomon's sister Eleanor, who lives in Mobile, will inherit a sixth of their mother's enslaved people—or, to be accurate, her husband will. On February 15, 1850, Solomon asks Eleanor's husband, Dr. Aaron Lopez, to assign him his share of the enslaved family in exchange for canceling Lopez's debts. Solomon writes that he's motivated not by personal gain but rather by "a sense of duty & humanity in not wishing the Negroes separated," pointing out that the value of Lopez's share of the enslaved family is worth less than the amount Lopez owes him. But Solomon's sister isn't interested in debt forgiveness. "To Sally's family I never will yield my rights, but by the decision of a jury," she declares.

For more than a year Solomon tries to make some deal, becoming increasingly enraged, in letter after letter, as his brother-in-law ignores him. Solomon finally gives up and now wants to be repaid, for debt that has gone unpaid for more than fifteen years. What started as a bluff—sign over your share of my mother's slaves at advantageous terms or else repay your debts—has become very real. Dr. Lopez's wall of silence doesn't crack. And so Solomon Cohen prepares to sue his own brother-in-law for a sum that he himself has suggested Lopez can ill afford: one loan for $460.73 of principal plus interest since 1833, the other for $280.77 of principal plus interest since 1834.

Justice is a word that Solomon initially uses in reference to keeping Sally's family together. Do his threats represent the lengths he'll go to in order to see that just end? Or is Solomon trying to restore his pride in the only way left? For now he feels he's the one to whom justice is due, hoping that Dr. Lopez will "reflect, and do me justice, both by act & thought."

I don't know how the matter ended. But Sally passes away a year after Solomon began his effort to acquire his brother-in-law's share of the family's human property. With typically muted emotion, Solomon closes a letter to another brother-in-law "Love to Sister, & tell her, that old Mom Sally is dead."

Fifty years earlier, Solomon's uncle Abraham attempted, in his will, to keep together a family he owned, though only until the death of his companion, a mixed-race woman known as Free Peggy McWharter, whom he himself might have freed from enslavement. Abraham, the older of the two brothers who'd come to Georgetown after their father's death, apparently saw no contradiction between living with a free woman of color and owning slaves. Of his twenty-one enslaved people, Abraham took care to name eight: "I give and bequeath to my executors hereinafter named, and the survivor and survivors of them, his executors and administrators, eight negroes, viz., Caesar, Rose, Harry, Binah, and her four children, Lucy, Judy, Billy and Tom, with the issue and increase of the females." Abraham placed these people, as well as his house at 55 Prince Street and all that it contained, in trust "for the benefit, use and behoof of Margaret McWharter during her lifetime," after which the estate was to be distributed among three of Abraham's nieces. McWharter died in 1806, and Abraham's legacy was judged so poorly written that it failed, passing instead, under the "residuary clause," to his brother Solomon Cohen Sr. and his nephews and nieces. But even before McWharter's death, Solomon Sr. and two other executors had already taken possession of the enslaved people specified in Abraham's will.

Solomon Sr.'s slaves passed to his wife, but it's impossible to know whether any of Abraham's slaves figure into the family that Solomon Jr., anticipating her death, tries to keep together in 1850. A genealogist named Sadie Day Pasha raised the possibility that the eight enslaved people named in Abraham Cohen's will were in fact his children and grandchildren. It would be illuminating to discover that Solomon Cohen Jr., in trying to keep Sally's family together, was motivated, as least in part, by family feeling—that is, love for his own mixed-race cousins. But it's too hard to connect the dots, and I can't find any references to Abraham Cohen, much less to his companion and any children they might have had, in Solomon's writing. What's certain is that the outcome of Abraham's will, and of Solomon's dogged deal-making, showed the futility of legal efforts to keep human chattel together and the uselessness of "a sense of duty & humanity" in tempering an inhumane system.

In his letter to Rebecca, Solomon allows himself to imagine the unimaginable—the end of slavery—which he fears the way the ancients did a solar eclipse: "How then can it be eradicated without inflicting death on us and desolation on our homes? The blotting of such a system, the blotting out of such an amount of labor and capital, would convulse the world." Solomon writes these lines at the very start of the war. Soon enough he'll know the apocalypse, though not quite as he imagined it.

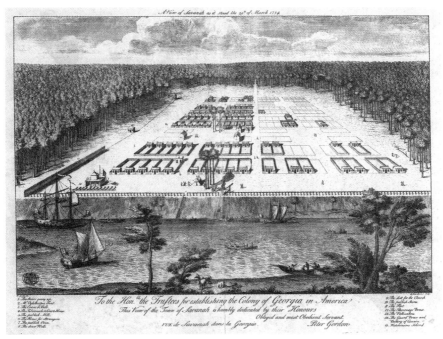

View of year-old Savannah with the progressive city plan laid out, looking south from across the Savannah River, March 29, 1734. Library of Congress, 97683565.

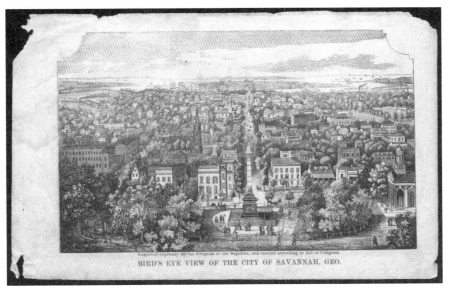

Bird's-eye view of Savannah, nicknamed the Forest City of the South, looking north, 1855. By the mid-nineteenth century Savannah had become a bustling port whose egalitarian founding ideals had been abandoned. Courtesy of the Georgia Historical Society, Georgia Historical Society collection of etchings, silhouettes, and other prints, GHS 1361-PR.

Cohen family portrait, ca. 1854. From *left*, Gratz, Miriam, Solomon, and Belle, with Miriam (Mamie) in *front*. Courtesy Georgia Archives, Vanishing Georgia Collection, ctm229.

Solomon Cohen, photographed in London after Gratz's death, ca. 1867. Courtesy Georgia Archives, Vanishing Georgia Collection, ctm227.

Miram Cohen's aunt Rebecca Gratz, shown here at fifty in a painting by Thomas Sully, 1831, was the founder of Hebrew Sunday School and benevolent institutions including the Philadelphia Orphan Asylum and the Female Hebrew Benevolent Society. Courtesy Rosenbach Museum and Library, Philadelphia, 2010.0027.001.

Solomon Cohen family house, corner of Liberty and Barnard streets, after it had become the city house of Mamie and James Dent and their children, 1880s. Courtesy Georgia Archives, Vanishing Georgia Collection, gly163.

Painting of an Aryanized Gratz Cohen, ca. 1925-45, by Anne Lee Haynes, that hangs in the Hofwyl-Broadfield plantation house. Courtesy of Georgia Department of Natural Resources, Hofwyl-Broadfield Plantation State Historic Site.

Photograph of Gratz Cohen as a young dandy, ca. 1860. Courtesy of Georgia Department of Natural Resources, Hofwyl-Broadfield Plantation State Historic Site.

C. D. FREDRICKS & Cº.

Carte-de-visite photograph of Gratz Cohen in his captain's uniform with a country backdrop, 1860s. Courtesy of Georgia Department of Natural Resources, Hofwyl-Broadfield Plantation State Historic Site.

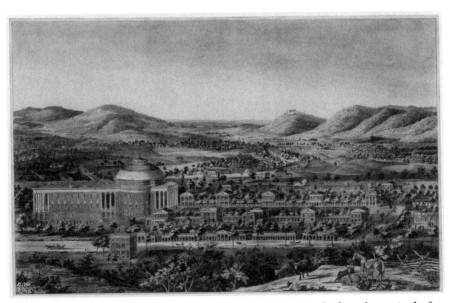

A loose page in Gratz Cohen's diary, ca. 1862, with a poem lamenting the departure of his enslaved valet: "Where he is now my spirit yearns to know / His loss has plunged me into endless woe." Courtesy of the Georgia Historical Society, Cohen-Hunter Papers, GHS 0161.

The University of Virginia, Charlottesville, 1856, six years before the arrival of Gratz Cohen, the first Jewish student at Thomas Jefferson's "academical village." Jefferson's plantation Monticello is on the hilltop in the background. University of Virginia Library Special Collections, u4773049.

BOMBARDMENT OF FORT PULASKI, COCKSPUR ISLAND, GEO 10ᵀᴴ & 11ᵀᴴ OF APRIL 1862.

Bombardment of Fort Pulaski, on Cockspur Island, by Union forces, April 10 and 11, 1862. Courtesy of the Georgia Historical Society, Georgia Historical Society collection of photographs, GHS 1361-PH.

General William J. Hardee's evacuation of Confederate forces from Savannah to South Carolina, across the Savannah River, December 20 and 21, 1864, as depicted in *Frank Leslie's Illustrated Newspaper*, March 11, 1865. Courtesy of the Georgia Historical Society, Georgia Historical Society collection of etchings, silhouettes, and other prints, GHS 1361-OV.

March Haynes, 1888. A deacon of Savannah's First
African Baptist Church and boat pilot, Haynes conducted perilous missions through the marsh to bring
hundreds of enslaved people to sanctuary on Cockspur
Island. Schomburg Center for Research in Black Culture, Manuscripts, Archives and Rare Books Division,
The New York Public Library, b22030888.

Belle Cohen (*center*) with her second husband, Eugene Corson, and Miriam Cohen at the Liberty Street townhouse they shared, 1885 or 1886. Courtesy of the Georgia Historical Society, Georgia Historical Society collection of photographs, GHS 1376-PH.

PART III
Sitting Out the War

12

Charming Friendship of Youth

Exactly a year after we bought the Liberty Street flat, a rally took place in Charlottesville, Virginia, to "Unite the Right," which comprised fascists of various stripes, right-wing militias, white nationalists, and neo-Confederates. Ostensibly these people gathered to protest the proposed removal of a statue of Robert E. Lee from a city park, but the larger anxiety they expressed was around the diminishment of white prestige in a multicultural society, Jews specifically being called out as culprits. Unless you banished these particular elements from American society, leaving a statue in a park wasn't going to appease the protesters. The dishonoring of Lee, himself opposed to statues and other monuments to the South's defeat, was an excuse for a display of white grievance and an exercise of white power.

A year later I was in Savannah preparing to visit Charlottesville to find out what I could about Gratz's college years. It was 2018 and the city of Savannah had joined in the national debate on the monuments. I never paid much attention to the Confederate Monument in Savannah's Forsyth Park, perhaps because, set on a mound and a hideous mausoleumlike sandstone base, the statue of a rebel soldier is so high up that you'd never even notice it if you didn't look up. Gun at his side and hands crossed at the waist, the soldier faces north, the enemy's home though not, in the end, the direction from which he attacked. The city decided to keep the statue but change the plaque to honor not just Confederate soldiers but all the Civil War dead. Rededicating the monument would include relocating the two busts at its base that had been moved there in 1910, thirty-five years after the monument was erected. (At least that was the plan before a Georgia state law passed, in 2019, providing "protection" for government monuments. So nothing changed at all, except that the Confederate Monument had been renamed the Civil War Memorial, something I discovered online and of which I can find no trace, nor of the proposed plaque, at the monument itself.)

I now knew who these busts represented, because of how they figured into the Cohen story. One was of Colonel Francis S. Bartow, the neighbor of Solomon Cohen's and commander of a regiment whose troops were among Savannah's first casualties of the war. The other bust was of Major General Lafayette McLaws, in whose division Gratz would serve as a volunteer aide in the last months of the war. McLaws was a name I'd long known in another context. A childhood friend lived on McLaws Street; all the streets in Habersham Woods were named after Confederate generals. This subdivision of great brick homes was developed in the late 1960s and 1970s. The timing was no coincidence. Confederate monuments popped up during periods when white domination felt under threat—Reconstruction and, a century later, the era of civil rights.

On the last day of my stay in Savannah, I took a walk through Forsyth Park. The story I was trying to learn was becoming quite relevant to current events—but of course it always had been. It was a hot spring afternoon and I circled the memorial and thought of all the other young men like Gratz, hundreds of thousands of the dead, and the quilt of remembrance made of their lives, big enough to blanket the South, durable, though stitched of some pretty fine material, the stuff of romance. And in the months and years after I'd returned to the very place I'd fled, it had become glaringly obvious, even to those who'd chosen not to see, that the fabric of honor and glory, crimson with martyred blood, in which the South had wrapped itself was getting a little threadbare, giving way here and there, tearing most spectacularly in Charleston and Charlottesville. There was something wrong with the way we remembered the Civil War and told the story of men like Gratz Cohen. A problem with the stories we told and those we did not, and at that point it was still unclear to me which problem was worse.

"My lameness prevents my performing the least military duty," Gratz has finally acknowledged. And so now, in the fall of 1862, he sets out on a more suitable path. He goes to college, becoming the first Jewish student at the University of Virginia.

Today the town runs seamlessly into the university, Main Street becomes University Avenue, but when Gratz was there, Thomas Jefferson's collection of buildings around a lawn was a bit out in the country. I go in August, when the hilly campus is quiet, but the place is still staffed, to do things like help a middle-aged man from far away track down the traces of a young man who studied here more than a century and a half ago. In the Special Collections library I find three autograph books bearing Gratz's inscription. Even before I locate his contributions, I'm moved by these collections of melancholy goodbyes, just as I was by Gratz's own autograph book, in the Georgia Historical Society. How clear-eyed these young people were that they would never see one another again.

Here's Gratz's entry, in his messy, upward-sloping hand, in George Albion Staley's book:

> I feel that no rhetoric is necessary to explain my feelings towards you,
> so I will simply sign myself your friend
> > Gratz Cohen
> > University of Va
> > Jan 6th 1863

> To Susie T. Brown:
> Could your clear, silvery ringing
> laugh sound forever in my
> ears. I would never fear the
> little blue devils, nor wish for
> sweeter music
> > Your friend
> > Gratz
> > U.V. June 21st 1863

But the autograph book of Elliott DeJarnette Gratz simply inscribes with his name.

Charlottesville and the University of Virginia in the Civil War, a 1998 monograph with a presciently search-engine-ready title, is available for perusal in Special Collections, but a librarian directs me to a bookstore where I might find a copy of my own. When I break for lunch I head into town and find the place. I tell the grizzled guy behind the counter what I'm looking for. "Ervin's book," says another person with a similar look. "Yep, that's Ervin's," says the first man. "Local guy," the second man tells me as the first one leads me outside and down alongside the building to a god-awful mess of a storeroom that mostly contains Jefferson's papers in various editions, stretching across shelf after shelf. Books everywhere, but not the one I'm looking for.

"Here's something," my guide says, handing me what turns out to be the *University Memorial*, the collection of sketches of alumni killed in the Civil War where I found the first biography sketch of Gratz Cohen set in print. I'd read this brief account online before I'd read his own words, or knew anything about him or his world—and yet I could tell it was only a story, and not an especially believable one. And now that I've set out to write my own, hopefully more convincing version of Gratz Cohen's life, the virtual book has become a material one, just as everything else about Gratz's life and times has become, over the months, more real to me. I pull open the rotting binding, turn the crumbling pages, but when I reach the entry on Gratz, his picture, protected by a single piece of clear film, is perfectly preserved, like a mosaic floor cleared free in Pompeii.

Gratz's gaze is so direct that the portrait comes off as psychological, though his expression gives absolutely nothing away, as befits a man whose short life was shrouded in mystery. Big brown eyes and cherub lips complement thick brows and a strong chin; the mustache, so vague in reproductions, is a definite arch over his mouth, though not fully grown in. It's a boy's face becoming a man's, and it's looking up at me from his century as I look down at him from mine.

I show the guy the picture of Gratz.

"Look at him," he says.

I explain who Gratz was, say I have a connection to him.

"Good for you," he says, though he can't possibly know what I'm talking about. I must have chosen the word *connection* precisely for its ambiguity, safely concealing the extent of my relationship to Gratz Cohen, which began when my husband and I bought the apartment but has only deepened since.

"It sounds like a fascinating story," he tells me.

"It is," I say. "But to write about a Confederate soldier who went to UVA a year after what happened here, it feels like a political act."

"Why does everything have to be political?" he asks, shaking his head. "Can't it just be historical?"

No, I think as I close the cover. I'll either be building a monument to this kid or tearing one down.

"It's too expensive," I say apologetically. "If I can get an advance on this book, though, I'll come back."

"That's all right," he says. "It'll be here."

In the fall of 1862, Solomon accompanies Gratz to Virginia, where they first stop at the Richmond home of Emma Mordecai, an aunt whom Gratz is meeting for the first time. He visits with other relatives in her home, but it's Emma, an unmarried woman who writes books and articles on Jewish subjects and serves as a volunteer nurse, who makes such an impression on him that she quickly becomes one of the people he admires most in the world—second only to his aunt Rebecca Gratz. In Charlottesville father and son check into a hotel, and soon Gratz is installed in one of the little rooms along the Lawn, the quadrangle at the heart of the university, where his college life begins.

The town and the university, while drawing students from rich Southern families like Gratz's, were strange to him. Savannah was beautiful; Gratz's first glimpse of Charlottesville left him unimpressed. Savannah was flat; Charlottesville was hilly. Savannah was hot; Virginia could get cold, an exotic climate he wanted his sisters to come experience with him. The Rotunda, where Gratz took classes, was grander than any building in Savannah, its exposed brick red, uniform, smooth, neat, and solid, unlike the soft porous mortar-smeared Savannah grey brick that builders liked to stucco over. The pavilions and colonnades along the Lawn of Jefferson's "academical village" were elegant. But Gratz's room, as in any other college dorm, was plain and basic: hearth, window, bed, desk. Travelers and even some locals found Savannah backward intellectually; Gratz now found himself among the South's brightest sons. Politically, the student body identified with the region where it came from and was keen on the Confederacy—but the school's administration objected, if only for its own financial interests, to the conscription of students.

In other words, Gratz Cohen was in a different enough place, and far enough away, to become himself without turning into someone entirely new.

Still, going to the University of Virginia in the fall of 1862 was a strange thing to do. This wasn't a military academy, like the previous educational institution Gratz had attended. This was a place where students had, for forty years, received a classical education in a pastoral setting, where they might have learned of the great wars of antiquity but without seeking any practical application from them. The student body was known for its rowdiness—most notorious was the case of Gessner Harrison, an alumnus and professor of ancient languages at the age of twenty-one, whose inability to control students culminated, in 1836, in being *horsewhipped* by one of them. But now Gratz was heading into violence of a different order. The previous August saw the Battle of Second Manassas, or Second Battle of Bull Run as it's more commonly called outside the South, which was fought just eighty miles northeast of Charlottesville. Although passage would have been relatively easy, considering the railroads between Georgia and Virginia were still in Confederate hands, going to Virginia when Gratz did was going into the heart of war.

Gratz would have prized the school's academic excellence, and its unrivaled class prestige in the South would certainly have appealed to Solomon. But there may have been another reason a Jew would choose Jefferson's university. His Statute of Religious Freedom, drafted in 1777 and adopted in 1786, states that "no man shall be compelled to frequent or support any religious worship, place, or ministry whatsoever, nor shall be enforced, restrained, molested, or burthened in his body or goods, nor shall otherwise suffer on account of his religious opinions or belief; but that all men shall be free to profess, and by argument to maintain, their opinion in matters of religion, and that the same shall in no way diminish, enlarge, or affect their civil capacities." It's the same kind of Enlightenment thinking that gave rise to the Fundamental Constitutions of Carolina a century earlier, which allowed religious freedom for Jews and other "dissenters" from Christianity, including Gratz's great-grandparents, the first of the family to move to the New World. Of the Jews specifically, Jefferson wrote, "I have thought it a cruel addition to the wrong which that injured sect have suffered that their youths should be excluded in the instructions in science afforded to all others in our public seminaries by imposing on them a course of theological reading which their consciences do not permit them to pursue." At the university that Jefferson founded, on the other hand, "we have set the example of ceasing to violate the rights of conscience by any injunctions on the different sects respecting their religion."

Jefferson wrote this in 1826, a year after the university's first classes were held, but it took another thirty-six years before the first Jewish student arrived. The University of Virginia hadn't lived up to its founder's ideals in other ways as well. Gratz had no role models, though an earlier first, twenty-one years before Gratz arrived in Charlottesville, might have given him pause, if he knew about it. In 1841 an Englishman named James Joseph Sylvester was made professor of mathematics, the first Jew hired by an American college to teach a secular subject. Sylvester was a brilliant and influential mathematician, but he became a victim of the anti-Semitism of the day. A Richmond Presbyterian newspaper lumped Sylvester's hiring in with that of a "Hungarian Papist," the pair of appointments "the heaviest blow the University has ever received." The paper's editorial board had seen this coming. "We have often said that as infidelity became ashamed of its own colors, it would seek to form alliances with Papism, Unitarianism, Judaism, and other errors subversive of Christianity." Sylvester arrived in November. With his long unkempt white beard and curls corkscrewing around his bald cranium, he was the very model of the genius mathematician, and he must have cut a strange figure on campus. He complained about the rowdiness of the students, and one in particular, whom, according to one account, Sylvester stabbed for insulting him during a lecture. The student's supporters in turn might have attacked the professor. By March 1842, less than six months after his arrival, Sylvester was gone.

There's no trace in Gratz's writing from Virginia of the kind of behavior on campus that drove Sylvester out two decades before. Local newspapers didn't put a target on Gratz's back as they had on Sylvester's. Nor was he taunted, the way Black students were when they integrated Southern high schools and colleges a century later. Gratz was more like his fellow students than not—they were all the sons of rich Southern aristocrats. Still, you can't be the first without any pushback, and I try to read between the lines of Gratz's letters and journal entries for signs that he might have been a victim of anti-Semitism. Gratz doesn't report anything like it, and in fact he praised Charlottesvillians as "a brave, generous, & simple people—each day I am struck by this and have to be grateful for some new act of kindness." But this is Gratz all over, always willing to see the best in people, though as with Abraham Lincoln, Gratz's very visible melancholia attracted people to him. "It has so far been my luck to find wherever I go friends kinder than the last," he wrote his sister Belle. Gratz would have eschewed any comparison with the president, but this one strikes me as true. One reason these men were treated tenderly, even by strangers, was that they were so obviously in need of it.

When he arrived, Charlottesville was a village of 3,000, composed mostly of modest homes arranged in a grid of around twenty blocks, with the railroad as its southern border. The street names were prosaic: North, South, East, Church, School, Water, Main. There was a town hall, a court-house, a jail. Gratz arrived the first week of October, a month shy of his eighteenth birthday. Of the hotel where he and his father stayed, the best in town, Gratz reported to Belle that it was "not by any means a Fifth Avenue." Gratz wrote his sister on Court Day, when "the assembly of starved horses & drunken men gathered from the surrounding country did not add any to the dirty red brick houses on a red clay hill, which compose the classic city of Charlottesville." He allowed, though, that the natural setting was pretty.

Attesting to just how provincial a place it was is a famous picture of the University of Virginia in 1856 that startles me whenever I look at it. The quadrangle, defined by the huge Rotunda at one end and the colonnades on either side, is in the middle distance. The little town of Charlottesville is behind it, with the rolling Southwest Mountains rising in the background. And in the foreground, on a precipice bound partly by a split rail fence, are cows and a horse. We're looking at the animals but not from so far away; they stand in for the viewer and put this one, at least, into an animal mindset, looking down dumbly and curiously at this thing set down in the middle of the country. Jefferson, himself a farmer, nods to the setting by incorpo-rating a little bust of Saturn, Roman god of agriculture, into the frieze of the first pavilion from the Rotunda. But you can't see Saturn's head from up here in this barnyard. From this angle the buildings seem to have no connection with their surroundings, managing to look both classical and futuristic. The university performed its function of preparing the region's youth for tomorrow by teaching the lessons of the past, setting students' sights, from their first view of the campus, on the architectural features that Jefferson borrowed from the classical and neoclassical buildings he loved.

But in the fall of 1862, the university was a lonely place, so deserted that visi-tors sometimes assumed it had closed up. In fact it was open for business, though business was bad, considering that faculty got paid for the number of students they taught. Owing to the war, the student population for the academic year of 1862–63 was a mere forty-six, down from sixty-six the year before, which was a ninth of what it had been the year before that. But even in such a small class, Gratz finds students with connections to home, including Jo Bryan, a nephew of Savannah slave broker Joseph Bryan, his best friend at the university. Then there's fellow Savannahian George Staley, who "rooms next to me—the ties of home have made us <u>very</u> intimate." The room on the other side of Gratz's is occupied by D. E. Huger Smith, whose intellect Gratz admires and whom he playfully calls "the greatest ass and ridicule of the university, you see he is from Charleston"— Savannah's rival picturesque port then and now. There's Tom Joynes and Edmund Harrison, a "very pretty plump & rosy cheeked boy," as well as a "poor emaciated atom of mortality named Roper, with plenty of sense." How happy Gratz sounds with these boys, all of whom he insists he's quite fond of, especially the ones he denigrates the most.

Now Gratz finds himself plunged into "that charming friendship of youth so full of pleasant memories when young hearts blend together, and desires tend to the same point, those are the days of Damon & Pythisiasis [*sic*]—no chilling influences of mature age come to blast; each age has its ties. Manhood—that of the loving wife. Middle age the offspring of our loins; but Youth alone knows friendship. The chain is broken, and the links can never again be reunited." Only during these college years—and in an all-male environment far from home—can Gratz have the intimate relationships that he realizes, perhaps for the first time, he craves. For Gratz, an intense loving friendship between two young men is the ideal relationship, and even as he's discovering its joys, it depresses him that it has to end.

It's not surprising that he turns to the Greeks for a model of this kind of friendship. He's come to this neoclassical academic village with the classics well represented in his seven boxes of books: Gibbon's *Decline and Fall of the Roman Empire*, the *Odyssey*, a seven-volume *Classical Library*, Gordon's *Tacitus*. And then as today, when you are looking for hot heroic men who are devoted to each other, you think of ancient Greece, Achilles and Patroclus being the most famous example, but Damon and Pythias in second place. As told by Cicero and others before and after, Pythias was accused of plotting against the tyrant Dionysius, who reigned in Syracuse between 405 and 367 BC. Sentenced to death, Pythias asks to return home one final time before his execution. The king turns him down. Damon then offers himself as a hostage, agreeing to be killed if Pythias doesn't return. Pythias goes home, but on his way back to Syracuse his ship is captured by pirates who throw him overboard. He swims to shore and races back just as Damon is about to be killed in his stead. Dionysius is impressed by how faithful these two are to each other and stays the sentence.

When I've finished my research at the Special Collections library, I walk the short distance to the campus that Gratz would have known. The student rooms lie along colonnades facing the Lawn. The day is warm but these walkways are cool, shadows pooling round the bases of the columns, and they extend so far out from the Rotunda that for a moment I feel I'm in a city, not just the "academical village" that Jefferson imagined but somewhere with boulevards, I suppose on the Continent. The grandeur somewhat makes up for the rooms themselves, which are small, about thirteen feet square, and to this day don't have a bathroom, though they're considered prestigious digs and it's competitive to get one.

I poke my head into an empty room where a young woman is unspooling a tape measure, and I see a space little changed from Gratz's day, and with only so many options to configure the furniture. There's a window on the wall facing the door, with room for a desk pushed up against it; the bed goes against the wall opposite the hearth. In that first autumn in Virginia, Gratz wrote a letter to his parents "sitting in my nice little carpeted room with a cheery wood fire crackling away, speaking its own language but speaking to me of home." The home he's talking about is a mansion, and the fact that this Spartan cell could remind him of it speaks of an adaptiveness that he'll demonstrate his whole life. In this college room he had a comfortable armchair and a baize-covered writing board, and I can almost see him seated there in the room I'm peeking into.

The subject of Gratz's first diary entry, perhaps written in a room just like this one, is Louis, his valet, who after at least one failed attempt has apparently escaped slavery for good. Looking for someone to blame, Gratz concludes that tormented diary entry this way: "Abolitionist. Emancipationist. Whatever he may call himself, can not one iota change if Nature has ordained it and it is unchangeable. God bless you, I say again, my poor Ebony Idol—My Sancho Pansa—Lil Black—My Shadow thou wast indeed—" Louis's escape surely had more to do with a desire for freedom than with the activities of abolitionists, whom Gratz seems to take as personal enemies, saboteurs of his relationship with his valet. Not once, but twice, does Gratz call Louis his ebony idol, an object of worship, if only to Gratz himself. In the promiscuous series of pet names that closes the passage, Louis is also a sidekick and a double.

In fact, from Gratz's entry on their "defence of the coast" you would never even know this pair left town, for Gratz doesn't find it important enough to record the duties he fulfilled as an aide-de-camp that winter, instead losing himself in a reverie about the man he performed them with:

> I cannot consent that this period of my life should pass onward like
> the waves of the ocean and leave no traces of its existence. Tis true
> it will not possess to me the interest of the past year & perhaps no
> period of my existence ever will again. Last Winter was indeed a
> little romance of excitement, of much pleasure, but its recollection is
> mingled with so much pain and can never be recalled without a sigh.
> Louis. Your name has stamped its self on my Life. In the doctrine of
> Counterparts my poor ebony Idol, you were mine and every event of
> that bright little life of mine last winter had entwined you with it; as
> the root of the Tree of Heaven spreads forth in every direction under-
> mining walls, under thick masonry until it can not be eradicated,
> so hath thou spread in every recess of my thoughts and thou art the
> emblem of the relation of thy race with mine.

In letters home Gratz referred to Louis as his valet or groom. But once he could express his feelings far from prying eyes, Gratz revealed Louis, if only to himself, as something much more. Whatever the doctrine of Counterparts is, Gratz seems to be calling Louis his soulmate, his equal, or even investing him with a higher status—an idol is the image of a god. And while Gratz always has a religious reference at hand, the Tree of Heaven in this case is a tree; not a lordly oak sheltering the tomb of a fair maiden or a noble warrior, recurring images in Gratz's Southern pastoral poetry, but a plain old tree, the invasive ailanthus. Louis has penetrated Gratz's very being.

The undated and untitled poem on the loose page tucked into Gratz's journal, which begins "Deep in my breast there is a load of pain," memorializes an unnamed man who serves the speaker in his infantry. The poem evokes the same feelings that Gratz describes in his diary entry—loss, but also betrayal, abandonment, by a man he believed was ever ready to "share my pleasure yet on bended knee." It's a more intense version of what an entire class of people will feel as the war drags on and institutions fall apart and beloved "servants" take off at the first chance they get. The lopsidedness of his relationship with his valet seems to come as news to Gratz, unwelcome, nothing short of a gut punch. He knew he had the power in the relationship but was unaware he didn't have all of it. Louis surely saw the military assignment on the coast less as a "romance of adventure" than as an opportunity to be free.

It's a man named David who now wakes Gratz Cohen at a quarter to six each morning with a basin of water. While Gratz dresses, David cleans his books, perhaps soot-stained from the previous night's fireside homework. Gratz takes breakfast and his other meals at a Charlottesville boarding house run by a Mrs. Ross, who has recently raised her rate to $5 a month. Prices are going up everywhere as supplies grow scarce, though unlike the average Charlottesvillian, Gratz isn't tightening his belt. To the contrary, in a letter home he writes, with apologies to his mother, that he has "never lived better, meals delightfully cooked abundant & of every variety, and dessert, even in these hard times." In a subsequent letter he includes the "bill of fare" from yesterday's dinner:

Soup
Fillet of veal stuffed
Roast chickens – Ham
cold beef & Mutton

                              Vegetables

Irish & sweet potatoes
Corn, stewed tomatoes

                         Salad
                       Tomatoes
                        Dessert
Stewed apples & milk

In the back of his mind, even as he's enjoying Mrs. Ross's cuisine, might be the arrangement his mother has made with her to care for him in case he falls ill. She suspected her delicate son was going to need it, and having this plan in place must have made her feel better about letting him go away from her to begin with.

Gratz takes German, Latin, and French, and a class called History and Literature. Latin is the subject on which he's most focused, drumming up drama in letters home about whether he'll pass the exam. He enrolls in a "natural philosophy" class without consulting his father, though he hopes, in a letter to his sister Mamie, that Solomon won't object. It's just one of many ways that Gratz begins to assert his independence.

He reads mock-heroic verses of Horace. He studies Racine's tragedy *Athalie,* its title character the widow of the king of Judah who has abandoned Judaism and attempted to eliminate the rest of the royal family, before being killed by the high priest. He reads Schiller's *William Tell,* about the Swiss struggle for independence from the Hapsburg Empire in the fourteenth century. It isn't just the ancient world that provides Gratz with models of great men performing heroic acts.

A couple of weeks after he arrives in Charlottesville, Gratz and a couple of fellow students visit Ashby Turner's grave. The Confederate cavalry commander with the luxuriant black beard was killed the previous June, at the Battle of Good's Farm, and is buried in the little cemetery on the university campus. Gratz plucks a couple of flowers for Belle and presses them between the pages of a letter to his parents, explaining that his sister should consider them sacred, having come from ground where "one of our heroic chieftains" was buried—a phrase in the idiom of the heroic literature he's studying.

During the war Charlottesvillians are always on edge, alert to both military reports and flimsy rumors, fearing invasion at any moment. Troops and refugees pass through the city, fallen sons are brought home for burial, and wounded and dying soldiers are fast turning the place into a hospital town—during the war years the twenty-block town with one of every other kind of municipal building has three hospitals. Typhus breaks out, as does measles, disease ravaging the town just the way it tears through camp. Armies are moving in the Shenandoah Valley to the northwest, but Charlottesville, while full of war activity, sees no fighting. It turns out Gratz has come to the right place to get what he wants—the romance of war without war itself.

Still, sitting out the fight is hard for him to get used to, and writing verse transports him to a more heroic place. A month after Gratz arrives in Charlottesville and exactly a year after a military review in which he participated, as aide-de-camp to General Harrison, he writes a poem lamenting how "changed the scene" has become for him, then going on to describe the review:

> Its birth it seems as if but yesterday
> Its pomp its glory & its aspect gay—
> My father's speech, the grand review
> When first oh Cosmo I began to know you

A month later Gratz writes in his journal: "My _____ I know not what to call him. Cosmo. He is on General Anderson's staff. May I see him soon."

Now, with soldiering out of his reach, Gratz finds a different kind of war to displace his feelings onto. He begins to see himself as the hero of his own family romance. The separation from his family—especially the women, his mother and sisters and aunt—affects him keenly. He's not exactly homesick, he confides to his journal at twilight toward the end of his first month in Virginia. What this child of his mother's relatively old age fears is the passage of time: "O relentless Time that thy sacrilegious hand will not spare the firm calm brow of my mother or the mild brightness of her eyes or guard the wrinkles from her lovely mouth." Time is the enemy and Gratz isn't around to defend his mother against it.

And then he gets to the point, the real source of his worry, the enemy that he actually could do something about if he weren't seated at a student's desk: "to think that the armed hosts of an infuriated enemy have sworn vengeance on the place of my birth, the home of the women I love." Surely Gratz feels guilty, powerless. But these aren't the emotions he attributes to the war. He asks himself, instead, "is it any wonder that I am sometimes sad." The war intrudes on Gratz's excitement about his studies and the relationships he's forming with friends. Of course it does. But the sadness he feels, the *blues* or *blue devils*, predates the war, going all the way back to his childhood. Gratz looks to events outside himself to explain a longstanding inner turmoil.

This might be the first instance where Gratz has made the Southern rebellion his own war, the struggle against an external enemy a proxy for the battle against the demons within. But it won't be the last time.

It's in this mental state that Gratz imagines he's gone into a kind of exile that could last nearly a decade. But by January 1863, three months after his arrival in Charlottesville, he's gone. The previous month in Fredericksburg, a town in the vicinity of Manassas but even closer to Charlottesville, a battle caused nearly 20,000 casualties, mostly on the Union side. It was a victory for Confederate general Robert E. Lee, though his conviction that young men, his own son included, should continue their education rather than be conscripted at this stage of the war was not shared by the Confederate States War Department. All men in the Charlottesville district between eighteen and forty-five were ordered to report for duty in March. Gratz hightails it out of there, heading for home, but a severe cold waylays him in Richmond, at Emma Mordecai's home. She tries to get him exempted, but despite his admiration for her capabilities, he has no hope that she'll succeed. "I was hardly ever more worried in my life," Gratz confides to his journal.

In Richmond, while trying to avoid conscription, Gratz runs into Cosmo, the officer he admired in the military review in November 1861. Cosmo is an unusual enough name that I manage to find out who he is. Casermo O. Bailey, born to an aristocratic Florida family, was based at a Confederate military camp outside Petersburg, Virginia, during Gratz's first year at the university. Of their encounter Gratz has only a few wistful words to report: "how we change—but it is all for the best I suppose."

But some good news comes his way. The university's appeal succeeds in getting its students a furlough (though not an exemption) until the end of the term, and so rather than having to flee south, Gratz returns to Charlottesville, safe now until July.

Though he's fallen behind in his studies, he slowly settles back into school life. "I even have hopes of appearing at the Latin examination," he writes Emma. But the demands of the intellect prove no match for those of the body. Toward the end of January, in the bleak Virginia winter, he comes down with pneumonia and pleurisy, an inflammation of the tissue around the lungs, which makes it a torture to breathe, much less cough or sneeze.

His friends send for the doctor. Ned Harrison moves his bed into Gratz's room, the monk's cell now even cozier. Ned nurses his friend with a mother's devotion, leaving his post only for class and meals. After nineteen days, Professor Socrates Maupin, a chemistry and pharmacy professor and faculty chair, finds Gratz well enough to be transferred to more comfortable quarters. Maupin and Colonel Alexander G. Taliaferro, the area's enrolling officer, bid to get him moved to their homes, but it's Mrs. Ross who wins out. There's a break in the snow, but Gratz is still too weak to make the trip on foot. And so one cold afternoon, still confined to his bed, he's hoisted up by his doctor, an unnamed student, and an unnamed Black man, then borne away by a total of *twelve* students.

Mrs. Ross installs him in her parlor, which she's transformed into a sickroom. The members of her household dote on him: "Students and professors' families were as kind and attentive as their good hearts prompted, the former offering their services when needed, the latter sending me little delicacies even in these hard times." Of course they do. Miriam and Solomon arrive and stay with him for two weeks until he's able to travel.

Gratz terms the trip home "a journey of suffering." The Cohens' stay with Emma Mordecai in Richmond was delayed because of a snowstorm, and for the entire trip south Gratz was afflicted with neuralgia, a nerve disease whose name was first coined in the nineteenth century and which would have made Gratz feel as if his head were being cleaved. The family reached home at the start of March, just as the Union navy attempted to capture Fort McAllister, a small earthwork fort on the serpentine Ogeechee River, near where it empties into the Atlantic just south of Savannah. The Union navy's earlier efforts had all been unsuccessful, and so this latest try was more stress-testing than anything else, to see how they could improve their warships, and sure enough the Federals were repulsed by Confederate sharpshooters in the marsh and guns in the fort itself throughout the night, and the next morning the Federal forces withdrew. The fort's mission was to defend the southern approach to Savannah, where Gratz had just come to recover, and while the Confederate victory at McAllister led to a general calming of the nerves in town, all he manages to record in his journal about his trip to Savannah was that it was "pleasant."

Since arriving home Gratz has only been sick with a bad cold, which counts as an improvement in his health. The grazing area to the south of the city—the commons on old maps—where he once rode his horse and picked bay leaves from the sweet laurel trees have been cleared, and the live oaks that shaded his childhood picnics with their mossy arms have been reduced to stumps, and on this grim plain, fortifications have been hastily put up. It's a shock, provoking feelings in Gratz even darker than the blues. But what woods are left are festooned with jessamine, its bright yellow flowers dotting vines twined in fantastical shapes all the way up to the treetops, and in the city center spring flowers perfume the air, and on the tree in the Cohens' back garden Belle counts 130 Japonica camellia blooms, with their deep pink petals and crimson hearts—and Gratz finds it all lovely and a source of "admiration for my home."

Still, in a letter to Emma that he writes during his convalescence in Savannah, Gratz explains how "strange & sad" it is for him to be "once more 'mongst old scenes & faces, like a dream of the past which has returned to us again." For Gratz this dream of his past, his childhood, is a nightmare, though just a few months earlier he was sitting in his twilit college room moping about how changed his loved ones would be when he next saw them, perhaps as long as a decade hence. Now, as Miriam scribbles at the bottom of the letter, he can't wait to get back to his "loved Virginia."

I find it strange and sad that his homecoming makes Gratz so unhappy, considering he's such a mama's boy and devoted son. Maybe that's it—returning to Savannah feels like regressing. Gratz was on his way to remaking himself, and now he's once again a lonely little boy. His half-forgotten old life soon becomes what is real to him and his life back in Virginia begins to fade, as if he has woken from a dream.

13

An Atmosphere of War

The odd feeling that he'd been dreaming, the one Gratz had when he first arrived in Savannah, returns when he's back in Charlottesville, at the start of April. The delirium of sickness, the bed-bound ride into town—surely it never happened, except here were clues that it did. Still affixed to the wall of his room is a notice—put up by whom?—calling for silence and limiting the number of students who could be there at one time. When he returns to Mrs. Ross's, he steps into her parlor and remembers it as his sickroom.

But the strangeness of reentry is tempered by the warm welcome he gets from his friends. Ned "pounces" upon him and drags him to his room for the night, until Gratz's is ready for him. Locke wanted Gratz to spend the night with *him* but Ned's invitation came first, and so what could Gratz do? The bed-hopping these boys did in sickness, they now do in health.

Gratz conveys all this in a letter to Emma Mordecai, with whom he just stayed in Richmond and who didn't think he should go on to Charlottesville, considering the "fearful" weather and Gratz's still delicate condition. But he went on anyway, dressed warmly and happily ensconced first in a cozy carriage and then in the "Ladies Car" of the train. On the ride he thinks "a good deal of Guy on my journey, what a beautiful example he is to youth of self conquest, that most difficult of all tasks, the noblest of accomplishments." Whoever Guy is, he's only one of several men in whom Gratz will find a beau ideal. The perfect guy—this is what Gratz himself is aspiring to become. But to get there he must conquer himself, as he would an enemy.

For the moment, though, none of that matters, for he's reunited with Ned and Locke and his other friends. Jo is away visiting a young lady. Gratz is thrilled to be back in the company of his mates and away from the reach of his family, though he assures his father that he will take care of himself and work hard—and that "your wishes shall be my law." Solomon Cohen was a lawyer, a man who put his future on hold until his father died, just as his own father did—the law of the father no less binding than the law of the land. But Gratz is a different sort of son, and his dramatic declaration of obedience to his father is hard to swallow, especially because, in the same letter, he lays the groundwork for perhaps the greatest act of disobedience he could perform at the moment—not pass his courses.

He's missed three months of school. As his bonds with friends grow—in sickness and in health, and always in war—Gratz is acquiring a very different education than the one Solomon sent him to Virginia to get. Meanwhile, exams are fast approaching that will test his comprehension of lectures that he didn't attend. No formula of filial loyalty, however spelled out in dutiful letters, can restore Solomon Cohen's power over his son, whose own heart is calling him with a force the distant father cannot match.

In Virginia Gratz gets a second spring, having been so cheered by the first one he experienced more than five hundred miles south. The ash trees planted in double rows on either side of the Lawn were still young and hadn't yet formed the canopy in place today, but their branches, fanning out above thin smooth trunks, were now clumped with green leaves, and robins serenaded those who passed below. It's in this bucolic setting that Gratz, still in good health, is studying languages and literature and sitting out the war, something he knows is wise considering his infirmities and delicate constitution, not to mention his very purpose for being there, to get a liberal arts education.

To make up for the time he missed, Gratz takes on a heavier load than the other students, attending nineteen lectures a week and reading an hour of Latin and another of German each weekday. And yet it's hard for him to concentrate, for the very idea of school is becoming more abstract. Things are falling apart, and the atmosphere on campus is starting to feel like a free-for-all. "My mind is completely unhinged," he writes his father, "indeed every one at the University is in the same condition." Gratz floats the possibility of going to Paris to study medicine next year, in case the college doesn't reopen in the fall. Never mind that he isn't taking a premedical curriculum and has never shown any interest in becoming a doctor; Joynes and Harrison might be going to Europe and he wants to accompany them.

His studies are interrupted by illness—migraines confine him to his bed for a week—and, surreally, by war. The young man who was on the point of fleeing south to avoid being conscripted, who prayed that the Yankees would stay well away from Charlottesville—now he goes out to meet them.

In Charlottesville, May 3, 1863, is a quiet Sunday. Most of the other students are at church and Gratz is trying to study. But the war is raging just sixty miles to the northeast. Confederate general Jubal A. Early has been left to hold Fredericksburg, while Lee is in Chancellorsville counter-ing the Union's Army of the Potomac under Major General Joseph Hooker. Two days later, on the night of May 5–6, Hooker withdraws, despite having troops that outnumber Lee's two to one; the Confederate general has won, but at a horrible cost of human life. During this week Union brigadier general George Stoneman, under Hooker's direction, is leading cavalry in central and southern Virginia, and it's rumors of these raids, which in the end achieve no strategic objectives, that Gratz and his fellow students are hearing.

Every available man, old and young, well and infirm—convalescents from the military hospital rise from their sickbeds for the occasion—join the students to form a company, rustling up any guns they can. But Gratz splits off from this motley group and takes off on horseback with a soldier he meets, a young friend of Jo's named Stringfellow who's on furlough from the army. The streets around the railroad are clogged with people trying to escape, slowing Gratz and Stringfellow's ride out of town. Finally they reach a bridge nine miles from Charlottesville—probably over the Rivanna, a tributary of the James—where they camp out in an older wom-an's home. In a bed he's made out of two chairs Gratz falls asleep in front of the fire before being roused, a couple hours later, by the news that the Yan-kees are a quarter-mile away. Gratz and Stringfellow ride down the road and wait. But the Union troops are actually ten miles distant and so the pair return to campus, refresh themselves, then ride to Monticello, where students are forming a company of cavalry and artillery. Gratz joins the artillery, spending the night under a covering of logs and pine brush. The next morning the enemy turns out to have taken a different route, and so Gratz goes back to his room and tries to pick up where he left off. And now, he laments to his father, he's *really* behind in German. Having replaced the Yankees as enemy number one, the exams are now approaching fast.

In retrospect, this aborted mission was just a continuation of what Gratz had been living, and Charlottesville had been enduring: war without fighting. Gratz could go through the motions of war without putting himself in any danger. But *he* didn't know he wasn't going to see any action. The bravery he displayed is hard to square with the kid who had, a few months earlier, begun to run away to his parents to avoid conscription. The delicate, sickly boy who requires endless pampering simply to be kept alive—now he's sleeping outside under logs?

He passes French and Literature. Fails German. Doesn't even bother to attempt the exam on Latin, the subject on which he's been focused since day one. This boy who as a child was photographed with a book on his lap that looks heavier than he is, this erudite teenager whose letters are peppered with references to *poissardes*, barmecidal meals, and the European fable of Mohammed's floating coffin—for the first time in his life he fails at an academic subject. And what's more surprising: he doesn't really seem to care.

In letters to his father he plays the obedient son. But in fact he's the one telling Solomon what he intends to do. He needs his father to send him money to get home after the school year, a lot of it just to be on the safe side, though he isn't sure yet when he's going to make it, preferring to stay on until all his friends are gone. Jo has joined the navy, Joynes has left for Petersburg. But Locke, who has invited him to stay with him after the term ends, gets sick, which gives Gratz the opportunity to move into his room for a week. In one letter home Gratz justifies his staying on at the university till the bitter end by how better suited it is than anywhere else for him to study. In another letter he complains that headaches are making study impossible. No matter—for the first time in his life, the bookish boy who's devoted himself to studying, sternly counseling younger relatives to do the same, has found something that interests him more, what you could call male bonding.

He meets young women as well, but when he writes his family about them, it seems to be for effect more than anything else, casting himself in a role he's supposed to play. He wishes that Belle could meet his lady friends to see whether he deserves his reputation as a "terrible flirt." He describes his male friends as people, full of blood and heat, while the women aren't even types, they're no more than names, Miss This or That. For all the social engagements he seems to have with them, Gratz never gets to know the women. They remain sisters of friends or daughters of the local gentry or military men, who are occasionally "pretty" but nothing more. It's only in letters home that these young women get much of a mention. In his journal, the one time we hear about prospective female romantic partners, Gratz is downright sniffy. When he returns to the university in the fall of 1863, he reports having left it the previous June "carrying with me the hearts of two young Ladies, E n L. and E B.W. & entangled in an engagement with the latter more agreeable to her than to me." Women were an entanglement, but he always managed to slip free. Of yet another young lady he archly notes, in a diary entry that November, that "the celebrated Miss Fannie Green the irresistable took special pains to interest me. I fear however that she won't succeed in her aims."

Meanwhile, Gratz basks in the atmosphere of war—not real war, with its shattered bones and spilled blood, but its ceremonial, chivalric aspects. In May, Stonewall Jackson's coffin passes through town and Gratz cadges a leaf from a cross of white flowers that women associated with the university have made and placed on the coffin, which Gratz finds shockingly small for such a war hero. It's there in the archive in Chapel Hill, this leaf, which Gratz wanted Belle, to whom he sent it, to treasure as a holy relic.

Next he attends a grand military review, the kind of thing he loves. He travels by train with a group of friends, mostly women, to Culpeper, Virginia, a prosperous wheat-farming community some fifty miles northwest of Charlottesville that was doomed, because of its strategic location midway between the capital of the nation and the capital of the Confederacy, to become a center of military action. After a series of battles, Robert E. Lee uses the county as a staging area for Confederate forces. Gratz rides for miles through barren countryside, with not even a post remaining to mark the enclosed fields where crops once grew. At the review, featuring more than two thousand horsemen, he's awed by the physical state of the soldiers returned from battle: "the handsome refined boys were rough sun burnt soldiers. Theirs had been the cradle of luxury. A youth of dissipation and pleasure. But oh God how nobly glorious were they now—hardly recognizable now to the friends of their younger days."

It's a change from the year before, when he wrote Belle, "Tis a heart wound when those who give every promise of nobleness and usefulness are cut off when just budding forth into manhood and beauty." Now, with their youthful looks gone, the men at the military review, some of them Gratz's friends, glow with an even greater glamour. And Gratz laments being left out. "God bless them & pity me who can not take my place by their sides," he writes, and I wonder if what Gratz really regrets is missing the chance to be so radically transformed, butched up, forged wholly anew in the fire of war.

There's an air of unreality about the Culpeper excursion. The staged military review, a ball with soldiers in uniform—these pageants are grand enough to give Gratz his fix of gallantry and glitz so that he doesn't need to fight himself. It's in high spirits that he returns safely to Charlottesville.

The deserted campus is growing more so by the day and still Gratz stays, until he's practically the only student left and remaining would make him feel too lonely. In June he reluctantly heads for home, stopping to see Emma Mordecai in Richmond and other friends along the way.

14

Sitting Out the War

His mind was unhinged, the threat of failing hovered over him—but in the spring of 1863, Gratz Cohen, who'd struggled since childhood with depression, was happy. Institutions—the Union, the college, the father—were falling apart or tucked out of view, their iron grips loosening up. It was fun: the young men were free to do whatever the hell they wanted, and mainly what they wanted was to be together.

But when Gratz arrives in Virginia in October 1863 to begin his second year, most of his pals have gone off to war. Although it numbers around the same as the previous year, the student body seems to Gratz inferior in every way. None of its members, he feels, rises "above mediocrity." In short, Gratz finds "a parcel of intruders" in place of his set, and he can't manage to conjure up last year's good times, as hard as he tries.

Jimmie Davis, a returning student whom Gratz hasn't mentioned before, now assumes a more important place in his life. Davis lives in town with another Jimmie, Rawlings, and their house becomes a home for Gratz whenever he wants to get off campus. Both are "very devoted" to Gratz, as he puts it in an extraordinary letter to his parents, in which he also recounts his streak of bedmates—what he calls his "usual luck." His childhood friend Frank O'Driscoll, enrolled now in the university, has come up from Savannah with him, along with Belle and their aunt and cousin, both named Cecilia. On Wednesday night Gratz sleeps with Frank. On Thursday, Jo, in town on furlough for the day, takes the place of Frank, whom Gratz puts in the room he had last year—there are a lot of vacancies. On Friday Gratz goes into town and Jimmie Davis insists he spend the night with him. Saturday night Gratz spends with Jimmie Rawlings. Compensating somewhat for the breakup of Gratz's set, all this company keeps his loneliness at bay.

Solomon and Miriam must have appreciated that their boy was so well cared for. He would never have written them about his bed companions if he thought they'd believe there was anything untoward about these relations. Gettysburg had seen fifty thousand casualties in July, and more recently the Confederate Army of Northern Virginia, pushed out of the North for good, had been fighting eighty miles northeast of Charlottesville, in Auburn and Bristoe Station. It was deep autumn in the Virginia mountains, death was all around, and I picture these boys clinging together, for comfort and warmth.

But for Gratz it isn't enough. These sleepovers are temporary connections, and the next day the loneliness returns, the blue devils find their way back in. If only the nocturnal press of bodies could extend into a different kind of connection by day, then perhaps the demons could be kept away for longer, maybe even for good. Call it what you like, but I have no doubt that Gratz's friends loved him. The only problem, for Gratz, was that they didn't love him the way he loved them. But the solution, the very idea of it, tormented Gratz more than the problem itself. To his journal he confides: "Jimmie Davis dear fellow, who loves me so, still is here & makes me a hero. May he never feel as I have felt but remain pure, innocent & guiless [*sic*] as now."

Guilt, shame, and sin are touchstones for Gratz Cohen, and they're all aroused by his feelings for men. "Shadows of the Past fall on my brain tonight. Shadows & memories of days which formed the romance of my life, commencing in the Autumn of the first war years, ending aye & forever in the summer following. . . . My sin was thy sin, oh sable wanderer, where eer thou art now. As tis the first remembered moment of my child hood, through after years, tho' parted now, we too must meet then. God enlighten & protect thee, God pity & forgive." It's the first time Gratz has written in his journal since he left Charlottesville in June, and he composes this entry almost immediately on his return. I imagine all this excitement and shame and guilt building up inside him, finding an outlet only when he gets back to his journal, tucked safely away hundreds of miles north of his family home. But for a confession, it isn't very enlightening. Gratz's sin goes unspecified, and as for his partner in it, "sable wanderer" is the same kind of language that he used to describe Louis in that rapturous diary entry in October 1862, the start of his first year in Virginia. In that entry he referred to the coastal adventure with Louis during the winter of 1861–62 as a "romance of excitement." Now it's the "romance of my life" that began that winter and ended "forever" the following summer.

But nowhere are Gratz's feelings more agonized than in the journal entry "Dated Forever," which he begins, shockingly for such a devout person, by asking himself "if there was a God?" Then he answers his own question:

> Truly none can answer that question better than I. In an hour of Phrenesy I called his curse down upon me now & hereafter. I was young & passionate, Reason had no control, but the all hearing Ear was not deaf, even to my youth. Man is a responsible being, a free agent, I called down a curse, it descended. I bear it within me, walking, sitting, sleeping—and will bear it till death, then it will drag my soul to ever lasting hell. I can not be totally depraved, it is not in the nature of my being—but virtues, good deeds, prayer, expiation & repentance avail nothing. On my brow is written "lost."

This passage, when I first come upon it, moves me to tears, and I realize how invested I've become in Gratz Cohen's story. He doesn't say why he feels irredeemably lost, but I can guess. His love for Louis foundered on the shoals of reality; he hoped his love for Jimmie Davis would remain unreturned so that at least one of them could remain "pure." Purity seems to be a goal shared by many young men of the period, as was shame over its unattainability. They also freely used the word "love" to describe attachments with other men. But for perspective, I read the diary of Harry St. John Dixon, a Mississippian who attended UVA the year before Gratz arrived. Dixon also spent nights in friends' rooms and like Gratz was nursed back to health by a devoted pal. But Dixon wrote constantly about women in his journal, recording meeting or just laying eyes on them whenever he went "down town": "Nature of the brute—women will make students stare." And Dixon did more than stare, relating his sexual encounters in a substitution code. Gratz's journal entries are encoded in their way, but I feel I can read them.

For his supposed depravity, Gratz asks to be cursed and God obliges—this is how Gratz knows He exists. But now that he feels cursed, he also, perhaps to his surprise, feels free—to do good works without worrying he's only trying to score points with God. With heaven foreclosed to him, there's a purity to any good that Gratz does: "I am not unhappy, I am totally careless. It is a pleasure for me to try to do good, not with the motive of those who try to gain Heaven by it, for me bribes avail not. . . . Let others be happy—I never can. Vive la bagatelle." Gratz says he's not unhappy, then contradicts himself by saying he can never be happy—but to me it's his pleasure that seems real. *Vive la bagatelle*—"Long live nonsense!"—strikes a carefree note not always present in Gratz's writing. He's freed himself, not from God but from His unreasonable demands. Under the terms that Gratz, growing up in an observant Jewish family in the Bible Belt in the mid-nineteenth century, understands to be God's, he's never going to be anything but depraved. And so he removes himself from consideration for God's chosen, instead consigning himself to the realm of a different kind of angel altogether. He's fallen, but he likes what he sees down in the dirt. This isn't exactly self-acceptance, but it is an act of self-determination. Now that he's given up trying to be so damn godlike, maybe he'll feel free just to be himself.

There's a lot going on inside. But Gratz soldiers through. If his first year at UVA was characterized by intellectual excitement and boys' adventure, year two is all about intellectual focus. Former classmates are gone, Federal troops are staying away from Charlottesville—and Gratz is buckling down. He's taking three challenging classes: moral philosophy, Latin, and Junior Law. Perhaps over the summer Solomon disabused him of the idea of running off to Paris with his mates to study medicine, for Gratz is now following in his father's footsteps, though he approaches the law not as a way to make a living or as an avenue to a political career but rather as a sort of master subject. To be a good lawyer, he's convinced himself, "one must endeavor to learn something of every thing." One must also be good. Gratz calls Law the "daughter of Theology," in that both disciplines teach of one's duties toward God and Man. In the law Gratz finds a way to be himself: a deeply religious intellectual.

He gets elected president of the Jefferson Literary and Debating Society. Founded in 1825, it's still around today, a jolly, preppy club. The Jefferson Society at the time seems to have been a more staid affair. D. E. Huger Smith, the Charlestonian whom Gratz playfully called "the greatest ass and ridicule of the university," remembered the society in his memoir as no "great display of eloquence," recalling also having been appointed to debate whether the English were justified in perpetually imprisoning Napoleon. Gratz's inaugural address, he writes his parents, "was principally on the Mind & the March of Intellect." Now there's an exciting Saturday night for you.

One of the only pieces of Gratz's that ever got published, and then only posthumously, was the address he gave, in his capacity as "monthly orator" of the Jefferson Society, to students leaving for war. He delivered it in verse and it wasn't staid at all.

In Virginia he's been writing poetry steadily. Gratz embeds poems in his letters, and a couple of freestanding bits of verse are included in Miriam's archive in Chapel Hill; but most of his poetry is committed to his journal, during his University of Virginia years. Some of Gratz's verse reflects the literature of courtly love to which he was partial, with knights and damsels running around castles. He was also heavily influenced by the Romantics, especially Lord Byron, whom Miriam loved too. Among the books Gratz takes with him to college are *Byron's Beauties* (portraits of the female characters in his poems), *Byron's Life and Letters*, and the poet's *Works* in eight volumes. Byron had sexual relationships with other men, starting from when he was just a couple of years younger than Gratz was at the time, but references in his letters would have been censored. Byron also had relationships with women, most notoriously with his own half-sister, and one of his female lovers called him "mad, bad, and dangerous to know."

Byron and Gratz were both aristocrats, but only in his wildest dreams could the religious young poet in Virginia live the life of his bohemian literary hero. If Gratz did dream those dreams, it was in his poetry. Though clearly unfinished, one of his best poems, set down in his journal and simply called "Adapted from Lord Byron," is addressed to a former lover with whom the speaker passed "that hour/ that mingled grief with shame," a moment during which the lover's name was engraved on the speaker's heart, just as Gratz wrote that Louis's "name has stamped its self on my Life." Gratz's poem concludes:

> Though never again on this side of the grave
> We will the same pathway pursue
> In regions beyond Lethes darksome wave
> May we the past renew.

The possibility of being reunited with a lover in death—this counts as a happy ending for a Gratz Cohen poem.

But if he was born in the wrong time and place to explore his passionate feelings for men, Gratz's timing was perfect to experience depression without shame. Sadness, and emotions in general, had real credibility in the nineteenth century, which was when depression began to be taken seriously as a mental illness, rather than as an imbalance of humors, and doctors and philosophers analyzed and categorized psychological disturbances and set forth cures. Gratz is aware of the latest scientific thinking on the "blues," though he acknowledges that this familiarity doesn't enable him to conquer them. What might have helped was writing verse. Romantic poets like Keats, still the rage in mid-nineteenth-century America, decades after his death, made melancholia the ever-present flip side of joy, something to be not just accepted but explored, experienced, as a way of tasting life itself. Writing melancholy poetry may not have cheered Gratz up, but it allowed him to plunge into his feelings of hopelessness rather than simply ignoring them.

Gratz's lyric poems explored his tormented inner life, but his Jefferson Society address had another, simpler goal: to urge the departing students on to battle. The version of the poem published in the *University Memorial* account begins this way:

> Go where glory waits you. 'Twas thus the poet said;
> The cry is echoed back to us in voices of the dead:

"Go, for your soldier brothers need you by their side;
Go, fight as we have fought and die as we have died."

If need there be, a thousand deaths were better than disgrace;
Better that every man should die than live a conquered race;
Better a grave on the battle-field, a martyred hero's fame.
Than all the acres in the land a legacy of shame.

With more than a year of war to go, the outcome already seemed clear, at least to Gratz Cohen: fighting was tantamount to sacrifice. The first three stanzas of his poem are spectacularly bloody, never even admitting the possibility of victory, urging the poet's fellow students to death rather than defeat. In the fifth stanza Gratz claims God will "lead you through," a bit of divine light breaking through the clouds that continues to shine in the next stanza, in which Gratz claims that "God doth give the victory and right o'ercomes the wrong." But victory turns out to be contingent, not so much on the justness of the cause as on the worthiness of the soldier, who must prove himself by embracing death. Call it being "transferred to Heaven."

Like Gratz's private verse, this poem is haunted by death. Surely most of his listeners heard the address as it was intended, a call to arms. But I hear something different. The chance of military victory is so remote in the poem that it seems to me the only victory Gratz Cohen can imagine—the true triumph here—is a personal one over the fear of death.

The part about dying to avoid being a "conquered race" is echoed later in the poem and explicitly described in racial terms:

Norfolk & New Orleans teach a warning,
Better the land should be one common grave
Than we the object of the Yankee's scorning,
The shackled subject of the negro slave.

Gratz quoted from other people's poetry in his own, and here it's an idea he borrows, that defeat meant whites would be giving up their liberty, certainly to the North but also to the people they had held in bondage. The horror of Black people becoming their own masters, and by extension the enslavers of whites, was conjured again and again by white demagogues in the region. Thomas Jefferson himself had done so, portraying enslavers in psychic bondage to the people they enslaved, though his cautionary tale, in Query XVIII of his *Notes on the State of Virginia*, imagines enslavers being "extirpated" if they *refuse* to emancipate their slaves, whose spirit, Jefferson notes approvingly, is "rising from the dust." (And in the world of business, whites at the time, facing crushing debts but without the legal recourse of bankruptcy, had no qualms about crying out for their own "emancipation" from "bondage" to their creditors.)

And so Gratz Cohen, former president of the debating society, stands before his fellow students at the end of the first term of his second year. Tuesday, January 20, is a very cold day, so the event probably takes place inside, perhaps in one of the faculty residences along the walk. The "Jeff," as the debating society is nicknamed, is holding a celebration for the departing students. The address is a special request, an afterthought—so the atmosphere is that of a party, not a lecture. Still, Gratz takes this duty seriously, doing his best to read with animation, meeting the eyes of his listeners, glancing at the text of his poem only occasionally. He knows by name the students who are leaving, he can't help looking out at them with sadness, for his loss and theirs, this audience of future ghosts. But there must also be envy in his eyes, and a little shame. He's just turned nineteen but he's staying behind, with the women and the girls and boys.

15

A Conscription Scare

In January 1864, Confederate generals Jeb Stuart and Fitzhugh Lee and their armies come to the Charlottesville area, lighting up the darkness, a second holiday to warm the frigid winter. It's a whirl of parties and balls and Gratz is in attendance. He's a handsome university student, brilliant and beautifully mannered—not to mention one of the few young men around still in one piece. The furlough that Confederate secretary of war James A. Seddon granted students at the university the previous year was not renewed, and the part of the original conscription law that allowed eligible men to pay substitutes to fight in their place has just been repealed. They've run out of options to avoid war, these privileged boys, and now Gratz's fellow students are disappearing by the day.

It's to recruit the ones who are left that Stuart and Lee are in town, and the local gentry put on the dog for these two war heroes. James Ewell Brown "Jeb" Stuart was blue-eyed and square-jawed, though his jaw was buried beneath a bushy beard and the roll of mustache that sat on top of it, a fat sausage curl stretching from ear to ear so assertively as to put to shame the manicured hipster handlebars of today. Stuart had a swash-buckling style, complete with yellow silk sash around his waist, a hat with an ostrich plume, and a saber. Lee wasn't such a peacock, though he had a nice beard too, if it wouldn't be quite enough to obscure in his round face the jowls he'd have in his later career as an elder statesman.

The atmosphere in town is suddenly as gay as a carnival, with so many social events that Gratz can't keep track of them all. He's especially impressed by a ball given by General Lee at the mansion of a local mucky-muck. Supper is elegant, the band delightful, and Gratz and his fellow guests stay until six the next morning.

But when Gratz returns up the hill to campus, a melancholy sets in. Sundays are the hardest. Although he attends a sermon or two, he doesn't typically go to church. People flit like moths round this golden boy, but on Sunday the campus empties out and Gratz takes advantage of the solitude to write letters and read Latin. Thomas Jefferson didn't want Jewish students to have to violate their consciences with Christian religious instruction. But did he ever anticipate the feeling of being left out of it? Could he have imagined the loneliness of the lone Jewish student, sitting writing in his room as the church bells sound in town? The student population is a fraction of its former numbers, campus seems empty even during the week, but on Sunday Gratz is left all alone with his thoughts.

It's religion he's thinking about, specifically his own. Having recently returned from a visit to her Richmond home, Gratz writes Emma Mordecai a letter in which he rails against Jews who don't know their own religion, partially blaming the "lifeless forms" of Orthodox Judaism for this ignorance. It's a simple, solitary gesture, a college student writing to a relative, but Gratz is entering into the crucial Jewish religious debate of his time, one that concerned the very future of American Judaism. Advocates of reform argued that in an age of tireless Christian evangelism and growing secularism, Judaism must evolve by abandoning calcified rituals and imprisoning religious strictures. Traditionalists believed, with equal fervor, that American Jews could resist assimilation only by embracing Orthodoxy.

Emma Mordecai was the perfect interlocutor, and maybe Gratz is continuing a conversation they'd begun by the fireside of her home, though she doesn't seem to offer fertile ground for Gratz's reformist tendencies. One of thirteen children born to a traditionalist father, Emma was the only sibling who remained an observant Jew, most of her brothers and sisters having converted to Christianity. Believing herself, like many evangelists, to be motivated by love, Emma's sister Ellen hounded her siblings, especially the women, to save their souls by coming to Jesus. After studying both options, Emma declared her mind made up.

The pretty young belles to whom Gratz was being introduced around Charlottesville couldn't hold a candle to this older woman with the fine mind, fierce opinions, and the keen ability to express her thoughts in writing. In January 1845 she penned an essay, the first of two, under the name American Jewess in the general Jewish periodical *The Occident*. Published nearly twenty years before Gratz met her, the essay, entitled "The Duty of Israel" and written in response to a friend who'd tried to convert Emma, seems to embrace the difficulty in following all the Jewish laws that the friend uses as an argument for conversion. But Emma ultimately urges her fellow Jews to find a more personal, spiritual relationship with God: "So few is the number of those who fill themselves with the spirit of those commandments, which as a matter of habit are repeated without reflection, and observed without feeling; so few are those who make the word of God their study that their lives may be led by it." Here was the common ground between Gratz and his aunt, the lifeless forms that the young man, playing the part of a Jewish Luther, rails against.

And it isn't just Orthodoxy that troubles Gratz. He laments the fact that Jews aren't using their wealth to support their own institutions: "It is a sad thing to think how little Isrealites do for their own religion, day after day we see them increase in wealth, yet no 'tithes' are brought for the service of Almighty God, who giveth all things, no costly temples arise for His worship, no asylums for His poor, no schools for His children, where they may learn His name & His works & all through this broad land there is not one Jewish newspaper to defend Isreal against the slanderous tongues of the press & the people." In fact Rebecca Gratz had been founding benevolent societies since 1801, when she wasn't much older than Gratz was. Isaac Leeser began publishing *The Occident* in 1843, and it pushed back pretty relentlessly from the start against Christian conversion efforts. Emma Mordecai's essay was right in line with this mission. But *The Occident* was a monthly periodical, and there was no more frequently published newspaper advocating for the Jews. Gratz wished he were in a position "to start a press to defend my slandered people and support their cause."

And so maybe this is it, the trace of the anti-Semitism that Gratz must have experienced as the first Jewish student at the University of Virginia. Neither in letters nor his journal does he ever mention being the direct victim of religious prejudice. But Gratz is much more likely to marvel over how kind people are to him than to register any slight; this is just who he is. Still, here it is, the acknowledgment of widespread bigotry against Jews, and Gratz's understanding that despite his status as a rich young Confederate like almost all his fellow students, the reflexive anti-Semitism of the day was aimed at him.

Even so, he manages to remain mostly upbeat. It's cold but there are long breaks between storms. To Emma he writes about how the "sunbeams dazzle on the snow & the roaring winds join the rest of nature in a hymn of uproarious praise," a prayer in which Gratz himself joins. He has a lot to be thankful for. He isn't stuck in bed, as he was this time last year. Nor is he in mortal danger, as are his able-bodied friends who've gone off to war.

Then suddenly it's over, that moment in January when the military fetes chased away his sadness and his fragile constitution was holding. First his health goes. On the last day of January 1864 he writes his father that "I suffered exceedingly from the heat, lost my appetite, had constant headaches & tho' able to go about could do nothing." There was no heat wave in Virginia in January 1864—Gratz had a fever. As usual he reports on his health as positively as he can: "I am now well again with my lips disfigured by fever blisters."

At the start of February, Gratz is ordered to report to Camp Lee, a training camp in Richmond. He's still visibly ill. The Confederate army is desperate for soldiers, and a new Exemption Act, enacted in mid-February, reduces the number of exempted classes, though the "physically unfit" still get a pass. But the act also creates in each county a board of investigation to develop the facts around exemption applications, to assist the enrolling officer—Colonel Taliaferro in Gratz's case, a man he already knows. A commandant of conscripts is designated to report any irregularities of the various boards, and no physician can sit on a medical board in his congressional district. The new boards grant certificates of exemptions to the disabled but report to the government those men capable of limited service.

Gratz goes before the board with a strong doctor's note in hand but is declared "not exempted." His doctor, a medical professor named John Staige Davis, is surprised by the result and consults with Professor Maupin. Dr. Davis writes him a second letter, while advising him to leave immediately for Richmond just in case. Colonel Taliaferro, whose houseful of daughters is always open to the university's eligible bachelors and who's taken a personal interest in Gratz, now finds his hands tied, so he suggests Gratz go before the board again. He hands over the second letter, he's reexamined—and this time gets a temporary exemption until March 1, when he must appear once again before the board.

Gratz panics, launching telegram after telegram to his folks and following them up with letters, some of them scolding Solomon for responding too slowly to his pleas. It's freeing to be hundreds of miles away from his father, but now Gratz is desperate for Solomon's protection. Just a little over a week earlier, confident his exemption would be renewed, he wrote his father, "I only wish I were able to burn mine." But now that his exemption might go away on its own, Gratz is whistling another tune.

I don't blame him. He's completely unsuited for soldiering and he has an education to finish. Although the *University Memorial* account of his life portrays him as a determined war hero, omitting any reference to his desperate attempts to avoid fighting, to me his defiance shows real grit, considering what it must have looked like, in February 1864, for a nineteen-year-old white Southern male to be living the life of the mind on a tranquil Virginia campus. A letter of protest written by the beetle-browed Confederate general Braxton Bragg the previous summer expressed a disdain that Gratz must have felt himself the object of whenever he walked down the streets of Charlottesville—or Richmond or Savannah. The army could have been increased by a quarter, Bragg wrote, if the friends of "timid and effeminate young men" didn't besiege the War Department asking for exemptions.

Nevertheless, Gratz wants to return home immediately and try his luck in Savannah, where he believes renewals of medical exemptions don't require reexaminations. But he awaits his father's advice. Should he come home? And what should he do if he's drafted? Reporting for duty seems not to be the answer he's looking for. In the meantime he tries to study, but in his head he's stuck in that cheerless office with his heart pounding in his ears and the suspicious eyes of the board of investigation upon him. Because horses are in short supply, Gratz has been taking his exercise by walking, thereby agonizing his feet, and simply standing in line waiting his turn to be examined is a torment to him. "I am unwilling again to appear before such an incompetent group of men & put my health and reputation in such irresponsible hands," he writes Solomon. The board members are "a parcel of foolish young men. The president of it is almost a dwarf and has been nicknamed 'Quilp'"—after the villainous dwarf in Dickens's *Old Curiosity Shop*.

From such a tribunal, Gratz has no hope of a favorable outcome. He's convinced they're intent on "playing me again the same trick." Some plan B must be executed before March 1, which is approaching fast. Now that the disabled are no longer automatically disqualified from being drafted into the army, Gratz's only hope for a permanent exemption rests on the application he has submitted to the secretary of war. From the Charlottesville area alone Gratz knows of "scores" of these exemption requests, so he has little hope of getting an answer before his deadline. He thinks it's fitting that the disabled hold clerkships or other desk jobs in the army; but here in Virginia, where the war is raging, he's sure he'll immediately be sent off to the front lines.

And he isn't the only one worried about his conscription. To his parents he writes, "All my friends have been devoted to me & it at least made me grateful to see with what concern black & white looked upon my prospect of departure." They know that once he leaves, he'll never come back. One way or another, he'll be gone.

Does Gratz know this as well? Ever since he saw, as a sixteen-year-old, Edwin Booth play Hamlet, he's been finding ways to get used to death— thinking of it as a jest, a noble sacrifice, a way to meet up with dear departed relatives. He's recently sat by his first deathbed, holding hands and smoothing the brow of a dying general, witnessing the shadows gather over his mind, the false finish in which the man thought he was already gone. Gratz found the experience beautiful, and "saw how easy it is for a Good Man to die." But his own death, now that he's faced with it, he wants to postpone. As he writes his father, "Life is so short & Death so cruel."

What worries him more immediately about going to the army is that he simply cannot fight. The very "idea of being forced into the army and the suffering I must endure in such a case is humiliation." Having to apply for an exemption is shameful enough, but having to prove his unfitness to the young men of the board of investigation is a "mortification to my pride & sensitive disposition."

Still, as anxious as Gratz is now, the one thing that keeps him calm is the certainty that his permanent medical exemption must come through, that surely the truth of his physical condition must get through to some authority somehow: "the constant pain which I feel assures me of this."

The previous spring Gratz postponed his departure from the university as long as he could, staying even as the campus emptied out for the summer, breezily explaining in letters home the various social engagements that would prevent his speedy return. Now, with the campus a "desert" in the middle of the term and the war raging around him, he longs to get back to Savannah. But Solomon wants him to stay and finish his studies. In mid-February, with the board of investigation deadline looming, Solomon gets on a train bound for Virginia. Whatever influence he throws around works. March 1 comes and goes. A friend of Gratz's, also unfit for active duty, has been conscripted and "expects to be put in the disactive service"— but Gratz is still attending classes. What's left of them: attendance at his course on law has dwindled from seven to four. But even with the threat of conscription gone, Gratz wants to go home, assuring his father that he "could & <u>would</u>" study at home as he's been doing at school—the opposite of what he once said, that the university was a far more hospitable place for study than home.

Gratz is desperate to avoid being drafted into the army, but whenever the occasion arises to defend Charlottesville, he jumps at it. The previous spring, an imminent raid on the town fizzled, but not before Gratz could ride out to meet the enemy. Now, at the end of February 1864, Albemarle County is the site of the only real action it will ever see in the war. In the skirmish at Rio Hill, four miles north of the university, Union brigadier general George A. Custer attacks a Confederate winter camp to divert attention from an attempt to free Union prisoners in Richmond. Twenty-eight-year-old Confederate captain Marcellus N. Moorman manages to fool Custer into believing his men are receiving cavalry reinforcements, and an accidental explosion of a Confederate caisson causes Custer's men to fire on one another. The rebel camp is destroyed but Charlottesville is untouched, and Custer's men retreat after about an hour—it's likely no one died.

It's a diversionary raid turned farce, and Gratz mentions it in a letter to Solomon: "Of course the raid disarranged every thing here & we hurried to the defence of Charlottesville, every moment expecting the attack, but the repulse by the artillerists changed the course & the speed of the raiders considerably." *I was there*—that's it. This young man who clings to his medical exemption like a life raft picks up a gun whenever the town is threatened. Did he fear only the rigor of the army, and with it the expectation he'd have to do something for which he was ill equipped, like spend time on his feet? Or was it death he feared, and so avoided putting himself into harm's way at Rio Hill? At the time of the skirmish, Solomon had already pulled strings to get Gratz's exemption renewed. However Gratz participated in Rio Hill, it was on his own terms.

The same themes play out as last winter, the old excuses pop up in Gratz's letters. Constantly sick, he misses lectures and can't keep up with his schoolwork. Dr. Davis is now prescribing for "torpor of the liver," a malady that seems to have had its heyday in the late Victorian period, with symptoms that include irregular bowels, flatulence, and a furred tongue. Additionally, Gratz's ears are ringing from the quinine he's taking. The doctor has also prescribed brandy, which Gratz measures out in spoonfuls from his last bottle of something resembling the liquor. His spirit flags, he's mired in self-pity: "I am truly unfortunate, not able to do my duty in any capacity; neither as a soldier nor as a student . . . my body has acted a treacherous part and can't be trusted. Mind is willing but flesh is weak." Gratz has dodged a bullet, literally, but the embarrassment he's managed to avoid on the battlefield he now finds on his quiet campus: "it is so humiliating and discouraging to be always behind."

Whether he's wallowing in his supposed depravity, imagining being unable to do his duty on a battlefield, or simply trying to pass his courses, humiliation lurks. And what is humiliation but public exposure, one's secret self hauled into plain view? The soldier who can't fight, the student who can't learn—this isn't just a matter of not being able to finish what you've started, this is, for Gratz, a moral shortcoming. An idea of unwholeness in the world codified as unholiness: unkosher, forbidden, not right. The fish without fins or scales, the land animal without cloven hooves. The beau left cold by the belles. I enter into Gratz's secret heart and feel the shame I knew as a young man, that queer adolescents still feel even in these more liberated times. For here is what it comes down to—the feeling of not being able to man up, not being enough of a man.

Increasingly Gratz is absent from the lecture hall and confined to his bed. When he doesn't have visitors, he writes. To Solomon he corresponds as the dutiful son, assuring his businessman father that his money is being well spent, making excuses for when his investment doesn't appear to be paying off. He tells Miriam that he's taking care of himself. To his sisters he writes as a big brother, advising them on their studies and passing along life lessons, and sometimes just gushing about his friends. But Gratz's letters to Emma Mordecai don't sound like a nephew's communications to a beloved aunt. They're respectful, but also extremely personal. In Emma Gratz has found a confidante, to whom he writes as himself.

The things he shares with her are intense. After a December 28, 1863, entry, Gratz no longer commits prose to his journal; he uses it exclusively for poetry. The kind of confidences he's been writing in his journal since he started at the university now show up in letters to his aunt. The cycle of sacrifice and purification that Gratz imposes upon the world around him—"I think of all the sin that must be expiated by the nation, but we have offered up our noblest & our best"—has sources in Judaism and Christianity and in older Western mythic traditions. But as the threat of conscription passes and Gratz finds himself, in a repeat of the previous winter, confined to bed, his interior life becomes increasingly unmoored from any traditions but his own.

Gratz considers himself one of the "Sunday children" of German lore, those spooky Sabbath-born kids who can see ghosts. To Emma he laments being laid up in bed but assures her that "when my situation is gloomy then my fairies come around me & as the clouds multiply, so do the fairies. I am always happiest when others are most miserable. Tonight in my sickbed I am joyous but in the midst of gayety, then unbidden the blue imps come, they whisper 'vanity of vanities,' they sit in my mind, & I see through their eyes back into the past, then into the future." Imagine how Solomon would have reacted to a letter like this. Emma was a pretty no-nonsense woman herself, as the diary of her hardscrabble wartime experiences attests, but Gratz was clearly comfortable sharing his weirdest fantasies with her. The fairies are his helpers. The blue imps put him in an unsettling position, but perhaps not a bad one for a poet, especially one drawn to the prophetic mode.

The blues come and go, but all winter Gratz is laid up with typhoid fever, which has killed so many people around him. It's caused by contaminated food and water, and it spread from one military camp to another, in both armies, especially in the first years of the war, when medical knowledge of infectious diseases was primitive. In addition to the fevers, Gratz's stomach is wracked with pain. When these two symptoms are absent, he feels he's on the upswing. "I can hardly call myself sick, and barring the headaches & loss of appetite, feel no inconvenience whatsoever," he writes Belle. But sometimes the pain is so great that he can barely sit up to write, in which case his handwriting is faint and messy to the point of illegibility. Sometimes he can't sit up at all, and dictates to a friend.

But his spirits hold up. There's little space for the blue devils in Gratz's room for he's rarely alone there, despite the departure of most of his friends. When Frank O'Driscoll, his childhood friend, leaves for Richmond, the very idea of it makes Gratz feel lonely, considering that Frank was a "kind & gentle nurse" and they were "arranged so nicely together." But Frank managed to adopt a cat, called Zoe, during his stay on campus, and once he's gone, Gratz amuses himself with this substitute's caresses; she especially likes batting at his goatee. Jo Bryan makes a surprise visit and the chatty pair are "like two girls together all the morning."

But it's Jimmie Davis who rarely leaves his side. When Gratz's twenty-five-dollar bottle of weak fake brandy, doctor-prescribed, runs out, it's Jimmie who shows up with the real thing, which is almost impossible to find, thanks to the blockade. It was Jimmie who loaned him money for the imitation booze to begin with; Gratz is in his debt in many ways. Jimmie is Gratz's nurse, creditor, smuggler, and companion. Jimmie is the friend Gratz hoped would never return his feelings, that he would instead remain guiltless and pure. Now the pair are inseparable and intimate. Jimmie knows the deepest workings of Gratz's body. The churning of his guts, the pounding of his brain. His sweats and smells. Despite moments of relative painlessness, the young poet with the vivid imagination can't picture himself well again. It wasn't exactly what he had in mind, but with Jimmie at his side, Gratz is happy.

16

The Last Summer

And then, in an instant, it's over. The intense friendships, the one-sided romances, the intellectual horizons, the opportunities to play at war—and the sheen of drama gilding it all. The freedom to be himself, or at least try, has vanished like a dream. Gratz is back home.

While Miriam and Solomon were in Virginia retrieving him—there was no point in their bed-bound boy remaining on at the university—Savannah, stressed out for years, reached a breaking point. Poor women whose husbands left to defend their homes now lived in households on the verge of collapse. The fancy goods to which families like Solomon Cohen's were accustomed were largely unavailable, but so were the basics, like grains and cooking fat, and what food could be bought was astronomically expensive. To head off "bread riots," as were happening elsewhere, Savannah had subsidized a program whereby foodstuffs were sold more cheaply in the municipal market. But reduced prices were meaningless to people with no money at all. And so in April three Savannah women, of Irish descent if not birth, picked up shotguns and took matters into their own hands, robbing stores for bacon and other staples. This dramatic tear in the social fabric, at a time when summer heat was on its way and epidemics of typhoid and other diseases were rampant, revealed the deep suffering that war had caused the average Savannahian.

But this isn't the city to which Gratz returns, not really. He notes that Savannah is in mourning for loved ones who've been killed or imprisoned or are unaccounted for. But the Solomon Cohens are inured to the economic hardships that poor families feel. This is partly why the letters Gratz writes Emma Mordecai in the summer of 1864 are so breezy. He's passing the summer "tranquilly." His summer job "is a pleasant one."

The way he reacts to the biggest thing stressing out the already tense city that fall is telling. There have been Federal prisoners in Savannah since the start of the war, but in the summer of 1864 Savannahians get a good look at a lot of them up close. Sanitary conditions in the notorious, overcrowded Andersonville prison near Americus, across the state to the west of Savannah, were horrific, with piles of the dead and those still alive severely weakened from cholera, diarrhea, and other ailments. With Union general William T. Sherman closing in on Atlanta, the Confederate army began to move the prisoners to the coast. In July six hundred Union officers were marched from the train station and past Solomon's house, before being held in a leafy stockade on the grounds of the Marine Hospital, across from the northeast corner of Forsyth Park. In September, 4,500 enlisted men descended from the trains and were marched, like the officers before them, down Liberty Street, though these pitiful-looking men were kept behind the jail, diagonally across the park, in a pen that was exposed to the sun and that a prisoner described as "a village of dog kennels."

To Emma, Gratz notes: "We've had a very pleasant summer & the weather now is lovely, much like the Indian summer I so loved in Virginia. This is something uncommon for us, the haziness of the atmosphere is increased by the clouds of dust raised by the tramping of the yankee prisoners through our streets. Andersonville no longer being considered a safe place, they are being removed here, to Charleston & Columbia." Forsyth Park, with its fountain and paths shaded by virgin pines, is where the city's gentry stroll, in war as in peace, and I picture Gratz among them, staring at the starved prisoners as great numbers of Savannah women throw them provisions. Gratz too feels sympathetic toward the "poor creatures" who "have suffered terribly," for which he blames the federal government rather than Andersonville prison officials. But the prisoners are only a distraction for Gratz in an otherwise agreeable season. He's made his peace with being home.

His summer job is as acting secretary of the Savannah district's medical examining board. Those "incompetent" young men who plagued him in Charlottesville, when his own medical exemption was imperiled—Gratz is now one of them, hearing cases like his own and making recommendations as to their validity to the enrolling officer. And it suddenly occurs to me that the fellow who was "almost a dwarf" and whom Gratz mocked in Virginia had probably been deemed unfit for active duty because of his height, and that Gratz, with his own disability, was this person's double.

Gratz seems to have made this connection himself, writing Emma that now "our country needs all her sons—even the lame and blind." He tells her about his new position immediately after Governor Brown has called out the reserves for the defense of Atlanta, which Sherman, after a series of victories over Confederate general Joseph E. Johnston in the area, is trying to capture. Brown also orders "all free male persons in this State between the ages of seventeen and fifty years, who are exempt from Confederate Conscription, and are not absolutely unable to do militia duty, which disability must be shown by the certificate of a surgeon properly appointed under the laws of this State, to report with the militias of their respective counties, as they are subject to State militia duty." With the stroke of a pen Brown has made it harder for men like Gratz to avoid what the governor calls the "bullet department." But with a father as connected as Solomon Cohen, this is exactly what Gratz manages to do, securing a desk job that allows him to do his duty to the best of his ability. Acting secretary of the medical examining board—perhaps the secretary himself has been sent for active duty—is a job to which Gratz is suited. In his previous two brief stints in the military, he's served as a general's aide-de-camp, with duties that included writing up orders. Producing reports is similarly up his alley, and he's able to do it seated, far away from whizzing bullets.

Gratz is safe, and glad about it. For perhaps the first time in two years, he doesn't feel conflicted about the way he's doing, or not doing, the war, writing Emma, "The position is a very pleasant one & is a sort of diversion for me, would that I could do more but since I can not, it is well to remember the lines of the poet, 'Man can not make but may enoble [*sic*] fate—by nobly bearing it.'" Holding a desk job is the reasonable way for a disabled person to serve in the army that Gratz felt was impossible in Virginia. While sense and sensibility, reason and passion, often seem at war within him, the young man who will one day be lauded as a war hero has for years been determined to sit out the conflict with a medical exemption. The bum legs he's endured since adolescence have become the very thing that can save him. Now that all hands are on deck, he recognizes his infirmity and does what he can. Indeed, he comes to see duty as just that:

accepting one's limitations. Instead of rushing to the battlefield, he heads to an office close to home.

Gratz's attitude toward his military obligations is healthy, but he himself still isn't. Naturally, he claims to be better, but admits that months of illness have left him pale, emaciated, and feeble. Strangers passing this representative of a departed demographic on the street might have wondered just what was wrong with him; but his friends might not have looked at him too differently. "Old friends would pass me by without recognizing me they say I am so changed," he reports to Emma.

The Savannah papers offer a steady diet of morale-boosting. Confederate successes are heralded, failures minimized. And I begin to see how Gratz's view of the war and the Northern enemies is shaped by the media. The papers are filled with accounts of the villainous outrages committed by the Yankees, not just admittedly scary stories of typical wartime behavior, such as hungry soldiers rifling through civilians' smokehouses and pantries and gardens, but also darker tales of children being bayoneted and white and Black soldiers gratifying their savage lusts on grandmothers, daughters, and granddaughters alike, even in the same household. Sherman himself admitted he wanted the South's population to feel the "hard hand of war" as a way of swaying public opinion and achieving victory sooner rather than later. But in the propaganda Gratz was reading that summer, the general's men were nothing but immoral exterminators.

According to the account of a Texas private printed in the *Savannah Daily Morning News* that June, "all the means that devilish malignity can invent, or Yankee ingenuity suggest, are resorted to to punish, harass, vex, and break the spirit of the people. He also states that printed orders from Sherman were found on the persons of some who were killed, directing that after the 7th of this month, any citizen or soldier, without proper authority, caught within three miles of the Railroad, should be immediately executed." Sherman's field orders said no such thing, it was property and infrastructure that he was hellbent on destroying—but no matter. Cartoons of the day provided images of this total destruction—house burned, wife raped and killed, even the dogs' throats slit. Like every other enemy in history, Yankees were portrayed as savage, ungodly, inhuman.

Or as Gratz, seeing the war in florid classical terms, calls them, "countless hordes of an implacable & unscrupulous foe which Hydra-like seem to increase the more as they are killed off." And yet he believes, as the newspapers do, that "the hand of Providence has sustained us in our noble efforts." For this reason, that God is on their side, the rebels simply cannot be defeated, and once the federal government realizes this, peace will come.

It's a strange way of thinking to us now, but one that found ample support in the papers Gratz was reading. In a "peace manifesto" issued in June and published in the *Savannah Daily Morning News*, the Confederate Congress proclaimed: "The series of successes which it has pleased the Almighty to bless our arms since the opening of the present campaign, enables us to profess this desire in the interest of civilization and humanity, without danger of having our motives misinterpreted. The world must now see that we can never be conquered. Will not our adversaries see that humanity has bled long enough, and desist from a longer perseverance in a wanton, hopeless contest?" We're winning, in other words, so how could our desire for a truce be seen as anything but for the common good?

The Confederate armies weren't winning, though Robert E. Lee's Army of Northern Virginia had achieved recent successes in that state holding back General Ulysses S. Grant, now commander-in-chief of the Union armies. But in Georgia, things weren't going so well for the rebels. Sherman had invaded Georgia from Tennessee in May, and all along the way he'd executed a series of flanking maneuvers against the Army of Tennessee, forcing Johnston, his antagonist, into retreating again and again. Sherman had more than twice as many men as Johnston, and the latter's apparent unwillingness to fight was alarming Confederate president Jefferson Davis at this critical point in the war. Chattanooga had fallen the previous November. Now Atlanta was in Sherman's sights.

In mid-July Johnston was replaced by Lieutenant General John Bell Hood, who performed as aggressively as expected against Sherman but at a cost of thousands of casualties that his army couldn't afford. The Battle of Atlanta, on July 22, initiated a siege of the city that lasted six long weeks. Milledgeville was Georgia's capital at the time but Atlanta was a railroad hub and industrial center; all the state's other important cities, including

Savannah, must have felt that if Atlanta fell, their date with destiny would be fast approaching. Savannah was already on edge, and in the summer of 1864, life continued as normally as it could.

Sherman was gaining ground; he had already seized control from Johnston of parts of northwestern Georgia, a land of rolling green mountains and valleys. Gratz regrets the loss of what he considers "the most beautiful sections of this beautiful state" but credits Johnston for having "maneuvered splendidly." Similarly, Robert E. Lee is "so calm—so nobly grand" and General Pierre Gustave Toutant Beauregard "gallant-glorious." It's a catalog similar to one he included in a letter to his father a year earlier: "Lee grand, noble—ay sublime. Beauregard the model general and chivalric itself, the darling of his troups. The stern and honest Bragg—and Jackson, with his zeal & religion, the idol of the people." With these thumbnail sketches, Gratz is quite consciously seeing the generals as characters in literature: "What a vast storehouse will this war prove to the future. Historian, Poet, dramatist & novelist, from what contrasts can they draw their heroes."

Gratz is following the war news, but as if it were installments of an epic or a novel, literature of the sort he's loved since he was a kid—tales of knights-errant and classical and biblical heroes—and has written himself. Surely this detachment helps him have such a peaceful summer. It certainly doesn't add to the minimal investment he has in the war as the secretary of an investigative board like the one to which he once appealed, a desk job he's been obliged to take.

The position is no more than a "diversion" for him, but from what? According to the *University Memorial* account, he studied law "under the tuition of his father." This is believable. Gratz studied law at the university and seemed to take a real interest in it as an intellectual pursuit. When he wrote Solomon to send him the Georgia *Code*, it was for an extracurricular comparison of the laws of different states. By now Solomon has retired from practicing law and, having continued as postmaster through President James Buchanan's administration, holds the same office in the Confederacy. He's also a director of the Bank of the State of Georgia. I can see the two men, in the evening and on weekends, sitting together in the mansion on Liberty Street, perhaps in the back parlor facing the garden and the lane, poring over the law books that Solomon has removed there. Father instructing, son taking notes. Solomon was all business, while Gratz never revealed a practical side, and I can't imagine these lessons satisfying the younger Cohen intellectually as his university lectures did, though he would have been his father's dutiful student.

Writing was Gratz's passion, and according to the *University Memorial* account, that summer he wrote "a work of fiction entitled 'Edith Brandon,' which, after being approved by the literary critic of the publishing-house of Evans & Coggswell, of Columbia, South Carolina, was in their hands for publication on most favorable terms." Gratz's heroine was "a young, high-toned, intellectual Jewess," Solomon wrote of the manuscript after his son's death. "He desired to have it published, but a strict incognito preserved." Solomon doesn't explain why Gratz wanted his book published anonymously, but other than a letter to the editor printed under a pseudonym in a Virginia paper, this would have been Gratz's first publication. A novel! I'm retrospectively excited for him, though skeptical of the timeline. Gratz would have had to be working on this book, which he never once mentions in his journal or letters, for some time, during sickness and school and war, if he could manage to finish it up and get a publisher in the space of a single summer.

"Stationers, Printers, Electrotypers and Engravers" was how Walker, Evans & Cogswell identified themselves on their invoices. Founded in 1821 as a stationery and bookbinding business, it became a publishing company as well in 1852. During the war Walker, Evans & Cogswell produced manuals and prayer books and the kinds of blank books Gratz would have used to take down the orders of the officers he served as aide; the firm also printed Confederate money and bonds. The Confederate government had only recently moved this printing operation to Columbia from Charleston, after that city became a target of Union shelling.

It's unlikely that a printer of strategic importance to the Confederacy would be actively working the slush pile of literary fiction while the Confederate States of America was fighting for its life. Perhaps a proto-*Gone with the Wind*, a compulsively readable piece of Southern propaganda, would have justified the printer's unusual allocation of resources at such a critical point in the war. Yet Gratz had written a "beautiful work the last summer he was with us . . . to illustrate the spirituality of Judaism," according to Miriam. If he finished "Edith Brandon" in the summer of 1864, submission and acceptance of the manuscript would have had to take place that fall, or at the very latest before mid-January, when Sherman was tearing up the railroads on his way north, for this scenario to be remotely possible, though if there's anyone who could have expedited the shipping, it was Solomon Cohen, postmaster of Savannah.

And then my folly occurs to me. The editorial process described in the *University Memorial* account sounds timeless: a manuscript is evaluated and accepted, a contract drawn up. But I've imposed upon it my own, modern fantasy of being published by a literary house. Walker, Evans & Coggswell was foremost a printer. Whoever its "literary critic" was, he would have been part of an outfit whose clients, mainly the Confederate government, paid for its services.

Whatever the terms of Gratz Cohen's contract with Walker, Evans & Coggswell, then, they would have expected first to be paid. And it so happens that Gratz had a father with experience in the publishing business, Solomon having negotiated with a publisher in Charleston to print books by Victorian Jewish writer Grace Aguilar, so that he could distribute them for sale in the South. I return to Solomon's correspondence with that publisher that I found in the Georgia Historical Society. Walker, Evans & Coggswell was based in Charleston before the war. The letters, written in 1851, don't mention the firm, but they're addressed to two men, the first being a Mr. Walker. Walker, Evans & Coggswell was founded by James C. Walker. Not only did Solomon have a longstanding relationship with this company, but one of the books he'd paid them to print, *Sabbath Thoughts*, was a posthumous collection of Aguilar's meditations for use on Shabbat. (The other was a memoir.) "Edith Brandon" may have been a vanity publication, but it wouldn't have been the firm's first foray into Jewish spirituality.

Solomon Cohen, the pragmatic man of affairs, was now trying to encourage his son's sensitive literary side. I suppose I shouldn't be surprised. This was a man who claimed to have indulged his son's every wish, who traveled hundreds of miles, more than once, to come to his aid. And there may have been something else behind the book contract. His military service abbreviated, his higher education in limbo, Gratz hadn't yet managed to complete anything, and here was a chance for the wildly successful father to help his son succeed at something. If only a publication had been enough for Solomon, or for Gratz.

Jewish spirituality was the subject of the longest poem Gratz ever wrote, to which he devotes the last thirteen pages of his journal. It's a rushing river of a poem, without stanzas or other breaks and only here and there a period. World history, the poem seeks to show, fulfills biblical prophecy, to which Gratz contributes his own prediction, one in which Jews are redeemed through suffering while in the process returning humankind to the "unity" of God.

The poem portrays Jews as scapegoats for other people's sins. Persecution has caused Jews to scatter rather than band together, but Gratz, speaking in the voice of God, offers a consolation to the people of Israel that, judging from his journal, he's withheld from himself:

> To him who tries to purify himself
> With genuine endeavor, who sorrows
> Over evil done with firm resolve no more
> To sin, to such a one believing in
> The power of prayer, whose soul demon
> Has punished to such a one give I
> Absolution.

Gratz's poem is addressed to his sister, probably Belle, and like Emma Mordecai's essay in *The Occident* attempts to instill pride in Judaism. Both Gratz and his aunt find fault with the current state of the religion, but Emma seeks a way forward in a spirituality based on adherence to the law, while for Gratz prayer is something more personal, the expression of a sincere desire for improvement.

This poem, though never published, can still be read in Gratz's fading hand, while "Edith Brandon" is gone. But after searching the most remote branches of the family tree, I find Edith Brandon herself. Or at least the faint traces of her life. She was Gratz's cousin, the granddaughter of his mother's aunt Lavinia, and of her life we know only that she died in infancy. Edith's family lived in New York and she may have been born around 1852, the year Gratz turned eight. Gratz's sister Belle went on to name one of her four daughters Edith, though there's no one in her immediate family tree by that name.

Gratz doesn't mention Edith Brandon in his journal and probably never met her, though if she did live and die around 1852, a date that makes sense on her parents' timeline, then young Gratz could have seen from close at hand how the death of their relative affected his mother, an experience that surely would have moved a boy like him. But the birth of "Edith Brandon" would have taken place more than a decade after Edith's death, and I wonder why Gratz felt he had to write about her, or someone with her name, in that last war summer.

As Gratz studies law and writes and slowly recovers from typhoid fever, domestic life continues around him. Belle, companion of Gratz's childhood, is eighteen years old and beautiful, practically Gratz's twin, and plays hostess whenever Frank O'Driscoll and Gratz's other friends come to visit. Mamie, the baby, is now fourteen and has just begun wearing long dresses. A daddy's girl, she monopolizes what little free time Solomon has with games of cards. Miriam refers to her children as her "trio" and notes in a letter to Rebecca that they are "fast climbing into man & womanhood." The melancholy tone of her letters lifts when she talks about her kids. Husband and trio and I send our love! Having her immediate family together enables Miriam to bear wartime, though it keeps her apart from her loved ones up north, including Rebecca Gratz. In letters Miriam barely mentions the war, but it's present in the urgency with which she strives to maintain family connections.

Throughout the summer Gratz describes his life as tranquil, pleasant. Even the weather complied, with cooler temperatures than usual. But this peaceful existence comes at a cost, for the prospect of a different kind of life, a more turbulent, passionate one, is gone. At the end of the summer Gratz writes Emma that he isn't preparing for college, as he normally would, because he won't be returning to Virginia, though it's still dear to him because of his friends and Emma herself. He doesn't explain why he isn't going back. The university was in session for the school year 1864–65, and in fact student enrollment increased slightly from the previous year. Perhaps Solomon balked at paying Gratz's tuition, but this seems doubtful, considering how invested, in every way, he was in his son's education.

Maybe after two years in which the sickly young man was largely absent from lectures, there seemed little point in trying again. But surely one reason that Gratz felt he couldn't go to Virginia was because it was too dangerous for him. There was no way he could avoid being conscripted and sent off to fight.

17

Taking the Field

The way Gratz Cohen is serving in the army, that last summer, is dull—a desk job, a diversion. Virginia is gone, and all that lies ahead is the long road of adulthood, the wife-kids-old-age future he once compared to the passionate entanglements of youth and found wanting. But he's come to terms with this, and with the fact that he's unable to fight. The distance he felt as a child from the other kids on the playground, even as he played among them, a remove he struggled to understand—all that is settled. The other boys have gone off to war and he simply couldn't, and he can accept this. For years he's known that his physical infirmities disqualified him as a soldier, something that his exemption confirmed and the medical board in Charlottesville had called into question. But now that Gratz himself is serving in the army in a position reserved for, as he puts it, "the lame and the blind," his self-assessment has been validated. His disability is official and permanent.

He writes of the peace within him and his hopes of peace for the country. At the end of the summer, with Atlanta under siege now for five weeks, Gratz still holds out for an end to hostilities—once, that is, the North accepts that the South can't be conquered. This is the morale-boosting theme promoted tirelessly in the local papers: the North might win the battle, or every battle, but they will never win the war. On September 13, a week and a half after Atlanta surrenders and the state's militia has been withdrawn from the Confederate forces, it's guerrilla warfare, not any impending peace treaty, that Gratz feels will keep the Confederacy's hopes alive: "in every thicket, on every mountain top, by every moving stream, the bullet of the concealed marksman will do its steady work until our freedom is achieved."

With the rest of the city, Gratz has been unsettled by the news he's been hearing of Sherman's successes in the northern part of the state. Confederate lieutenant general Hood has evacuated Atlanta, torching military facilities as he left, and in early October Confederate major general Samuel G. French tries and fails to capture the Union army's rations or cut off their supply line where the railroad runs through a deep man-made cut in the Allatoona Mountains northwest of Atlanta. But in mid-October Gratz is strangely calm, to which he credits his belief that though Lincoln will surely be reelected, antiwar sentiment in the North will foment nothing less than a revolution, "the grand finale to the struggle."

Northern papers were indeed full of respected voices calling for a truce, and Northerners were weary of a bloody war, well into its fourth year, that many hadn't supported in the first place, for economic and other reasons. Some of what I find in the *New York Times* from October 1864 could easily have been printed in Southern newspapers, such as letters from Southern citizens recounting Yankee atrocities. Some of what the *Times* reported in fact had come from Southern newspapers, including extracts from Georgia papers on the humanitarian crisis unfolding around Atlanta. But the Northern papers also gave Sherman the star treatment, reporting rapturously on his capture of Atlanta (he "thrilled the nation," stated the *Times*) and on the might of his army and his likely plans to capture more Southern territory. If Northerners were losing support for a war with no end in sight, the Sherman juggernaut now convinced many that federal aims— reunification and, now, the abolition of slavery—could soon be achieved. With Atlanta occupied and the very heart of the Confederacy in Union hands, Lincoln will coast to victory against a Democratic Party whose platform calls for negotiations toward a truce. But Gratz is convinced that "we are as far if not farther from being conquered, than we were at the beginning of the war," a resiliency that cannot help but exhaust support for the war in the North.

And here too Gratz returns to the theme of his own rottenness: "I wish that I deserved, Aunt Emma, your good opinion of me, but searching myself I know I do not, it is so difficult to be true & noble & good, to rise above our mortality, to be of the earth & not corrupt. Sometimes the world seems to me to be 'out of joint,' wrong throughout from beginning to end. Truth, a myth, & our prejudices our only guides, but even in spite of all this, I do not doubt a sustaining Providence, who sees not as we see, nor judges as we judge." What Southerner of Gratz's class wouldn't have felt the world was out of joint in the fall of 1864? But he seems to be writing about something other than the fighting in Georgia; it's his inner state that concerns him. Emma Mordecai must have scratched her head over this passage. But it's clear to me why the world in which Gratz Cohen finds himself, with its limited options for the kind of life he wants to live, the one he tasted in Virginia, would feel all wrong to him.

And so he goes back to that other option with which he's been trying to accustom himself: "Thus we journey on, drawing at once a sweet & bitter draught from life's goblet till the silence of death settles forever on our varied lives. There are times when to look back brings no pleasure, when the future yields no hope but we jog on, trifles occupy us & when the end comes we are surprised & would linger, as we murmur 'how soon.'" How intimate this nineteen-year-old is with death. But I don't think he wants to die. He just can't find a way, in this world, to live.

The High Holidays arrive. The Solomon Cohens' festive Rosh Hashanah meal may have come straight out of Miriam's own recipe book, a collection she began in 1828, when she was still Miriam Moses, with dishes such as "Koogle," which involves a loaf of bread and three-quarters pound of suet, as well as calf's head stew and roast chicken basted in a gravy spiked with brown sugar. There's a shortage of kosher meat, but surely a man like Solomon would be able to procure it. Perhaps they dine with Octavus Cohen and his family in their mansion a few blocks away.

For services Gratz and his family walk the block to the little synagogue on Perry Lane and take their places of prominence in the sanctuary; Solomon Cohen has been the congregation's president for eight years. From outside come the clop and squeal of the horse-drawn trolley, the chatter of passersby, the birdsong in the trees, all the everyday sounds of the city to which the congregants will contribute their voices. The religious service continues as it always has, the traditional forms of worship on which Solomon insists and that no longer move his son at all. Despite Gratz's preternatural calm and the signs of daily life all around, it's a season of sadness, and the sermon would have reflected the grief of the community and its hopes for peace in the coming year. Many of the congregants' sons are away at war or have been killed; everyone is somehow involved in the war effort. Like Miriam Cohen, most of the members of the synagogue

have relatives up north—and at any rate feel a connection with their fellow Jews north of the Mason-Dixon line. Synagogue records show that
the congregation was concerned, during the war years, with matters like
ensuring a supply of matzoth and kosher meat, rather than taking a stance
on slavery.

With what they're hearing about the burning of Atlanta and the sav-
agery of Sherman and his men, I wonder whether Solomon, or anyone else
in the synagogue that day, believes he'll be sitting in that sanctuary in a
year's time.

By the end of November, the city is preparing for a previously unimagined
attack by land, though its increasingly alarmed residents are still hoping
Sherman might choose another target, up the coast. By the time his army
arrives, on December 10, 1864, rice fields and canals have been flooded to
make the swampy land to the west and north of the city harder to navigate,
and batteries and entrenchments have been put up on dry land, where trees
have also been felled as a barrier. Sherman shows up with 60,000 infantry
and 6,000 cavalry. Facing them, under the leadership of Lieutenant General William J. Hardee, are 10,000 men, mostly older and unaccustomed
to fighting. Savannah mayor Richard D. Arnold has backed Hardee up,
ordering every remaining man to the defense of the city. It doesn't seem
like much is standing between Sherman's men, ragged and hungry after
their monthlong march to the sea, and a good meal in town, but they're
held off for ten days.

In the meantime, Sherman contacts the Union warships off the coast
after capturing the long-impregnable Fort McAllister, on the Ogeechee
River to the south of the city. At the mouth of the Savannah River, Fort
Pulaski has been in Union hands for more than two-and-a-half years.
Hardee knows he's in trouble and Sherman calls on him to surrender. He
refuses, then, two days later, when Sherman is in Hilton Head conferring
about how to capture the Confederate forces, Hardee is evacuating them
from Savannah.

Hardee's men march through the city the dark cloudy night of December 20, then cross the river into South Carolina on pontoon bridges and
plank roads padded with rice straw, Confederate warships burning, by
Hardee's orders, on the water behind them, fire and smoke shooting up into

the night lighted only by a quarter-moon. It's hard to imagine thousands of men and wagons and cannon in motion being quiet, and Union brigadier general John Geary, who will serve as Savannah's military governor during its occupation (and, later, San Francisco's first mayor), suspects something is afoot. But Hardee's troops manage to pull it off, successfully defending the South Carolina marsh as they make their way through it, leaving behind a civilian population of 20,000 and cotton worth $28,000,000. Hardee later explained he hadn't burned the cotton because its distribution in warehouses across Savannah would have meant burning down the town.

The evacuation I can picture, but what's hard to understand is how Sherman let an army get away right from under his nose. Afterward, he expressed disappointment. But at the time he seemed to have other aims: the capture of the city, food and rest for his men, whom he wanted to keep in one piece.

By the time Hardee's men left the city under cover of night, Gratz was gone, departed midway through the siege of Savannah along with the rest of George Harrison Jr.'s brigade. Gratz's friends had "spared no remonstrance to induce him to stay home," according to the obituary by Samuel Yates Levy, Octavus Cohen's brother-in-law. Levy had been a captain in the Confederate army, serving mostly around Savannah, and a prisoner of war for a full year. He would have had his own reasons for making a martyr out of Gratz Cohen—and softening the blow for his parents. But Levy had known Gratz since he was a child. And what Levy recalls is Gratz's "natural delicacy of frame and of constitution" and "his gentle hand and heart." Levy, a bookish man, admiringly credits Gratz's "constant and unceasing study" for increasing his natural delicacy, making him even more unfit to fight.

Did his family too try to get him to stay home? More than two years earlier Rebecca had also found him unsuitable as a warrior, citing his youth and frailty. As for Miriam, was this the cause for which this Philadelphia-born woman was willing to sacrifice the son who'd been wasting away before her eyes? But Miriam—trapped in an ideal of womanhood at the intersection of two patriarchal cultures, Jewish and Southern—would have deferred to Solomon. Maybe General Harrison Jr. had promised him that with Gratz as his aide-de-camp, the same role Gratz had played three years earlier for his father, he'd be able to keep an eye on him. This was a plum role for trusted relatives and loved ones, who enjoyed the protection of the general's shadow. An aide-de-camp was also a scribe, and this was what really suited Gratz to the role: he knew how to write. Perhaps Gratz, whose letters from college were full of efforts to seduce his father into doing something for him, worked his charm on Solomon once again.

Unlike his father and grandfather, Gratz saw no reason to wait for his father's death to strike out on his own. He'd left home again and again—and intended to do it once more. "Upon the fall of Savannah . . . he no longer placed any restraint upon his wishes, and took the field"—this is Levy's explanation for why this young man now comfortably sitting out the war he's been desperately avoiding, who moreover is gaunt and frail from more or less constant illness, goes off to do battle for a cause that is looking increasingly lost. Or as the *University Memorial* imagines it, "When remonstrated with, and reminded of his physical inability and sufferings, he replied, 'The enemy have invaded my home, and I must aid in its defence. If I can't stand, I'll kneel and fire my rifle.'"

I picture parents and son in the front room of their house, the more formal parlor for a discussion of utmost seriousness. It's nighttime and cold outside, but nothing like those last two winters in Virginia. Candles flicker in their holders, and in every direction Gratz can see himself twinned in the rattling window glass, so thin and pale that he practically glows as he announces his wish to leave his home to defend it. He needed his father to agree for him to volunteer that first war summer at Fort Pulaski, when his only opponents were mosquitoes and horseflies. Now that Gratz, three-and-a-half long years later, has abruptly switched from being resigned to sitting out of the war to plunging in, the stakes are much higher and he needs no one's permission. But as much as he's become his own man, he's still a dutiful son, especially under his father's roof, and would never join up if Solomon put his foot down, as he's more than capable of doing.

Just the month before, Solomon picked up his pen to request, indeed insist, on a medical exemption for reason of physical disability. The letter was addressed to Major General Henry C. Wayne, in Milledgeville, and dated just a few days before he and his fellow Confederates abandoned the capital as Sherman approached. Solomon Cohen was a man of influence, over the years he'd recommended professional men, as well as candidates for political and military office, and he expected results. This request for exemption was on behalf of one Charles Rothschild, who walked with a cane and was afflicted with neuralgia. The letter was accompanied by a medical certificate from Dr. Richard D. Arnold, the mayor of Savannah, himself.

Gratz seems to be in no better shape than this Charles Rothschild.

Miriam surely manages not to cry. For Solomon it's reflexive to display no emotion whatsoever. Maybe he remembers the time six-year-old Gratz came to him in the same parlor, the boy so tiny against the huge front door, announcing his intention to explore the worst parts of the rough city on his own. Sounding then much as he does now, his voice quivering with put-on bravado. And what went through Solomon's mind then—better the boy be dead than cowardly—is perhaps what passes through it now. His delicate, gentle, sickly Romantic poet of a son who cried at the death of a bird, whom he had to rescue again and again in Virginia—here finally is the chance to prove himself a man.

I picture Solomon blessing his departure.

PART IV
Things Fall Apart

18

As We Have Sown

Green Pond, Coosawhatchie, Broxton Bridge, Cheraw, Fayetteville, Averasboro, Bentonville—near-forgotten places, most of them, dots on the map of Gratz's route, with Frank O'Driscoll at his side, through the Carolinas and toward his destiny. Pencil, paper, pen, ink—all were scarce, and so Gratz wrote in his head and committed the result to paper whenever he could. We have only two letters from him that last spring of his life, but from them, a letter of Solomon's, and the vast historical record I manage to re-create his itinerary. The dots that are harder to connect are the ones that make up Gratz Cohen himself. He's like a pointillist painting—you have to have just the right perspective, the perfect distance, to get him to cohere.

The right distance—that's what I'm in search of that cool drizzly morning at the start of March when I leave Savannah, sailing across the Talmadge Bridge, which spans the south channel of the Savannah River. (Wikipedia tells me it's the Talmadge Memorial Bridge, but no one calls it that.) It's a cable bridge that's higher and airier than the Corps of Engineer model in place when I was growing up. And another thing has changed: the city of Savannah has put up signs pointing to the SAVANNAH BRIDGE. It's up to the Georgia General Assembly to change the name, but in the meantime, one can only hope this local act of fiat sticks. Eugene Talmadge was the populist governor of Georgia for three terms, starting in 1933, the year my father was born. My grandfather once saw old Gene Talmadge with his trademark red suspenders make a speech in front of the Desoto Hotel—torn down and replaced in 1968 by the Desoto Hilton Hotel, now just the Desoto Hotel again, still just a block from my place—in which the governor declared he'd "never met a n----- worth more than a dollar a day." I don't know how Grandpa responded—I get the story secondhand, from my dad—but the crackers applauded heartily.

On the South Carolina side of the river the same goods and services are available as when I was a kid. You cross the bridge to buy fireworks or get a lap dance or get laid. Two neon dice flash in perpetual tumble on a sign outside a trailer down the road. Every bit of terra firma in this soupy land is devoted to things you can't enjoy on the Georgia side of the river, other than the produce you can purchase from a stand, seasonally. Now I'm driving just over the speed limit on this narrow two-lane road and still cars are racing around me. This isn't a state that thinks highly of authority, even its own.

In 1860 South Carolina didn't need dens of iniquity or the country's fourth highest rate of automobile deaths to display its independent spirit. On December 20 it became the first state to secede from the Union, and Sherman never for a second forgot it as he trudged through its Lowcountry just over four years later. His army's two wings had seemed to be targeting Augusta, two hundred miles upriver from Savannah, and Charleston, on the South Carolina coast, and the rebels split up to defend both approaches. Sherman's men poured between them. The peach trees would begin blooming as the general made his way through the Carolinas, but death was the only harvest anyone reaped that spring.

Hardeeville, where I get onto I-95 north, was officially station #9 on the Charleston & Savannah line, just twenty miles by rail from Savannah. Today this place offers the traveler gas and fireworks, and somewhere around here was a car dealership where as a kid I went with my father and grandpa to buy a car. It was in Hardeeville that Lieutenant General Hardee (no relation to the town's founder) released the volunteer battalions and the men he'd forced into the army in Savannah. But by then, Gratz and his brigade had already moved on, farther down the line.

Coosawhatchie, South Carolina, station #7, is a town I'd never heard of until I read the name in a letter Gratz wrote shortly after arriving at the University of Virginia for his first year there: "We were so gloriously successful at Coosawhatchie." Robert E. Lee had had his headquarters in the town until earlier that year, 1862, and Gratz must have been referring to one of the small battles that occurred there. Gratz got to see the place for himself on his march through the Carolinas, mentioning it in that last letter to Emma. In the first two weeks of 1865, Harrison's brigade defended the railroad bridge in Coosawhatchie.

On January 5, Harrison wrote his superior Lafayette McLaws: "The enemy are shelling to the right and left of my line, but more heavily than usual on my left. We are replying slowly on the right." And to Assistant Adjutant-General Captain R. W. B. Elliott, reporting on what was perhaps a sonic weapon: "Enemy has been beating drums in their camp all day, and much more chopping than usual is heard about their picket-lines. They have shelled us more than usual to-day. With the general's consent, I will open on them with ten or twelve guns to morrow morning." And this line to McLaws on the 14th, Harrison's last day in Coosawhatchie: "Enemy have Negro pickets in my front this morning where they have heretofore put white men." The sight of Black men in uniform was so strange and even enraging to Confederate soldiers that it often elicited some remark, and not always as neutrally put as Harrison's.

A big sign announces the Coosawhatchie exit off I-95, but there's nothing much there when I arrive. I'm just a few minutes off the interstate but a world away. There's the Coosawhatchie Baptist Church (DOWN ON MY KNEES, LEARNING HOW TO STAND) and the Second African Baptist Church (JESUS LOVES YOU). There's a sign for the Bridge of Coosawhatchie just before the actual bridge over the little river, but I think the sign refers to what looks like an abandoned motel. Another sign, just beyond, jauntily reads

←BIBLE STUD
*WED 70

The railroad tracks are still there and apparently in use. There's an official historic site marker at the rail crossing, indicating that the town was named for the Coosaw tribe. British troops burned Coosawhatchie during the Revolution and destroyed the bridge in a 1779 raid. The town had its heyday as a seat of government until 1840, and the Civil War seems to be the last big thing that happened here.

I get back on I-95, then turn off onto Highway 17 north. The country here is beautiful, pine forest close up to the road, then breaking to reveal vistas of creeks snaking through the marsh, here and there ghostly near-limbless trunks of trees, bare or draped with moss. I imagine Gratz would have been struck by the beauty of the place while wondering, as I did, exactly where he was. The landscape is just different enough from the Savannah Lowcountry to give you the eerie feeling that you're not quite home. On my way to Green Pond (station #4), where Gratz spent Christmas 1864, I pass a sign for the Booker T. Washington Center, then cross the Harriet Tubman Bridge, over the river where she helped lead Union raids on plantations in June 1863, freeing some 750 enslaved people.

"I need some consolation, dear Aunt Emma, this dreary Christmas eve," Gratz wrote from his camp at Green Pond. "I left Savannah a few days after the siege commenced, with Col. Harrison on whose staff I had volunteered for the defence of the city & he was ordered to take command at this point a station on the Charleston & Savannah Rail Road which it was necessary to keep open to prevent Savannah being cut off from the only channel of egress yet open to her and a portion of that (about a mile from here) within easy range of the yankee batteries."

It doesn't surprise me to learn that Solomon Cohen was on an "executive board" of seven men that helped make the direct rail route between Charleston and Savannah a reality. He played many parts, but they all served the larger goal of building the Lowcountry civilization that his son was now risking his life to defend. Sherman was trying to destroy the Charleston & Savannah Railroad, which connected the two cities, to cut off Hardee's supply line. Green Pond is closer to Charleston than Savannah; Gratz was sixty miles from home. For days he sits amid occasional shelling waiting for a river of reinforcements to roll by to help defend Savannah. But when the great flow finally arrives, it's coming from the wrong direction—his own corps, led by Hardee, is retreating from the city they've just abandoned.

Gratz has no news of his family, but he's heard of the atrocities committed by the Confederate army in his hometown: "a portion of Wheeler's command mad with liquor & left behind was sacking the street & burning the houses." If this was what his own side was doing, Gratz can well imagine what the arsonistic Yankee monsters he's been hearing about will do to the city they've just entered, a delegation including the mayor having officially surrendered since Gratz left. He wonders bitterly what the holidays must be like for his family there, "what part they are to play in the Christmas festivities of a mob of lawless soldiers. . . . What horrible saturnalia will they make of it tomorrow men who for the past month have been enjoying the pleasant pastime of burning the homes & devastating the farms of Georgia?"

But despite picturing the worst for Savannah, Gratz quotes Sherman as having said, "I will go through Georgia with gloves when I cross the Savannah I shall take them off." To cross the Savannah River is to leave the city and the state, and in fact it was Sherman who restored calm to the town, plagued not only by Wheeler's troops but also by widespread civilian looting. Sherman ordered that "families should be disturbed as little as possible in their residences" and normal life should be encouraged, and when the city's aldermen requested that the enemy soldiers respect the property and lives of the citizens and protect the honor of the ladies, General Geary complied, stating that any soldier who violated these orders would be put to death. The little black book about the city that my father gave me notes no instances of rape or murder, but does lament that the "mildness and justness" of the "conquerors" soon gave way to "petty persecutions" such as the requirement that citizens carry a pass with them as they pursued their daily pursuits, without mentioning that this was exactly what its Black population, now fully liberated, had been required to do under civilian rule.

Whatever he imagines, Gratz concedes that his family's fate is now in God's hands. It's what lies ahead, whatever that might be, that he considers truly hopeless. His fellow soldiers feel the same way. They're tired and many of them no longer see the point of continuing on. And yet Gratz feels that "we can not turn back now with dishonor behind us, we have at least honor in front."

To Emma, Gratz reports that "frightened women & children issuing from the doomed city came to our H.Q.s, asking for wagons to carry them on their journey away from the yankee shells which were falling in this neighborhood." The suffering of these people affects him deeply. But there's nothing he can do for them, nowhere to tell them to go.

Was volunteering to defend the city, by keeping the railroad open, the same kind of impulsive gesture that Gratz had made, twice, in Charlottesville, rushing out to protect that town against raiders who never showed up or whom he never came into contact with? Maybe. But when the Confederate reinforcements he was expecting to see pass Green Pond never turned up, he must have known he was in it, the war, for real. He was no longer defending his home, but what did he think he was doing? He doesn't sound like someone who's gotten in over his head. He sounds, again, calm. Resigned to fighting even as, just that summer, he'd been resigned to not fighting.

And he indulges in self-pity: "I am a refugee with no home but the camp in which I shall remain as long as my health permit. I can hardly realize the situation & like the old woman (whose situation was nothing compared to mine) I ask myself again & again 'If I be I.'" The reference might be to a nursery rhyme, understandably now obscure, about an old woman who goes to market to sell her eggs and falls asleep on the King's Highway, has her petticoats cut by a peddler, wakes shivering, and cries out, "Lauk a daisy on me, this can't be I!" Her own dog no longer recognizes her. Gratz can't understand how he came to the rude conditions in which he finds himself; he can't even seem to find himself.

I try to enter into Gratz's bewilderment as I drive back and forth along the one road through what no one would call a town. Green Pond: a senior center, a Baptist church, and a tiny post office right next to the railroad. In just the few minutes I'm here, three or four cars pull up to the post office and three or four people go in, as if trying to set a record for how many people they can fit in there. When he got here Gratz found little more than the railroad he was sent to defend, the same rail bed that I'm looking at.

Cheraw, pronounced as it's spelled, memorializes the Native people that the town of the same name displaced. Here, in the northeastern part of South Carolina, General Harrison's mission has changed, from defending the railroad to joining up with other Confederate forces to delay Sherman's advance.

Beginning with the capture of Columbia, on February 17, the last two weeks of that month were marked, for the Confederates, by a sense of uncertainty and impending doom. General P. G. T. Beauregard ordered Hardee to evacuate the Charleston garrison on the same day that Columbia fell.

Neither Beauregard nor any other Confederate commander knew where Sherman was heading. Acknowledging that the hour was "dark,"

Beauregard wanted to concentrate his forces in Chesterfield, seat of the county where Cheraw is located, and ordered Hardee to move all his troops there. Later, with the expectation that the enemy was heading to Charlotte, Beauregard ordered Hardee to that city, but by way of Cheraw, where he could move infantry and artillery by rail, and his wagon train and surplus artillery by the road. Then Beauregard changed course again, ordering Hardee to head to Charlotte by rail via Wilmington and Raleigh.

But the fall of Wilmington, on February 22, caused Beauregard to countermand his earlier order and direct Hardee to Charlotte via Cheraw after all. By now Sherman's plans were becoming clearer: he seemed to be heading straight to Cheraw. Of Hardee, Lee told Beauregard to "hasten him forward" but to delay the enemy's movements by obstructing roads and burning bridges. Beauregard also ordered Hardee to destroy supplies before Sherman could get them.

Harrison's brigade was some seventy-five miles northwest of Charleston when the order came to head toward Cheraw, so they had a head start on the rest of Hardee's Corps, taking whatever dirt roads they could find to skirt the swampy Lowcountry terrain. I found no letters from Gratz describing this leg of his journey, but as he makes his way north, he must be imagining Columbia in ruins, something he's surely now heard of but hasn't seen for himself. As I head north to Cheraw myself, bypassing Columbia well to the east just as Gratz did, I wonder if he's worried about his manuscript. Nowhere does he ever mention the publication his father has arranged. By this point has he abandoned the idea of a future literary career, or any future at all?

Gratz, Sherman, "Edith Brandon"—how often have I moved the pieces around the game board in my head! The manuscript, bound in brown paper, makes its way from the desk in Gratz Cohen's childhood room and across the Savannah River, then all the way north to Columbia, in the center of South Carolina, where the editor with whom Solomon has contracted waits at his desk in the offices of Walker, Evans & Coggswell. All this before Sherman even leaves Atlanta to blaze his way southeast across the state of Georgia, heading straight for Savannah, where the highly flammable manuscript can no longer be found. Gratz himself departs just before the city falls, advancing into South Carolina as part of Harrison's brigade. Famously, at least in my hometown, Sherman wires Lincoln that he's sparing Savannah, instead giving it to the president as a Christmas present. The rebels don't know that the general has a bigger target in mind, the capital of the first state to declare secession.

It's the kind of setup that makes you believe that a certain fate awaits all things and that it cannot be avoided. On the day in mid-February that Columbia surrenders, Gratz is forty miles south, in tiny Orangeburg. As Harrison's brigade heads northeast toward Cheraw, Sherman sticks around to destroy anything of military significance in Columbia.

It's unlikely that Sherman was responsible for the fires that burned most of the city the night of February 17–18; at least partial blame goes to the Confederate soldiers who torched warehouses of cotton as they retreated, and the powerful winds that night. As for Walker, Evans & Coggswell, now that this printing firm was almost wholly in the service of the Confederacy, including serving as its mint, Sherman would have set his sights on the building where it was located—and where the manuscript of "Edith Brandon" sat waiting to be typeset and bound. Instead of remaining in what would turn out to be the safe haven of a desk drawer in Savannah, "Edith Brandon," like Gratz himself, traveled straight into the fire to come.

By February 26, almost all of Hardee's men had arrived in Cheraw. But the bad weather that delayed Sherman's march through the state worked against the Confederates as well. Most of Hardee's cavalry were slowed by the overflowing rivers and creeks and washed-away bridges, and without these men Hardee was in turn hindered in learning of Sherman's movements. Hardee's Corps, in which Gratz served, totaled about 10,000 newly organized and mostly inexperienced men. Meanwhile, Sherman, fresh off his recent victories, was heading their way with a force of 45,000, according to the estimate of Joseph E. Johnston, now Beauregard's superior. Robert E. Lee had just reappointed Johnston, sidelined after his meek performance against Sherman in Atlanta, to command Confederate forces in the Carolinas and build what Johnston would call the Army of the South.

I drive up to Cheraw on the actual anniversary of Sherman's occupation. It's pouring just as it was then. In fact the Great Pee Dee River was so swollen in March 1865 that Sherman had to stay in town longer than he'd planned, though he and his men didn't really seem to mind spending time in gracious Southern towns. I've even got a guide, an advertising guy who works for the city, a big-hearted, open-minded native named Dale Davis who tells me he's realized, perhaps to his own surprise, that Sherman wasn't evil, he was just doing what he needed to do. It was a job and he was good at it, I agreed. He was an excellent ravager, Uncle Billy was, and in this case his special skills served the good goals of keeping the Union together and freeing the enslaved. After the war he got another job, ravaging the bison and Native Americans out west so the railroad could come through.

Dale has a key to every public building in town. He takes me to Old Market Hall, where enslaved people were sold. He shows me the top floor of Town Hall, which was an opera house and a dance floor in earlier incarnations, including when Dizzy Gillespie, the area's famous local son, was a teenager, before he left for New York. We go upstairs to what is now a courtroom, and Dale tells me that Dizzy played trumpet up here—for social events to which Black people naturally wouldn't have been invited.

The outside of Town Hall is inscribed with Masonic symbols because the building was partly paid for by the Masons. But their money went only so far. Like the house Gratz grew up in and my townhouse in Savannah, Town Hall is scored to look like blocks of stone. But unlike Solomon Cohen's brick buildings, this one is made of wood. In front it's got a beautiful ironwork exterior staircase running behind big white Doric columns, echoed by the smaller white columns of the same order on the little Greek Revival building next door, now the Lyceum Museum. This sweet one-room building began as a chancery court, became a private meeting room and library, served as quartermasters' headquarters for both sides in the Civil War, and now contains exhibits of Confederate money, cannonballs, swords, and this note found scrawled in the minute book of the Merchants Bank, a Georgian-style redbrick building on the other side of the Lyceum that once held the second largest safe in the state:

Remember my Southern friends when this foul Southern war is over that you invested your surplus spunk in a very poor war when you got it into your head to secede you have satisfied yourselves that after all the Yankees are not so very hard to live with. You perhaps have satisfied yourselves that southern Rights was best attained by sticking

to the old Union. Remember when you look at the deserted track—
through Georgia and SC that Maj. Gen. William T. Sherman was your
best friend.
    By one almost a Southerner
    Cheraw SC was entered By the Yankees on the 3rd of Mar.

If Columbia was a special target for Sherman, imagine what he thought
of Cheraw, located in Chesterfield County, which issued the state's first
secession resolution. The lawyers' pens with which the deed was done are
behind glass in the Lyceum, and Dale opens the case for me to get a better
look. Nobody was going to get a better look at the courthouse where the
document was signed, in the nearby town of Chesterfield—Sherman made
sure of that.
    A few days earlier, on February 27, Harrison's brigade was ordered "to
proceed tomorrow morning on the Cheraw and Camden road and take
position seven or eight miles from Cheraw" and "report military information" directly to Hardee's headquarters. "We reached Cheraw about the
1st March," Gratz wrote Emma, "this was the first town our troops had
entered since they left Savannah. The place was so pretty & the people so
kind that we all hoped we might be allowed to defend it."
    On his way into town Gratz would have seen big homes with wrap-
around porches, followed by the columned and pedimented buildings
downtown. He grew up with neoclassical architecture in Savannah and
lived in it at the University of Virginia, where it signified nothing less than
Western civilization itself. What relief this city boy must have felt at being
once again in a grid of elegant homes and grand municipal buildings and
churches. The town itself would have been a lot busier than it is today, with
a commercial scene smaller than but similar to what Gratz knew in Savannah. Rice was king as you got closer to the coast, but around here it was all
cotton. The Great Pee Dee River is unnavigable just north of town, and so
it was here that cotton from the interior of the state was shipped downriver
to Georgetown, on the coast.
    Dale and I walk down the road from the city center to the austere pre-
Revolution Old St. David's Church, with the nation's first Confederate
war memorial in its graveyard, then past the seafood store and the Baptist
church and down to the park on the river, with a boat ramp and picnic

area. This place is deserted like everywhere else downtown. The river is flat and brown and slow moving and lovely, and Dale tells me you can get in a kayak and just drift downriver to the town of Society Hill. There's a bluff on the other side, but here the land falls seamlessly into the water. In a recent hurricane the river rose well into the green bowl of the park, but left no trace that I could observe.

But what I really want to see is the depot. The coastal elites and planters downriver figured their valuables would be safer in this little out-of-the-way town in the interior. But the very fact that the place was being used as a storehouse, including of ammunition, might have contributed to Sherman's decision to target it. And certainly it was a strategic site in the state's economy.

Scenes similar to the one Gratz witnessed appear in other accounts, but for him it distills nothing short of the truth of the war. Rather than leaving it to Sherman, now only a day away, the Confederate army opens the warehouse, and suddenly it's a free-for-all, which Gratz describes in vivid detail:

Before we left it, the depot, which was filled with stores of every description, sent to Cheraw for safety, was thrown open to our troops. I have never seen such a sight as ensued & hope it shall never be my luck to see such another. A crowd of soldiers & citizens, women & children, black & white rushed in. In their eagerness to seize the plunder they looked like a band of demons let loose. It was a picture for an artist. Avarice, Selfishness, Greediness all had dozens of prototypes there. The stores in the depot consisted principally of Old Wines, fine French China, glass & valuable Books belonging to private individuals; sugar, flour & other government stores, which were soon disposed of among the crowd. Fine old sherry & Madeira wine drunk up like water, by a body of men who would infinitely [have] preferred mean Whiskey. Exquisitely painted French China dashed to pieces on the ground or sent off to play its part in some soldiers mess and then share the fate of its companions. Bohemian glass was likewise treated and saddest of all the Books. You can imagine how I felt to see them thus abandoned. I saw among them a fine Law library & a splendid

collection of French books. I took some of the latter, also a book of
letters published in London in 1657, valuable on account of its age.
I suppose the books belonged to some man of taste & letters—

Nowhere does the gulf between the rich young volunteer aide-de-camp
and everyone around him, soldiers and citizens alike, yawn wider. How
preposterously unsuited for war is this effete boy, how constantly scandal-
ized he must have been! For this is war too, the plundering part of it no
less than the combat. And suddenly Gratz's paralysis breaks and he does
what he's judged the others for doing, and takes some booty for himself,
Providence having put some French books and an old collection of letters
in the way of someone who could appreciate them.

But in addition to these treasures, what Gratz has just gotten is a lesson.
The rabble is greedy and uncouth and it's in society's interests to keep them
down: this is the conclusion that Solomon Cohen, civilization builder,
might have drawn. But it's not the one his son learns.

> Such scenes are sad, but they teach a moral. Would that we all might
> learn it & imprint it on our hearts. Our punishment is heavy upon
> us; but not heavier than we deserve. Years of pride and luxury, of ill
> spent lives and fortunes, must be atoned for & then will come peace
> & independence. To me the hand of God is traceable in every event
> that happens to us and our final success thro' His mercy certain. As
> we have sown, so have we reaped. The haughty aristocrats of South
> Carolina who deemed but few men good enough to sit at their tables
> and drink their wine, at Cheraw & other places saw that very wine
> drank up by a crowd, most of whom they regarded with just the same
> feelings as a Russian noble does his serf. The wealth which every rich
> man, as God's steward, should expend for the improvement of his
> fellows, they employed for their own enjoyment, has gone from them,
> and the Books, China, Silver, Glass which it purchased, are burnt or
> scattered in the hands of friends & foes. This is our tribulation, but a
> day of retribution far more horrible will come to our foes.

Gratz isn't haughty but he's a snobbish aristocrat himself, an aesthete—
and yet it isn't, ultimately, the broken glass and china that grieves him, or

even the breakup of the world that these fine goods represent, which is the one he's volunteered to defend. It's the world itself, the injustice of it, that he finally sees, here in this pretty little town more than two hundred long miles from home. Inequity, he comes to see, is iniquity.

You don't have to be religious to see the war as a play of sin and retribution: the obvious sin upon the land, the entire country and not just the South, was slavery. Black people were the most unequal group of all, yet Gratz groups them with the other looters. He doesn't distinguish between the women clamoring for flour to feed their families and the men pouring Madeira down their throats and the soldiers smashing plates the likes of which they'd probably never seen before. They all look like demons to Gratz. And he finds them all justified in their actions.

Gratz never gets as far as recognizing slavery as cause for God's punishment, and certainly his upbringing would have given him no reason to go there. But his understanding of the immorality of the very system that produces a few treasure-hoarding elites and hordes of desperate poor strikes me as significant, especially coming from a well-off young man like Gratz Cohen. And if it isn't the immorality of the system itself that he sees, it's something close to it, now that he realizes how the rich are using their money: on baubles rather than the betterment of society. The economic underpinnings of the war, the cliché "a rich man's war but a poor man's fight," was coming true to Gratz with each step he took from home, the march through the Carolinas a journey through the region's stratified society and the endless suffering of the poor, as well as a tour of his own privilege. Gratz considers himself a refugee, his misery bringing him closer, in every way, to people with whom he would have had little contact before.

Gratz wants to defend Cheraw—but a stand on the south side of the Pee Dee River isn't meant to be. The next big battle is coming into view for General Johnston, and it's going to be in North Carolina. That's where he needs to amass men if he's going to have any chance against Sherman. A fight in Cheraw would be a rout for the Confederates.

Heading to Fayetteville, North Carolina, Hardee flees across the Great Pee Dee, burning the bridge behind him. "That night for 5 or 6 miles, to our encampment, the heavens hung over us like a crimson canopy," Gratz writes. "The poor little town was being burnt."

The business district was indeed burned, the result of an accidental explosion of captured gunpowder that the fleeing Confederates had abandoned. The depots with their fine wine and china are no more, but downtown there's Carolina's Treasure Barn, where I go after saying goodbye to Dale. Under the place's soaring rafters you can buy perfectly good factory-made secondhand dressers and end tables, as well as framed posters of ducks and ships and Indians, wicker furniture, and grandmotherly sofas and armchairs, and Coca-Cola–branded items like a café table and chairs. I could buy something small, I guess, but I can't really think of anything I need.

Reversing the order of the Carolinas Campaign, I next head south, toward Ehrhardt, South Carolina, another town I'd never heard of, my destination a hunting lodge called Broxton Bridge Plantation, to see a reenactment of the Battle for Broxton Bridge, a conflict I wouldn't have known about had Solomon not mentioned it in a letter after Gratz's death. This battle is now considered part of the two-day Battle of Rivers' Bridge, during which 1,200 Confederate soldiers tried to head off some 7,000 Federals on their way to Columbia, seventy miles due north. The two bridges spanned the Salkehatchie, a narrow waterway through swampland swollen by rain.

On January 23, 1865, from his headquarters at Broxton Bridge, Harrison described the soupy terrain to Captain Elliott in a letter that he very well may have dictated to Gratz: "the swamp varying from ten paces to half a mile to the run of the river on the east side. The river in most places is swimming. The swamp is soft but not boggy; could with some difficulty be penetrated by horsemen in many places; in many places footmen could cross by felling timber, which is very thick. The swamp is low and upon an average about 1,200 yards wide. At this time it is almost entirely inundated. In many places other currents than the main stream are running several feet deep."

Harrison's brigade was well entrenched by the time of the arrival, on February 2, of Union major general Joseph A. Mower, who tried and failed to cross Broxton Bridge before moving upriver to Rivers' Bridge. On February 3 Federal troops waded into the swamp, for hundreds of yards maneuvering around cypress knees and the trunks of tupelo and oak, straight into enemy fire, but managing to flank Harrison on both sides and, after

several hours of intense fighting, forcing him to retreat. In the only engagement of any consequence in the state at that point in the war, the rebels
ended up delaying their opponents' march to Columbia by a day.

In a calmer moment, Gratz took out his Bible and read the 27th Psalm
of David, which begins:

> The Lord is my light and my help;
>   whom should I fear?
> The Lord is the stronghold of my life,
>   whom should I dread?
> When evil men assail me
>   to devour my flesh—
>   it is they, my foes and my enemies,
>   who stumble and fall.
> Should an army besiege me,
>   My heart would have no fear;
>   Should war beset me,
>   Still would I be confident.

In the margin of the Bible, alongside the psalm, Gratz wrote:

> How comforting is this beautiful Psalm to a refugee and a soldier at
> this trying hour
> Near Broxton's bridge—Colleton District So. Ca. Jany. 20th 1865. G.C.

"He was in the Battle of Broxton's Bridge," Solomon concludes in a letter written just over a year later, his son's few scribbled words alongside a
lesser-known psalm of David the evidence that he was there, in the war, by
the bridge—in life.

The reenactment of the Battle for Broxton Bridge gets rained out. It's
pouring on the day it's scheduled, just as it was on the day of the battle,
154 years ago, but staging the conflict under such conditions must have
seemed a bit too realistic for the organizers. With Broxton Bridge I would
have visited every site in South Carolina that Gratz wrote about. But I'm
not doing it in the same order—Green Pond would have come first, then
Coosawhatchie, Broxton Bridge, and Cheraw—and even if I were, so what?

If I could somehow ride from Savannah to North Carolina on horseback, in a driving rain and in uniform, would it make me feel any closer to Gratz Cohen than I already do? Learning his path through the Carolinas is easy. The real mystery is why he so drastically changed the course of his life, and in the process brought it to an end.

19

Trial by Water

I have a work event in Charlotte, then take off for the Smithfield area, in central North Carolina. I make the same trip by SUV that the Army of Tennessee made by train in February and March 1865 to join up with the hodgepodge of other troops that "the skillful and experienced Joe Johnston," as Sherman called his old antagonist, was assembling. I get off the interstate, head down two-lane roads. Horses, cows grazing in pastures, red clay soil, lots of trees. Loblolly pine the farther west I get, more candelabra-armed than the longleaf ones that towered over my childhood home. It's late April and neat little azalea bushes, mostly an orange-red, are in bloom around people's houses, two months after they flowered in Savannah.

On the main street of a little Cape Fear River resort town, I pass old buildings marked by modern influences, like the place with the sign out front saying BUILD YOUR OWN QUESADILLA, before this little flowering of urban life gives way to country. I end up, purely by chance, in what might be the right spot, or at least pretty close to where Gratz wrote his last letter. I've crossed the river on Highway 217, at Erwin. It was on this bank that Gratz was camping, and I'm in the right county—Harnett—and just about the right distance from Raleigh as I pull into the parking lot of the nature trail on the other side of the bridge. I have my pick of spaces. It's a nice park, with picnic tables and clean bathrooms and good broad wooden walkways leading down to the river. A gorgeous spot on a beautiful spring day, but I'm feeling creeped out, having seen both versions of *Cape Fear*. The river itself does nothing to quell this feeling of danger. It's brown, muddy, and loud, with trees—pine, sweet gum, box elder—growing right up to the water's edge and beyond, the river parting around them to form little eddies and cascades as it rushes to the ocean. The river isn't especially broad but it does seem fearsome, in its speed, and claustrophobic, the way the trees close in on it on both sides. It's also very straight, giving it an unnatural feel.

Driven out of Fayetteville by Sherman's army, Hardee's men crossed the Cape Fear River on March 12, burning the covered Clarendon Bridge behind them. While Federal troops were destroying buildings in Fayetteville, Gratz and the rest of Harrison's brigade were moving northeast along the river, "from swamp to swamp," as he put it in his final letter. While Johnston was amassing his scattered forces in Smithfield, midway between Raleigh and the railroad hub of Goldsboro, Hardee was tasked with delaying Sherman in the lowlands between the Cape Fear and Black rivers. The Union commander wanted to capture Goldsboro but he sent a second wing, under General H. W. Slocum, in the direction of Raleigh to confuse Johnston. That was Hardee's other mission, to find out Sherman's true destination. The daylong battle would take place at Averasboro, and Gratz was writing in a moment of calm two days earlier.

Here was Gratz's trial by water, and while he admits to constant pain in his feet, he feels that his new "mode of life" hasn't yet done him "material injury." He plans to leave before that happens. He's touched that Emma's brother George, a man he barely knows, has invited him to his Raleigh home to recover if he needs to. This is his escape hatch, the capital city that Sherman, thanks partly to faulty maps, believes the rebels plan to defend anyway, leaving his route to Goldsboro, well to the southeast, wide open.

At Fayetteville Sherman sent away three hundred sick soldiers, a luxury Hardee didn't have. But if there's anyone who could bail, from battle or the army itself, it's Gratz Cohen, and he knows it. Yet unlike many of the demoralized men around him, Gratz sticks around, because "if I cannot live honorably, I hope God will give me strength to die bravely." The Southern code of honor may have included persevering in the face of adversity and never giving up the fight, but while Gratz has, in the past, regretted not being able to fight, he never believed there was anything dishonorable about it. You want to shake this kid, press him into telling just what he now feels is so dishonorable about the way he's been living. And why he needs to get himself killed for it.

The Averasboro Battlefield museum, in a town called Dunn, has a cheerful cranberry-colored roof and one of those tricolor OPEN flags that you see outside country bakeries and antique stores. Inside, after welcoming me to (and incidentally teaching me how to pronounce) ah-VAY-ruhs-buh-ruh, a docent asks, "Are you local?"

I shake my head. "I'm from Savannah."

"Well, that's local!" she excitedly replies.

Savannah is 285 miles away.

But despite my initial confusion, the docent's response was what I must have been looking for when I said where I was from—indeed when I put on my T-shirt with the name of a Savannah coffeehouse that morning. I wanted to be talked to like one of them, and she doesn't disappoint.

"Are you a history buff?" she asks.

"Actually," I say, "I have a relative who fought here—and died in Bentonville."

"Awwww," she and the other lady working there commiserated.

Gratz wasn't my relative, but it's too late to backtrack now.

The docent leads me to the first room of the museum and shines a red laser light onto a map, one that's familiar to me now, though I still don't really know how to read it, showing troop movements throughout the day. Then she points to a drawing of a mostly cleared field with a few pine trees around it. I've seen this picture before and thought it illustrated the destructive effects of war on the land. But this was what the 8,000-acre plantation called Smithville looked like before the battle was fought. After the war, with slavery over, the Smiths couldn't farm all that land and ended up using it for naval stores—smelting loblolly pines for tar and pitch, using the resin for rosin and turpentine.

"They're the sappiest pines," she says. "I think that's how you put it."

Then from out of nowhere: "We held them back." She was referring to the fact that the rebels managed to delay Sherman's left wing for at least a day, buying Johnston a little time.

"We came close!" But the docent isn't talking about Averasboro, not anymore; she's talking about the war, all of it. "Considering at the start of the war we had no industry!" she goes on, far away now from the topic at hand. "Or army!"

"Or navy," I put in.

"Or navy!"

We meant she and I and all Southerners. If I'd said I was from San Francisco, I might have gotten a different tour. Yep, I thought, the South lasted a good long time, it put up a hell of a fight, considering.

I want to ask the docent if she thinks slavery would have ended without the war, but instead I just nod and go into the artifacts room, with its displays of CONFEDERATE BULLETS and UNION BULLETS and IMPACTED BULLETS, which remind me of thumbprint cookies filled with chocolate.

According to the *University Memorial* account, Gratz "received from the commander of another brigade a warm and public commendation on the field for his gallantry and cool bravery." I can't verify this, though Harrison's brigade did play a key role at Averasboro, holding off Federal cavalry from flanking the Confederate brigade defending Hardee's second line. Before sunrise on the 17th, Hardee and his men were gone, on the road to Smithfield, having left campfires burning behind them to make it seem as if they were still there.

I take the driving tour and dutifully pull over at each marker. I photograph the slave cabin that's been hauled from somewhere else, and the nearby monument to the members of McLaws Division, to which Gratz belonged. I stop at each of the three Confederate lines, stand at the edge of fields, look out at the treeline. There isn't a lot to see. To describe what I felt, I could do something manly and mute, Hemingway-esque, and simply cut away to an old tree. Or to the rain. But it isn't raining the day I visit, as it was much of the day and night of the battle, and in fact I don't feel much. At least not what I expected. In this pretty country I can't really sense Gratz's presence—but I'm intensely aware of my own. I'm alone in the landscape, and far from home, regardless of how neighborly the battlefield museum docent feels toward me. The ghosts of the men who fought here, the gallantry they displayed, the sacrifices they made for a cause they believed to be noble, the parts they played in the divine plan—no, what I feel is something duller than all this, nothing much more than a sense of waste.

20

The Thickest of the Contest

I pass more Protestant churches than the sparsely populated countryside would seem to be able to support, one after another, and THANK YOU JESUS signs in front yards among the American and Confederate flags. After a few miles on I-95 I exit and head down two-lane roads, my GPS going in and out, mostly out. I feel like the family in "A Good Man Is Hard to Find" as they search for a long-ago and, as it turns out, faraway plantation, trying one country road after another until the only one left is where their terrible destiny awaits. But of course it was Gratz's fate, not mine, that lurked in these unlikely parts. I recover from my wrong turn, and the whole trip from one battlefield to another takes only around forty-five minutes. Gratz left Averasboro with the rest of Hardee's Corps in the wee hours of March 17 and was on the battlefield in Bentonville before noon on the 19th, having rested along the way near a place called Elevation. Averasboro, Elevation, Bentonville: vanished towns all.

On a tour of the Harper House, the farmhouse that served as a Union hospital during the Battle of Bentonville, the docent does not lament that "we" lost the war. He wants to tell us what happened here, from every perspective, and he speaks with a historian's carefulness, never assuming anything that cannot be documented. The Bentonville battlefield is bigger and more developed than Averasboro, and it was Bentonville where Johnston made his last stand, the Confederate army's final attempt to stop the Sherman juggernaut.

The downstairs rooms of the Harper House have been furnished as they might have appeared when the house was a hospital. Each of the two parlors downstairs is set up as an operating room, with tables draped in grey blankets and blood-drenched rags and lots of scary tools. What didn't have to be staged are the traces of bloodstains on the floors.

After touring the re-created slave cabin out front, I ask the docent if he thinks slavery would have ended without the war.

"That's a good question," he replies. "But how long would it have taken? Ten years?"

He shows us the 1860 census slave schedule with the ages of the three enslaved people in the Harpers' household. No names—something I've already observed in the slave schedules for Solomon Cohen's census records. But the names of the Harpers' enslaved workers are known: Lucy, her son Alexander, and his wife, Clarsey. "Unfortunately," the docent continues, "we don't know much about them. And since it was illegal to teach them to read or write, they didn't write anything themselves. Theirs would have been a very valuable perspective that unfortunately we just don't have."

Dozens of books chronicle the battle in minute detail, and every day is March 19, 1865, at the Bentonville Battlefield historic site—but it's through Margaret Mordecai, Emma's sister-in-law, that I learn what the day was like for Gratz Cohen. It was the Raleigh home of Margaret and her husband, George, that could have been his sanctuary. Later, in a revealing letter to Emma, Margaret provided the only reliable account of Gratz's death.

It was bound up with Frank O'Driscoll, a different kind of male character in Gratz's story. He was with him in Virginia as well, and Gratz mentions him in letters and journal entries, but never as an object of affection, like Louis or Jimmie Davis, or as a beau ideal, like his uncle Gratz, or as a crush, like Cosmo the officer he first admired from afar. The O'Driscolls lived on the same block of Liberty Street as the Cohens, and their kids grew up together, though Frank was two years younger than Gratz.

Like Gratz, Frank left little trace in a public record that was full of his father's accomplishments. Both fathers came from South Carolina—Solomon from Georgetown, William from Charleston—and moved to Savannah in 1838. Like Solomon, William was a lawyer who gave up his practice to become a businessman and banker, striking it rich in the boomtown economy. William, an enslaver, worked as a cotton and commission merchant, with offices on Bay Street near Solomon's. A director and president of the Bank of Savannah, William also served as the Belgian consul in Savannah, representing Belgium in transactions that came through the port, though unlike Solomon, he never held elective office. And there was another connection between the two men: Solomon was William's landlord. William lived between Solomon's house and the as-yet-unbuilt townhouse my husband and I would one day buy into. In 1858 Solomon wrote William that rents had increased in the years since he moved in and offered a new rent of $800 per year or $700 for a lease of three or five years. Whatever William O'Driscoll had been paying, he apparently accepted the new terms; he's listed in the 1859/1860 city directory with the same address.

Maybe Gratz thought of Frank, three years his junior, as a little brother. Or simply as a shadow. Frank was "stout and rosy," and I imagine he was fascinated by his brainy sensitive friend, taking his cues from him and following him from place to place. Frank certainly showed up when he was needed, just as everyone else in Gratz's orbit was required to do. When Gratz returned for his second year at the University of Virginia, 1863–64, he found that most of his friends had departed for war. But this lonely year was made bearable by Frank's presence; it was his first and only year at the university, where the seventeen-year-old studied Latin, modern languages, and math. The two were "arranged so nicely together," Gratz reports to his parents. And though Gratz doesn't mention him in the letters he wrote from the field, Frank was with him in the Carolinas in the first months of 1865, all the way to the end.

Four years earlier, when he was doing his first military service and encountered no foes deadlier than mosquitoes, Gratz wrote Belle that as a Sunday child, he believed he was always watched by fairies. I wonder whether he woke up every Sunday, the Sabbath for most people around him, feeling lucky or protected by these pagan spirits. This particular Sunday, March 19, 1865, couldn't have felt all that special to any member of Hardee's Corps; they were starving and exhausted.

They'd marched for fifteen miles on Saturday, not camping till after dark, then leaving the next morning at three. They were still some five miles from Bentonville, and Johnston expected them first thing in the morning. He was amassing forces to fight Sherman's army while it was divided into two wings. Even by consolidating Confederate troops in Georgia and the Carolinas as well as what was left of the Army of Tennessee, Johnston had only 20,000 men, while Sherman, once he could gather his forces, had three times that many. It was a long shot, requiring a perfectly timed one-two punch—quickly crush Sherman's left wing at Bentonville, then move on to defeat his right wing at the railroad hub of Goldsboro, all with the goal of preventing him from meeting Grant in Virginia.

Hardee's men crossed the bridge over Mill Creek, entering Bentonville from the north, around nine on a sunny day, the first in what seemed like forever. Did Gratz, who always remarked on the weather in letters, even notice? Did he breathe deeply of the fresh air perfumed by pine and peach trees in blossom, or pause to listen to the chirp and warble of the birds? He certainly heard the din of the battle already raging just to the south, and he must have felt this was the big one, the decisive conflict that would end the war and that he was determined not to miss. But it was all in God's hands now. Along with the constant fire in his feet, Gratz would have been in a state of such physical deprivation as to feel something indeed righteous, the unmooring of his spirit from his tormented flesh.

Gratz and the rest of Harrison's brigade fell out at the church to rest, feasting on hardtack and fat bacon. The village of Bentonville comprised a dozen unpainted mud-and-wood cabins near a creek. Johnston had his headquarters here, on the farm of Mr. Benton himself.

Later that morning, Confederate general Braxton Bragg, signaling potential trouble on the battle's southeastern front, asked Johnston for reinforcements for his subordinate Major General Robert F. Hoke, who was fighting Federal forces south of the Goldsboro Road, the same one I drive down myself on a self-guided tour of the battlefield. North of the road, where the farms and the town were, was terra firma. South was a barely penetrable mess of wet and dry, hard and soft, light and dark, sharp and blunt: a thicket made of the tough roots of blackjack oak, razorlike brambles, dense pine forest, marsh, swamp, streams swollen from rain. Hoke's men had positioned themselves on relatively firm ground, successfully holding off the enemy, who were stuck in more treacherous terrain. But Bragg worried that should the front be extended to Hoke's left, he wouldn't have enough men to cover it. Hardee ordered Major General Lafayette McLaws—commander of the division that included Harrison's brigade—to head down there and connect with Hoke's left.

For Gratz Cohen and Frank O'Driscoll, that brilliant morning in the village of Bentonville now took shape around a single question: whether or not to take their own horses into battle. "For they had a choice belonging to them," Margaret Mordecai would write Emma. I could stand in these North Carolina fields and stare out at the trees for hours and never feel as I do when I read Margaret's spidery hand. Perhaps because she was a woman of great humility, she steps aside and recounts parts of Gratz's last day as a story, complete with dialogue, avoiding the bland summarizing characteristic of letter-writing then and now. And suddenly I'm there, moved in the sense of feeling transported in time and place, standing with these boys as the sun warmed their bones.

"Frank," Gratz says, "let us ride the horses we were on when we left home."

"I feel so much attached to that horse," Frank replies, "I don't want to mount it lest it be killed."

To which Gratz might have replied that he was attached to his horse as well, in a very real way, having once written "The story of the centaur was not such a fable as it seemed."

We don't know which horse Gratz rode from home, but the only horse he ever mentioned in letters was Belle, who shared a name with the sister who was his confidante long before he met his aunt Emma. Two years before, Gratz wrote his father a letter in which he tried to persuade him not to sell the animal when he was away at college. They spoke different languages, the pragmatic businessman father and the romantic idealist son, though the latter tried out the vocabulary of the former—"if she can not be sent off to some plantation or given to some one till I return, as this is so expensive now I will consent to have her sold but I cannot say willingly"— before losing focus and ascending, for the rest of the letter, into the ether: "In my long rides how many petty sorrows have been unburthened before her, which none have ever heard. I imagined she sympathized; I knew she'd never betray."

In the end, Margaret writes, "Gratz yet seemed to desire it & Frank and he rode on the horses that Gratz wished."

It was a slog to the battleground and it took some doing, in the rough terrain, for McLaws's four brigades to get into position to the left of Hoke's line, with Harrison's and Colonel Washington Hardy's brigades in reserve in back. The fighting was still taking place well to their right, and so McLaws set his troops to building earthworks and killing time.

In the meantime, the Confederates were routing Union troops on the Cole plantation north of the road. At 2:45 Johnston ordered the Army of the Tennessee to advance, the sheer suddenness of the attack startling General William Passmore Carlin's men into a hasty retreat. Shrieking like banshees, the rebels suddenly appeared at the top of the ravine, surprising their adversaries in the swampy bottom, firing at them and tearing up the very slope they were trying to ascend on the other side. The Federals' escape was further impeded by a high fence. Their wounded were moved from the Morris farmhouse, the makeshift Union hospital now heavily shot up, to the Harper House, down the road.

The Morris farmhouse is gone but the site of the farm is my first stop after leaving the visitor center. It's a sunny spring day, the cultivated fields serene under the warm Carolina sun. There's a sketch of the place, made by a *Harper's* artist traveling with Federal troops, showing the Union XX Corps configured on a mound among a couple of dozen loblolly pines standing well apart from one another. Cannon and horses on the left, a thick line of men extending out of the frame to the right, gunsmoke puffing out before them and before their opposite number on the other side of the field. The pine trees are gone now, and so is anything else that would make this spot feel like the battlefield in the drawing.

The signs talk a lot about the Union guns, the twelve cannons of the XX Corps and the additional nine belonging to the XIV Corps, as well as the muskets hidden in the woods to the left of where I'm standing and the ones wielded without any cover behind me. The cannons threw canister and spherical case shot, both of which are illustrated on a sign, white drawings on a blue background that remind me of Rauschenberg's ghostly white figures on exposed blueprint paper. Canisters contained layers of lead or iron balls, which were great for mowing men down. Spherical case rained these balls down over enemy heads. The muskets shot Minié balls, that innovation in ammunition that was easy to load in a rifled long gun and shattered bone on impact.

I'm interested in the angle of the guns, and in the guns themselves, and what came out of them, because it was on this field on the Morris farm where Gratz Cohen would ride up, facing muskets and big guns, and more muskets to his right.

Shortly after noon McLaws got word that the battle would be shifting in his direction, and so he moved some of his men into position, including "a line of skirmishers in a direction towards the rear of the firing." But before they could get in line, McLaws received word to come back to the other side of the Goldsboro Road to join up with the troops Johnston was gathering there, a movement "which was commenced at once, without a moments [*sic*] delay," as McLaws wrote in his journal.

And so Lafayette McLaws, with his thick wavy hair and bush of a beard swallowing up his mouth, turned his men to the right, retracing their steps but in reverse, counterclockwise, as if to move backward in time as well. Except on that day, Gratz had postponed his destiny by heading into the soupy land south of the Goldsboro Road, and it was only as he moved backward along that clockface of a battlefield that his time began to run out.

In the field on the Cole plantation, McLaws saw Johnston, commander of the Army of the South, among other generals. This was where, McLaws knew, the rebels had routed their enemies earlier in the day. And so he was surprised that the coast wasn't clear, that in fact shells were bursting overhead. He moved his men behind the earthworks built earlier in the battle in the woods to the north of the Cole field, and then, when the firing stopped, sent them out to collect the guns of the dead on the field.

The sign I'm looking at, in front of a field bounded by a quaint split rail fence, marks the five Confederate attacks against Union positions that afternoon.

This series of charges seems to me, a novice at war, like an awful illustration of the definition of madness, to do the same thing more than once and expect a different result. A group of young men from Confederate states moved from my right to my left across the field until they were thrown into disarray or "torn to pieces," as another sign at the Morris farm notes, by groups of young men from Union states. And then the Confederates, what was left of them, crept away. This was the pattern, and the young men who enacted it, from late afternoon until after night fell, begin to seem interchangeable, as they were to the Union rifles and cannons facing them. Trying to follow the arrows and bars on the battlefield maps, the ones illustrating movements of groups of men, and even the narratives is challenging, like reading an account of a chess game when you don't play chess. My mind drifts and I think of the Confederate soldiers, each of them with his own memories and hopes and desires, and I wonder what they wanted, and to what ends they thought they were being used, when they stepped out onto that utterly exposed field in these last weeks of war.

Two brigades of Brigadier General William B. Taliaferro's Division went first. Brigadier General Stephen Elliott Jr.'s troops, from South Carolina, moved quickly and orderly out of the woods to my right and "were met with rapid volleys of grape and canister shot, besides a heavy rifle-fire," according to a witness. Colonel William Hawley's men from New Jersey had a clear shot at them from their right, while Brigadier General James S. Robinson's troops from New York, Ohio, and Wisconsin pummeled them from directly in front. Within about fifty yards of the Union line, those Confederates who hadn't been killed in the crossfire "suddenly wavered, halted, and then retired with the utmost precipitation," a panic that the witness found "incomprehensible as it was inexcusable." Next up, Colonel A. M. Rhett's brigade, who advanced, twice, against the Federal soldiers on the Morris farm, the 13th New Jersey joined by the 82nd Illinois in flanking the Confederates from their right. At sundown Rhett's men charged again, this time being showered by canister rounds from the cannon stationed on the far side of the ravine, between the Federal soldiers shooting at them from their right and those firing straight at them. Major General William B. Bate's four brigades next took their chances advancing on Robinson's men. Federal cannons were pouring forth their destruction from both sides of the ravine, the ones on the near side throwing case over the heads of Robinson's men out front, who were joining the fire from the ground.

McLaws reports that "the musketry recommenced with great fury" just before he was ordered to send two brigades straight into the firing. Harrison's was one of the two he chose.

Those young men from Georgia passed through Bate's line, the very last brigade to serve as cannon fodder for the very much dug-in Union

XX Corps on the other side of the wide-open field at the Morris farm. The world was draining of light. In an otherwise prosaic and strangely detached account, McLaws describes the moment with an eerie beauty: "The sun was declining rapidly and the smoke settled heavy & dense over the country. A fog also came on, which added to the smoke made it impossible to see but a very short distance. The firing was very rapid for some time after my Brigades went forward, but gradually ceased as the darkness increased." McLaws doesn't mention that cannon and musket fire made for a bloodbath for the Confederates, including his own brigades. In fact the number of men killed during the three days of the battle was low compared to the famous conflicts of the war—Chickamauga, Antietam, Gettysburg—names seared on our collective consciousness, each representing a sickening loss of life. The woods around Bentonville made for good cover, and it was easier to hit a tree than a man. But there were no trees in that field on the Morris farm.

Harrison's men had to step around Bate's, for by this time those who remained of the latter's four brigades were flat on their stomachs, having easily been repelled by Federal fire, like the units before them. Harrison's brigade advanced a few paces to form a new front line, but relentless gunfire from the Morris farm caused them almost immediately to drop to the ground themselves. "Had these fresh troops been thrown in an hour earlier our victory would have been more complete and more fruitful of advantage," Bate wrote, though in fact he had accomplished no more than the soldiers who preceded him.

Gradually in the darkness McLaws withdrew his men to the earthworks on the other side of the ravine, hidden in the pines.

That afternoon, according to the *University Memorial* account, General Harrison sent his aide-de-camp, Gratz Cohen, on a little reconnaissance mission, a perfectly typical thing for a commander to do to prepare for the day's action. A doctor had tried to keep Gratz off the field entirely, according to the account. Though the dialogue sounds as canned as the rest of the quoted speech in this portrait, it fits with Gratz's medical history:

"You are too sick, Mr. Cohen; you cannot endure the fatigue of this battle," said the Surgeon of the division.

"Let me share the danger and the glory of this fight, and I will follow your advice always afterwards," was the reply.

Even the wounded Wilfred of *Ivanhoe* is sensible enough to follow the advice of his doctor—the beautiful, brilliant healer Rebecca, who was possibly named after Gratz's great-aunt—and stay put when the Norman castle in which he's imprisoned comes under assault by his fellow Saxons, a fight Wilfred is eager to join. But Gratz, who got deathly ill every winter, must not have been bedridden if he could convince the doctor and General Harrison himself that he was fit for battle. I wonder if he managed to convince himself—or if he knew the doctor was right and saddled up that morning anyway.

But according to the *University Memorial* account, Gratz never made it to the battle itself, that series of Confederate assaults on the Morris farm. Even the reconnaissance mission didn't do him in; it was the aftermath of that ride that proved fatal. To his commander, presumably Harrison, Gratz delivered good news: the enemy was in retreat. "He had just finished his report," according to the *University Memorial*, "when he was instantly killed by a bullet through his head, the smile resting on his beautiful face even in death."

It's true that on the afternoon of March 19, when Harrison's men were doing little more than waiting in the swamp, Federal troops were being routed on more solid ground above the road, the Cole farm. But there would have been no enemy in position to kill Gratz after returning to give his report. Harrison's men were in the back, with no one and nothing but impassable terrain behind them, and even the two other McLaws brigades in front of them were off to the side of the action.

Samuel Yates Levy, in the obituary he printed in the newspaper he published, the *Savannah Daily Herald*, doesn't mention the reconnaissance mission or the report. Instead he has Gratz dying by leading the charge, an even more heroic end than in the *University Memorial* account: "foremost in the front and in the thickest of the contest, animating the men by voice and example, he fell dead, without pain or suffering." I don't know the sources of the *University Memorial* account—Solomon was probably one of them, if not the anonymous author himself—but Levy, a Cohen relative, surely would have had access to a firsthand account. George P. Harrison Sr. was not just a business client of Solomon's but also a fellow Savannah elite, a member of its tight-knit community of movers and shakers that included the extended Cohen family. When his son, Gratz's commander George P. Harrison Jr., came home, the Cohens, who'd entrusted their boy to him, naturally would have been given a full accounting of the circumstances of Gratz's death. He probably didn't die at the start of the hostilities, as Levy writes—unless you count the very end of the first day as the "very commencement of the battle." But it seems far more likely that he perished on an exposed battlefield, as Levy claims, than after delivering a report behind Confederate lines.

This is not the Gratz Cohen I've come to know, the young man who was willing to do anything to keep out of active combat, even as recently as the previous summer. But it does sound like the Gratz Cohen—ecstatic with sickness and pain, caught up in his own martyrdom—of those last letters written on his path through the Carolinas, however he assured Emma he would take care of his health. And on March 19, 1865, with the sun sunk like a lead ball behind the treeline, Harrison's brigade was indeed "foremost in the front and in the thickest of the contest."

Was Gratz with them? You certainly wouldn't have expected him to be leading the charge. This wasn't an aide's role, even one who wasn't inexperienced, disabled, and sick. But where Gratz should have been was nowhere near the path of war to begin with; everyone knew it, even Gratz himself. Where he ended up, the life in which he found himself, was a continual surprise to him. The reconnaissance mission itself would have been dangerous—a man on a horse was an easy target and a valuable one, for he could have been carrying general's orders. Was he in fact struck immediately on his return? Or did he survive long enough to join up with Harrison's men in that last-ditch effort to make all those Confederate advances count for something?

Gratz could easily have wandered into the wrong place at the wrong time, a lone human being nowhere reflected in the precise movements of men represented by arrows, rectangles, and lines on maps drawn years after the fighting had ended. These renderings don't capture the smoke, the draining of the light, the disorienting noise. But I think Gratz knew exactly where he was. After giving up Virginia and the heightened, more realized life he lived there, he no longer felt he had anything to lose—except what was left of his treacherous flesh. *Self conquest, that most difficult of all tasks, the noblest of accomplishments.* Maybe Gratz did abandon all caution and fear and charge straight ahead, right into enemy fire.

PART V

Revelation

21

But He May Not Have Mentioned

After slipping out the night of March 21 across Mill Creek at Bentonville, leaving behind in the village those too sick to travel, and in the fields and woods, like a macabre trail of crumbs, hundreds of the dead, Johnston led his men, the better-off wounded and the merely exhausted, to Smithfield to recuperate. The general, discouraged but undaunted, wired Lee for help in taking on Sherman. But Francis O'Driscoll was done. The eighteen-year-old, a volunteer, had something more important to do than fight a hopeless war. He'd taken Belle—his own beloved animal had been shot out from under him—and ridden the fifty miles northwest to Raleigh, to the home of George and Margaret Mordecai.

Imagine what that ride to Raleigh was like for Frank. The landscape of sorrow through which he traveled was as varied as the physical terrain of swamps and overflowing streams and dense pinewoods that he traversed. Mismatched, rider and horse, and who knows how easily Frank could appeal to the Lord or find peace in His secret motives, as Gratz would have? Frank might not have had Providence, but he had certain cold facts. He'd lost his own beloved horse, he *knew* it was going to happen, that fresh sunny morning three days earlier. The poor substitute of Gratz's horse was now the sole audience for Frank's tears—and for the rehearsal of what he'd say once he got to Raleigh, where Gratz's relatives didn't know they were waiting for the news.

Why do I think Frank was riding Gratz's horse? There's no evidence for this at all. Margaret's letter to Emma points out that Frank's horse was killed but doesn't say what happened to Gratz's. I suppose I respond to the terrible symmetry of the situation: Frank survived, but not his horse. Gratz died, but Belle did not.

And if Belle was the horse Frank rode to Raleigh, then she too would have been bereft, and found comfort in her role as confidante. It was familiar to her, the human voice around her as she moved through the world. The "petty sorrows" that Gratz said he unburdened to her now thundered in the full-on grief of his best friend. The nice boy who'd lived in his luminous neighbor's shadow his whole life.

Frank might have known that Gratz had relatives in Raleigh from spending the past three months by his friend's side. Or perhaps Frank learned of Margaret and George Mordecai from the letter he found when he rushed to Gratz's body "very soon after the fatal ball was shed," according to Margaret. And so instead of the Jewish prince, it was his Gentile best friend who showed up at the door of the Mordecai residence.

He wasn't the first stranger to appear. How they knew to come, I don't know, but that Greek Revival mansion on a street of temples to wealth was full of wounded men, the sickest of them out of sight in their rooms that evening while the relatives come to care for them crowded round the supper table alongside those soldiers able to do the same. And among them now Frank O'Driscoll, with nothing wrong with him but an empty belly. He must have felt this too, survivor's guilt, without even the comfort of having a term for it. Frank alone with his thoughts amid the commotion and Margaret too busy to do more than glance his way, much less have a word with him. And so after supper, when the dining room was empty and Frank had gone upstairs, she sent for him to come down to talk.

Margaret was an heiress and devout woman, physically weakened for ten years now from the loss of her only child, a stillborn. She was a lifelong member of the Church of Christ—George, a captain of industry and bank president, had converted to Christianity on the death of his father, the same year, 1838, that Solomon Cohen moved to Savannah after the death of *his* father—and so she was primed to see Gratz as a martyr. But perhaps Margaret's religiousness predisposed her also to the liberating power of the truth. That's what she wanted from Frank—the truth.

After riding up that afternoon and cleaning up, Frank had met with the master of the house, in the sanctuary of George's study. This was the official part of the stay, where Frank stated the purpose of his visit and George questioned him on the details. The movements of men on the battlefield. The timing of that last advance. The burial, technical details of, nature of prayers pronounced. The display of articles Frank found on the body where it fell, as well as the catalog of those that had been snatched before he could get there. And then the older man shook the younger's hand, called for him to be shown to his room, and sat down again at his desk. He took out a fresh sheet of paper, dipped pen into ink. The addressee everyone's confidante, his sister Emma Mordecai.

All this George conveyed to his wife, who still felt something was missing.

Where did the older woman and the young soldier sit? Perhaps at the same table that had been so crowded earlier in the evening. A candle between them, maybe a pitcher of water and two glasses, likely nothing stronger than this.

From Margaret's letter I imagine the scene. The candlelight illuminates Frank's face from below, the gaunt sleepy childish visage gone red and demonic looking, a thought Margaret quickly pushes from her mind. She pours him a glass and urges him to drink. But at first Frank won't talk, no more than to punctuate her own remarks with a syllable or two of his own. An unpracticed interrogator, Margaret is the one doing all the talking. She feels what she believes Frank is feeling, what Emma surely will when she reads her husband's letter.

How it must pain you to recall the events of that terrible day, Margaret says.

Yes ma'am, Frank replies.

But for the sake of those who loved him, if you could, while it is fresh in your memory—

Yes ma'am.

That day, that afternoon, for I understand it was in the afternoon when your dear friend fell—

End of the day, yes ma'am.

And then nothing but the silence of the room. It's quiet a long time. Margaret's already halting words have run up against a wall. And as she collects her thoughts and tries to hold back tears, it happens. Out of the dead intractable silence, sound. Frank O'Driscoll has begun to talk.

The news soon reaches him, traveling straight to his ears, for everyone knows these two are a pair. It's almost full dark now and the things in the world have lost their authority, and now one of those things is his friend. The body crumpled where it has been shot off the horse, the items secreted around the corpse—everything has been freed of its borders, dissolved into the dark. Although Harrison's was the last group of men on the front lines that night, and they hit the dirt and retreated soon after taking their few steps forward, fighting continued well after dark, fire flashing through the smoky air till around 9 p.m. Simply going through Gratz's things, Frank could have been killed himself.

Normally, an army's medical corps would wait till the battle was over to retrieve the dead from the field; men equipped with stretchers would come, people who were trained to do this sort of work. But army regulations couldn't keep soldiers from retrieving the bodies of their friends and loved ones. Frank, according to Margaret's letter, didn't wait. He rushed to perform the terrible labor of getting Gratz's body back to safety, behind the treeline. Frank's feet sank into the mud, but his friend's bones might as well have been filled with air. And so maybe that much was a relief, moving the body to safety was something he could do. Horror, shock, grief, loss, failure might have registered on his face. Perhaps also pity for the wounded moaning around him, or hatred they were still alive. Maybe the enormity of Frank's new responsibilities allowed for no distracting emotion, nothing that could swerve him off course.

Back behind Confederate lines, relatively safe now, Frank read the letter that I myself now have read, the last one Gratz ever wrote. It was addressed to Emma Mordecai, not him, but what did that matter now? Toward the end of that letter Gratz writes: "I have heard nothing from home since 16th Jany—inclosed I send a letter, which you may be able to send on its way by flag of truce." But there was only one letter among Gratz's things, which might have been how Frank knew someone had already gotten to the body. I'm hungry for this and all Gratz's lost correspondence, but I can't imagine a thief in cross fire taking the time to examine either of his two last letters. We don't know how they were arranged among Gratz's effects; perhaps the letter to Solomon and Miriam was inside the 1657 English book of letters. Or maybe, after reading it, Frank threw the letter to Gratz's parents into the fire.

The old book of letters, the French *bouquins* Gratz carried with him from Cheraw—where did they all go? Later, Solomon would pore over the scribblings in the margins of Gratz's Bible, taking these annotations as holy word. But Margaret reports only that Gratz's effects included "a book." As for the letter to Emma, maybe Frank gave it to George to mail to his sister. She would go on to copy out this "last letter" and send it to Solomon and Miriam. The last one they'd received from Gratz was dated March 6, eight days before this final letter to Emma, written five days before his death.

It might have taken him a while to start telling, but Frank had left his room prepared to show, and now he takes out Gratz's card case and opens it up on the table. Considering how Gratz liked fine things—remember the French dictionary bound in morocco that Mr. Knapp gave him at Fort Pulaski—this one was probably elegant. I wonder if in his haste the thief simply overlooked it in the folds of Gratz's clothes. Inside the case are "various little scraps of paper on two of which original religious sentiments were written confessing devotion to and trust in God," as Margaret would write. "On one of his cards various faces were sketched."

In the candlelight each scrap and card is passed across the table. The "original religious sentiments" I can imagine, for Gratz's letters were filled with them. Maybe by "original" Margaret means not quoted from the Bible, for Gratz's religious ideas, while an interesting mash of Judaism and Christianity, were actually pretty standard. God punishes us all, not just our enemies, for our sins. Providence decrees our fate. In death we'll meet our beloved departed. These were comforting thoughts for Gratz, for they imposed order on the chaos he lived through, gave sense to the madness around him. Made his suicidal decision to go to war seem like part of God's plan.

It's the drawings I wonder about. What they looked like, whose likenesses they were meant to capture. Cosmo the Confederate officer, Jimmie Davis in Charlottesville, Louis? Or were they of the women he loved, his mother and Belle? As for the cards themselves, the things the case had been designed to hold, these would have been Gratz's cartes-de-visite.

Gratz's picture on this card was taken on the same set of the Charleston studio where other Confederate soldiers had their portraits made. In the full-body view shown in that photograph, Gratz looks dapper in his captain's uniform, his right hand tucked inside a long coat tied with what looks like a tasseled curtain rope. In one version of the portrait, his elbow is propped on the base of a Greek column whose full height is never revealed in any of the soldier portraits. A balustrade is set up against a wall, possibly curved, papered with a country scene. A thin-trunked tree rises elegantly on the wallpaper over Gratz's left shoulder, the smudges over his right possibly representing distant mountains. The floor has a diamond-shaped pattern probably meant to conjure marble; perhaps the subject is supposed to be standing on the porch or loggia of a great country house. Though thin and of slight stature, Gratz looks surprisingly healthy, and more baby faced than in the reproduction in the *University Memorial*. He's dwarfed by the fake column and the fake tree. I wonder how long he had to stand there and if his feet hurt. His expression gives nothing away.

Margaret notes the drawings but doesn't speculate on their subjects; nor does she have anything to say about the photograph on the calling card. Do words pass between Margaret and Frank along with the cards and scraps, or do they behold these articles in a reverential silence?

When they're done Frank collects the scraps and cards and carefully puts them back in the case, as if in some order, and returns it to the pocket it has barely left since he first picked it up.

Near the Bentonville visitor center there's a cemetery with the remains of 360 unknown Confederate soldiers. Several vivid accounts of the battle describe the bodies of soldiers left on the fields and in the woods, a sight made more macabre on the battle's final night, when gunfire set ablaze the pinewoods and everything in them, flames shooting into the night sky even as rain fell.

And yet not only was Gratz's body not abandoned, it was carried safely behind Confederate lines and, according to the *University Memorial* account, moved to the Benton farm in Bentonville, just to the north, where Johnston himself had his headquarters until the afternoon of March 21, when he and his staff were forced to flee on foot a Federal charge. Frank buried him there—another of the horrific tasks suddenly forced on him—and marked the spot so carefully that he and Solomon could find it a year later. Did he do so with a cross or something more discreet? I imagine Frank quickly mumbling the only words he knew that might be appropriate for the occasion, unaware of what prayers a Jew might require but hoping that his, heartfelt as they were, would somehow count.

And so Gratz's charmed life continued into death. Frank saw to that.

By the side of the road, I stand at the marker in what was once John Benton's yard and think about Frank for a while. Frank the callow one who existed in Gratz's story to keep him company at college and on the path of war. The aimless one whose life took on purpose with Gratz. Who later assumed his role as an agent of history with aplomb, having the presence of mind to cut off a lock of hair before committing the body to the earth, creating a relic for those who would seek to make a martyr of Gratz Cohen.

Or this: Frank sawed it off with affection, a personal gesture without thinking of how it would resonate in history, cutting the lock simply to have something by which to remember his friend.

But Margaret doesn't need Frank to tell her about the burial. He's already provided the details of the "interment so well done" to her husband, who's written them down for Emma. Margaret hasn't read George's letter, but he seems to have briefed her. Anyway, this isn't what she's after.

Margaret Mordecai wants to know how it happened. How Gratz died. That's what she's after, the truth. She expects her letter to be read second, as a corrective to her husband's, or at least a supplement, though the two letters will probably travel together en route to the Virginia farm where Emma is living.

"But he may not have mentioned," Margaret writes.

It's for Emma that Margaret is sitting across from Frank in her home; she truly believes the truth will set her sister-in-law free. Margaret's letter isn't meant to soften the blow of her husband's. On the contrary, she knows it will deepen Emma's suffering in the short term, do her "no good"—but ultimately set her free.

The truth is holy, though it isn't what any of them wants to hear.

Margaret takes it all down. "That afternoon his noble young friend was shot & entering the back of the head it is supposed in the confusion of battle it was by our own people, so Mr. O'D said for he added Gratz was facing the enemy."

In my head I'm there in that big house in Raleigh repurposed as an infirmary, there in the quiet broken only by the snores and sighs and moans of the wounded, the silence even deeper now that Frank has said what he had to say and Margaret has reached across the table to grasp his hand.

I'm there with these ghosts because they aren't just comrades in suffering, they're allies in the truth.

Frank answers whatever questions he's asked. It doesn't occur to him to lie and make his friend's death more noble than it was. The legend-making would begin later for Gratz Cohen, just as it would for the region he came out of. Frank rushed to Gratz "very soon" after he was shot. We don't know how he learned what Margaret calls the "grievous intelligence" of how his friend died. But Frank was there on that field of death, he was there.

It is supposed Gratz was shot in the head by another Confederate soldier. It is supposed it was an accident, and certainly what we know about the conditions that Harrison's brigade faced at the time, their visibility reduced by thick smoke and the falling of night, makes this explanation plausible. Perhaps, even when faced with this more determined interlocutor, Frank still had not, could not, reveal all. Or maybe he just didn't know; he wasn't an eyewitness to the crime.

At any rate, unlike the secular-minded scribes who wrote the two other accounts of Gratz's death, Margaret has no need to make him a war hero to turn him into a martyr; it's his faith alone that sets him apart and gets him to heaven.

"I know that you will mourn his loss from the bottom of your heart," Margaret writes Emma, "for the sake of his bereaved, devoted parents with whom no one in this sorrowing world will feel a deeper, tenderer sympathy than you my dear kind hearted sister." Emma made the rounds of Richmond hospitals, tending to often gruesomely injured patients with the same sangfroid with which she must have cared for Gratz in the winter of 1862–63, when he spent two weeks recuperating in her Richmond home. His journal is a minute chronicle of his emotions, whereas the strength of her writing lies in its cool observation, whether of wildflowers on a walk or bloodstains on a dining table used for amputations. She writes about her own feelings this way, with an austere detachment, as if feelings too were facts. Her journal covers the year beginning May 1864, but the pages from mid-December 1864 to April 1865 haven't survived. When she does refer to Gratz in the pages of her diary that remain, on three occasions before he died and none after, it's in passing and with rather less than an aunt's affection. He is her "dear young friend," his letter "very sweet." The final time she refers to him, in November 1864, she could be talking about a stranger: "Mr. Cohen [*sic*] removal to So. Carolina is much regretted by all his friends."

But Gratz's death breaks through Emma Mordecai's composure. Neither George Mordecai's letter nor his wife's reached Emma before she learned the news from another source. Her niece Annie sent her a note that's in the Georgia Archives but in such bad condition that I can't read it. Emma's subsequent letter to her sister Ellen is perfectly legible, however. Gratz idolized Emma, and she, for her part, feels "it an undeserved honor & distinction to have been regarded by such a being as I was by him." And she acknowledges, perhaps to her own surprise, "You have not exaggerated my sorrow at his loss," then imagines what Gratz could have become: "the most earnest teacher, the ablest defender, the brightest example of 'the Law which Moses gave to the children of Israel, the Inheritance of the congregation of Jacob.'"

What I try to imagine is whether Gratz's racial attitudes, inescapably shaped by his father and birthplace, would have changed if he'd survived. If the enlightenment he underwent on the path of war would have continued after it, as the region he loved was given the opportunity to remake itself.

Margaret, Frank, and Emma were now heirs to the truth, but there's something they probably didn't know: the role Octavus Cohen Jr. might have played in this chronicle of a death by so many foretold.

One of Octavus Cohen Sr.'s folders in the Georgia Historical Society contains business correspondence, presidential pardons for him and his wife "for taking part in the late rebellion against the Government of the United States," and a printed-up poem called "The Lay of the Last Rebel" that's supposed to be funny and whose narrator insists he doesn't want a pardon:

> I am a good old Rebel,
>   And that's just what I am:
> And for this land of freedom
>   I do not care a damn.

I'm very glad I fit them;
   I only wish we'd won;
And I don't want any pardon
   For any thing I done

There are also two requisitions for military supplies—haversacks, canteens, and knapsacks—that are associated with a different Octavus Cohen, his son and Gratz's first cousin Octy, a lieutenant and acting ordnance officer in George P. Harrison Jr.'s brigade, which included the 5th Regiment of the Georgia Reserves. These requisitions, dated January 5, originate from a station "near Coosawhatchie S.C."—Octy was stationed in nearby Pocotaligo—and are formal documents, certified and approved.

But a third requisition, dated January 23, is more urgent. Signed by O. S. Cohen in "Broxtons Bridge" and addressed to a Captain Barrett in Branchville, this request is in the form of a hastily written note. "Can you send me tomorrow," it begins, then lists ammunition including 600 rounds of "12 Pdr Napoleon Spherical Case," 300 rounds of "12 Pdr Napoleon Shell," 100 rounds of "12 Pdr Napoleon Canister," 100 rounds of "12 Pdr Napoleon S. Shot," 40 rounds of "12 Pdr Howitzer Shell," and so on, before closing "Please answer immediately." Coosawhatchie—Harrison's brigade defended the railroad bridge in this South Carolina hamlet during the first two weeks of 1865. Broxton Bridge—Harrison's men were there toward the end of January and the first week of February, the month before Gratz was killed.

Gratz and Octy were only sixteen when they started their military service at Fort Pulaski, both of them petted by the older troops. But Octy had the military career that disability had denied Gratz. Octy served as quartermaster to Harrison Jr. in the Georgia State Troops and was appointed second lieutenant to a regiment defending Charleston. He was Harrison's aide-de-camp at the Battle of Olustee, the largest battle Florida saw, in February 1864. This was the same position that Gratz would take in December, while Octy assumed new duties for the same brigade. Octy looked out for Gratz at Fort Pulaski, and now, I can't help thinking, he's ordering the ammunition that might be used to blow a hole through his first cousin's skull.

22

Memorials of the Mighty Dead

This authoritarian father, merciless legal adversary, unflinching states rights advocate, poker-faced businessman, stern synagogue president, contemptuous dismisser of fools, defiant defender of slavery—Gratz's death cracks him open like an egg, and all the gooey stuff runs out. To Emma Mordecai, that universal confidante, Solomon declares himself "almost frantic" and ponders: "I cannot understand the dispensation that removed from earth our darling, & left me to mourn, & exclaim with David oh my son, would God I could have died for thee. He was so pure—so talented—so certain to benefit his race—so gifted that he must have been a shining light among men, & I—my task is done. But I will not complain." These sentiments, he makes clear, are for Emma alone to know; he's shared them only with Miriam and her. Solomon doesn't want anyone else, and certainly no man, to know that he harbors such natural emotions.

The next day Solomon feels the need to explain his unusual outburst. "Men, mingling with the world," he continues to Emma, "are forced to suppress feeling, or they would become ridiculous, & this very suppression makes me, at times, fearfully sad." Sad not just for the death of his son but for the rigid masculinity, its product the fantasy that an oversensitive boy could redeem himself with a manly death for a noble cause, that got them both into this predicament to begin with.

But if this devastating loss and his newfound understanding of the perils of manliness showed on his public face or otherwise affected the way he carried out the duties as a citizen that he'd performed his entire adult life, there's no evidence in the public record. The public Solomon Cohen after the war sounds exactly as he did before it.

In the years leading up to 1861, Solomon's ambitions to build a shining city on a sun-scoured fever-ridden bluff had been realized, though the conflict had brought the boomtown to a halt, isolating the place from the

greater world and so making its raison d'être as a port obsolete, the silty
river, always tricky to navigate, made impassible by the boats sunk for that
purpose, and the railroad and telegraph lines torn up. Now, with the city
under military occupation and local government continuing to function,
the railroad is being rebuilt and the river cleared of the obstructions laid
by both sides. Banks reopen and commerce along the riverfront starts
up again. That's the easy part. An entirely different relationship between
white and Black people now needs to be invented, a new social and political
structure, and Solomon realizes that the city's future depends on the states'
relationship with the Union, beginning with the terms under which they
could be readmitted to it. And to affect this relationship, Solomon must
play on a larger stage than Savannah, Georgia. It's the House of Representatives on which he's set his sights.

He's a seasoned politician, a states rights man from way back, and
now that Solomon Cohen is the father of a martyr, his position as *one of
us* is unassailable. Whenever a suspicion arose that he wasn't committed
enough to the cause, he managed to convince his detractors otherwise. In
spirit he'd always been with the secessionists—that's what he said to save
his ass with the rebels. Now, in order to represent Georgia in Congress, he
has to do the exact opposite, convince the federal government that he'd
been for the Union all along. In a letter to President Johnson that's part
of his amnesty claim, he writes that he had no choice but to go along with
the wishes of his state: "I was opposed to secession—did not attend any of
the preliminary meetings—nor did I vote at the election for delegates to the
Convention—but when the State called, I obeyed her mandate."

Solomon writes this in July 1865, but by September, with state elections
approaching, he still hasn't received a decision. His son will become known
for dying, but Solomon Cohen is nothing if not a survivor. And his claim
to President Johnson is in fact truer than what he said to avoid being ostra-
cized, or worse, by his fellow Savannahians. Solomon wanted Georgia to
stay in the Union, though on terms he knew the federal government would
never accept.

With his pardon apparently in limbo, Solomon has good reason to be
nervous. Even though the man to whom he is appealing—the Tennessean
Andrew Johnson, who as Lincoln's vice president assumed the presidency

after the assassination—is, as Solomon would say, *sound* on the question of states, and specifically white, rights, there's a clause in Lincoln's Proclamation of Amnesty that threatens Solomon's pardon. It's the very first exception, making ineligible for amnesty "all who are, or shall have been, civil or diplomatic officers or agents of the so-called Confederate government." Solomon was postmaster, a civil office, under the Confederacy, continuing in the same position he'd held before the war.

In his letter for amnesty, the Honorable Solomon Cohen distinguishes, legalistically, between an officer *of* the Confederacy and one *under* it. An example of an officer under it and so not responsible for the decisions of the government? Postmaster. Never mind that the Proclamation of Amnesty itself made no such distinction; Solomon Cohen could make an argument out of what should have been in a law as well as he could parse what was actually in it.

And Solomon is technically disqualified by being a member of another exempted class, this one created, in his amnesty proclamation of May 29, 1865, by President Johnson himself: Solomon is worth more than $20,000. At first Johnson appeared tough on the leaders of the rebellion. But knowing where the new president's sympathies truly lie, Solomon isn't afraid to admit that his personal property was worth well over $20,000 before the war, and that he wouldn't take double for it now. His railroad and bank stocks are now yielding nothing, as are all those Confederate bonds he bought to support the cause; his slaves, he feels, have been "robbed" from him. But unlike the region's planters, Solomon diversified his investments, enslaved labor having been only one of his income streams.

In September he writes to Frank P. Blair Jr., who recommended him for amnesty in the first place, to help address the "peculiar circumstances" of his case. This is the same man, a major general in the Union army at the time, who after the capture of Savannah Solomon queried about maintaining his property and profession during the occupation. Blair was a lawyer and congressman representing Missouri, and he went on to become the (disastrous) Democratic vice-presidential candidate in 1868, but during the war he led Sherman's Seventeenth Army Corps on the march to the sea and then north through the Carolinas, where Gratz would meet his end, fighting on the other side. An unlikely ally, Blair would seem to be, but while he was ardently antislavery, he was no supporter of Black equality. And he was a relative, distant kin through Rebecca Gratz's late sister-in-law, Maria Gist Gratz, a Christian.

In a letter to Blair included in his *Memoirs*, Sherman tartly responds to Solomon's query.

> 1. No one can practise law as an attorney in the United States without acknowledging the supremacy of our Government. If I am not in error, an attorney is as much an officer of the court as the clerk, and it would be a novel thing in a government to have a court to administer law which denied the supremacy of the government itself.
> 2. No one will be allowed the privileges of a merchant, or, rather, to trade is a privilege which no one should seek of the Government without in like manner acknowledging its supremacy.
> 3. If Mr. Cohen remains in Savannah as a denizen, his property, real and personal, will not be disturbed unless its temporary use be necessary for the military authorities of the city. The title to property will not be disturbed in any event, until adjudicated by the courts of the United States.
> 4. If Mr. Cohen leaves Savannah under my Special Order No. 148, it is a public acknowledgment that he "adheres to the enemies of the United States," and all his property becomes forfeited to the United States. But, as a matter of favor, he will be allowed to carry with him clothing and furniture for the use of himself, his family, and servants, and will be trans ported within the enemy's lines, but not by way of Port Royal.

In other words, if Solomon Cohen, whom Sherman labels a "rich lawyer," wants to quit the occupied city—something he must have inquired about, perhaps to be closer to Gratz—he's welcome to leave with the clothes on his back and precious little else.

Now, nearly a year later and six months after the death of his son, Solomon has sworn fidelity to the United States, and the only thing stopping him from playing his part in the next phase of civilization building—or as Solomon would see it, civilization preserving—is his pardon. That's what he needs to go to Congress to support President Johnson in his efforts against what Solomon calls "the surging waves of Northern fanaticism . . . to do justice to the South to protect her rights."

Like a magician, President Johnson appears to take away with one hand while giving with the other, making an exception to his own exception by granting Solomon (and many others) a pardon. The *Savannah Daily Herald* of November 4, 1865, leads with Solomon's speech of October 30 at the state's Democratic convention. The month before, he was elected, along with two other prominent Confederates, as representatives from Chatham County to the state convention. (The rebel candidates got roughly *nine times* as many votes as the Union ones did.) In early December the Georgia General Assembly will ratify the Thirteenth Amendment, outlawing slavery, and Solomon is typical of his legislative colleagues in accepting emancipation as a done deal and a condition for Georgia's readmission to the Union. This is a bitter enough pill to swallow, but now the state is being asked to accept another condition, which will become section four of the Fourteenth Amendment: " . . . neither the United States nor any State shall assume or pay any debt or obligation incurred in aid of insurrection or rebellion against the United States, or any claim for the loss or emancipation of any slave; but all such debts, obligations and claims shall be held illegal and void." Remember Solomon's calculation, in a letter to Rebecca Gratz, of the value of all the slaves in the Southern states? And what about the millions of dollars worth of cotton abandoned to the occupying forces in Savannah alone? Would these losses be considered debts that the federal government was expected to pay? Section four of the Fourteenth Amendment was a way to forestall such claims.

But the Fourteenth Amendment, today the most cited of all constitutional amendments, more significantly granted citizenship to the formerly enslaved. Repudiation of debt, Solomon feels, is a slippery slope, and will soon be joined by the North's "fanatical" demands for "negro suffrage, negro equality, social and political." Whatever white Southerners thought emancipation would look like, this isn't it. After all, even the Northern states haven't granted Black people social and political equality.

In November 1865, Solomon is the top vote-getter in Georgia's First Congressional District, which includes Chatham County. This grandson of an immigrant Jewish shopkeeper and unpaid rabbi seems to have overcome every hurdle toward realizing the next stage of his political ambitions as a member of the United States House of Representatives. To Emma he claims that Gratz's death has robbed him of all earthly ambition, that he reentered politics only because his fellow citizens demanded it—but now that he has won, he's prepared to move his family to Washington. Someone, after all, has to combat the "mad malignancy" of the Radical Republicans.

But neither Georgia's House delegation nor its two newly elected senators, including former vice president of the Confederacy Alexander H. Stephens, are allowed by the Republican-controlled Congress to take their seats. Stephens is held up as an example of the South's chutzpah in choosing the leaders of their rebellion to sit in the legislative body of the government they'd rebelled against. Solomon gets cast out along with this much bigger fish, the kind of man from whom he tried to distinguish himself in his application for amnesty. In the end it doesn't matter whether Solomon was *of* the government of the Confederate States of America or *under* it. His political career is over.

It's a good time to go collect what's left of his son. And so at the start of February 1866, Solomon Cohen and Frank O'Driscoll travel north through the cold Carolina countryside on the path Frank and Gratz took nearly a year before. Considering the state of the rails at the time, the pair would have had to take various forms of transportation, though remarkably, they made the 600-mile round trip in two weeks, apparently undistracted from their mission by the need to rest.

On this "sacred mission," as Solomon called it, Frank is "as kind and considerate as possible." What has the younger man told the older of his son's death? Solomon boasted to Emma that on the battlefield Gratz could always be seen where the bullets fell the thickest—this Solomon learned from members of his son's brigade. But in their correspondence with Gratz's last confidante, letters that never stray far from the subject of their son's death, neither Solomon nor Miriam ever references the version of the event that Frank told Margaret Mordecai.

Whatever accounting Frank has given Solomon, does the latter, as they ride together, want to hear the story again? Is there anything left to tell? Is Frank sick of telling or could he do so for the rest of his life?

One thing I do know: Frank has already asked Solomon for Belle's hand.

Belle, only a year and a half younger than Gratz, the siblings inseparable as children, growing up in the squares, sleeping together at least
till Gratz was twelve: this was the girl whom Frank wanted to spend his
life with. The three of them had grown up together, Frank's family neighbors (and tenants) of the Cohens in the rowhouse a couple doors down.
The ghosts of these children still played on the sidewalk—and the ghost
of Gratz couldn't have been excluded from the new couple. Imagine that
relationship, a threesome, with Gratz always between Belle and Frank as
they walked arm and arm through the world. It must have been especially
strange, considering Belle was a look-alike for her brother. Or perhaps not
so odd to Frank, who after all wanted to marry her. He must have known
what he was doing, knew it would be a way to gaze on his dead friend's face
for the rest of his life.

There's no evidence that seventeen-year-old Frank asked for Belle's
hand before volunteering with Gratz. Did he broach the subject immediately after he returned, now in a much stronger position with Gratz's
relics in hand, the things he himself had harvested from his friend's body
before committing him to the earth, all these labors done at great personal risk? Frank might not have known that Solomon was, as he put it,
"as much opposed to intermarriages as any one I ever knew." But Frank
had known the Cohens his entire life, knew Solomon was a strict and
religious man.

Did Frank have to summon the courage, then, to ask the stern father for
permission to marry his fair daughter? Or did he feel invincible, imbued
with the moral authority with which Solomon would later credit him? I
believe it's the former. Frank was always in Gratz's shadow, as cozy and
reliably affectionate as the kitten he left behind when he quit Charlottesville to go on a short trip. Frank assumed the job of devoted caretaker
that everyone else did in Gratz's life; it was just his rotten timing that he
happened to be the one in the role when Gratz's luck finally ran out. Frank
would have approached his friend's father with humility and respect.

But Solomon had changed. He'd become less intimidating, though not
diminished—Gratz's death seemed to make Solomon fully human, at least
in his personal life. He no longer felt he had to bully people into going
along with the plan. Now it was a young man asking him to go along with
his plan. Solomon was in a terrible predicament! What choice did he have

but to allow his elder daughter to marry this Gentile, considering what Frank had done for his boy? The engagement was a done deal before the two men left on their gruesome journey.

In Goldsboro Solomon hires a carriage to take them to Bentonville. For nearly a year John Benton, on whose farm Gratz was buried, has watched and tended the grave, and Solomon finds the coffin in perfect condition but the outer box slightly decayed. He has a new box built, its seams sealed with rosin boiled with turpentine—pine products that are a specialty of the region—and the box filled with powdered charcoal. During the twenty-four hours he spends in Bentonville, he eats nothing. Food, he believes, would only choke him.

The funeral took place on February 13, 1866, a Tuesday. Friends and acquaintances were invited to gather at the house on the corner of Liberty and Barnard to depart at four for Laurel Grove, the first city cemetery open to people of all faiths. Here is how Solomon describes the burial to Emma: "Mr. Jacobs came to us, as I had requested & officiated at the burial of my son. The services were very solemn, & very appropriate. All classes of the community—high & low, Bishop, Priest & people united to do honor to the memory of our darling. And it was right for he was no common person." Mickve Israel had no rabbi at the time, so the Reverend Jacobs, either Henry or his brother George, would have come from New Orleans at Solomon's request.

Three months later, on Wednesday, May 9, Belle and Frank got married. The Honorable W. R. Fleming, judge of the Superior Court, presided.

Time passes, sad events are succeeded by happy ones—but the extent of Solomon and Miriam's loss only becomes clearer with each day. At least Solomon has something else to focus on, regaining his professional stature. But Miriam can think about only one thing. She isn't well, she isn't at all well, and the doctor prescribes nothing more than exercise, for Miriam's isn't the kind of malady that medicine can heal. Solomon obliges by taking her on walks, which help—but at home there's nothing she can do to make life bearable.

The big house on Liberty Street has become a cage, as it contains her son's books, clothes, boots, toilet articles, writing, *objets* . . . Their presence reminds her constantly of Gratz's absence, and yet she cannot stay away from them, and she will keep most of these things until her death, dividing them up between her daughters, who she knows will treat them as the precious relics they are to her. His writing especially draws her. I wonder if Miriam read his journal and if so what she made of it. From a letter to Emma we know that his juvenilia, dating from as far back as when he was eight, strikes her with wonder at the sophistication of his thinking and the elegant way he expressed himself. None of this writing survives. The possibility of judgment by strangers made her fearful of sharing it with anyone who didn't know and love him. But she wanted Emma to read it. Emma would appreciate every word of Gratz's writing the way she appreciated him.

Gratz starts to seem to Miriam not just good, but perfect. In every measure—the pureness of his thought, the justness of his judgments, the strictness of his self-examination, his concern for the happiness of all beings—he was exemplary, unlike anyone she's ever known, and in this way her own son comes to seem strange to her. He was unique among men, and maybe more, something beyond human. Angels come down from time to time, the Torah shows, to test us and show us how to live, sojourning among us and then returning where they came from. Perhaps Gratz, belonging to God, was never really hers.

But this idea can comfort her for only so long. Miriam feels stuck in a perpetual present, with no hopes for the future and a past that slips from her grasp. Rather than dulling the pain, the passage of time only reveals how attached she was to her son. Six months after Gratz's death, Miriam writes Rebecca:

> God alone knows what my mental sufferings have been from the first to last—each day do I feel more poignantly the loss of our precious son, each day reveals to us how entirely our earthly hopes & happiness were garnered up in this loved being—& oh how dark & desolate the future is to us without him to lean on in our old age & to protect our darling daughters when we shall be no more. Dear Belle & Maimy do all that devotion can dictate to soothe us. Their loss is no common one for their beloved brother was every thing to them. So gentle, so loving, & so wise in all his counsels, so perfect in all his ways that he was an example to his young friends. I feel dearest Aunt that I am

trespassing on your feelings, & as I can only write or think on the
one subject that fills my heart I must now leave you.

Solomon too remarks that time can't heal this particular wound and
describes his feelings, to Emma, in similar terms to his wife's:

> This is a sad season with us, and it really seems that both Miriam
> and I become each day, more deeply impressed with the extent of our
> loss—and more sensibly alive to our loneliness—we murmur not, for
> God still spares us our two daughters—healthful, affectionate, gentle
> & intelligent—but our beloved, our only son is no more. Our hope
> is taken from us—our pride, & hope are crushed. He was to be our
> friend, our adviser, & to whom all things were to have been commit-
> ted, one on whom we could lean in the decline of life, and to whom,
> when death was near, we could have committed the care of his sisters.
> Oh it is a terrible blow, & time seems only to exercise its force.

Solomon busies himself directing activities such as rebuilding the railroads
and clearing the river. And he's a corporator of the new Georgia Joint Stock
Land and Immigration Company, whose goal is "procuring agricultural
labor, facilitating immigration and promoting the commercial interests of
the State of Georgia." This company will advertise daily in the Savannah
papers, seeking to attract white labor from outside the South to do work
done by formerly enslaved people. Most freed Black people, it turns out,
have other ideas than entering into contracts with their former enslavers
to do the same work they'd done before. Once readmitted to practice in
US courts, Solomon will restart his legal career by practicing a different
kind of law, representing the region's planters and other businessmen in
bankruptcy proceedings.

But Miriam needs a change. If Gratz's things won't vanish, if the spaces
he traversed in the house and the walls upon which he gazed insist on
remaining, then she herself must leave. Solomon, observing "the wasted
form of my wife" and suffering himself from "the black pall that Death
has spread over my home, & heart," rents the house out to a nephew. Solomon and Miriam consider a move to Europe. Or a new life up north—but
Solomon has heard of the rude treatment of Southerners in that part of the

country. So instead they travel, to North Georgia, Baltimore, Philadelphia to visit Rebecca Gratz.

And the town they leave behind begins to become something other than the little civilization that Solomon Cohen helped build. He hoped to go to Washington to support President Johnson, but with Southern representatives excluded from Congress, the inevitable has happened. In March 1867 the Radical Republicans in Congress pass a Reconstruction plan, over Johnson's veto, that would reorganize the South's political structure by enfranchising Black men. The South would have to change. That spring Republicans sponsor mass rallies in Chippewa Square, and Black people, some of them armed, pour in from the countryside to demand their new rights and hear speeches from politicians seeking their votes.

In April 1867, Solomon and Miriam, with Mamie and their niece Georgina in tow, leave for New York, to set sail for the Continent.

There's something other than grief and the changing landscape of their hometown that draws Miriam and Solomon Cohen to Europe that spring: the birth of their first grandchild. Ten months after her wedding, Belle O'Driscoll gives birth to a girl, named Frances, after her father. Fanny is born in Paris, where Belle and Frank have moved temporarily with his parents. A historian of Savannah Jewry suggests to me that Solomon might in fact have appreciated the removal of his daughter to Europe, so that the scandal of the synagogue president whose daughter married a goy had time to die down. But intermarriage between Savannah Jews and non-Jews was increasingly common, and may have represented the ultimate step in the acceptance of Jews by the larger community that men such as Solomon Cohen more generally sought. He might not have liked Belle's marriage to Frank, but it would have only strengthened the Cohen family's place in Savannah society.

On Wednesday, May 8, the Cohen party boards the steamship *Malta* bound for Liverpool. Their European tour will last fourteen months, and Miriam and Solomon will document it in travel journals, account books, lists of artworks they saw and people who received them, even catalogs of articles of clothing and bars of soap packed. How different an experience it is to read these extremely legible documents, put together in peacetime, than to decipher Gratz's journal, its scribbled, sometimes obscure and even

obscured entries recollecting intense emotions, and not always in tranquil-
ity. Miriam and Solomon's cooler, fact-filled travelogs describe the same
places and contain passages so similar that taken together, they can feel
like a kind of secular New Testament—the Book of Solomon, the Book of
Miriam. These two journals alone show that Miriam and Solomon were
true partners, with more than just their shared history in common; theirs
was a match of intellects, both deeply grounded in high European culture.

The same story, told sometimes in the very same words, and yet different moods hover over the two accounts. It's the Old South whose loss
Solomon laments as he travels across the Continent. Notre Dame de Stras-
bourg, completed in 1439, inspires him to reflect on the "senseless rage of
the radicalism of the French Revolution," when the cathedral's tower was
almost destroyed. This is a man who venerates religion and the established
order, and soon his thoughts run to the person he considers the United
States' very own Robespierre, Charles Sumner, the Massachusetts senator
who was an antislavery activist and is now a leader of the Radical Republicans in Congress: "Sumner in his madness, or hatred of the South, would
pull down virtue, intelligence, civilization, to a level with vice, ignorance,
& semi barbarism. But there is a just God, who has declared 'Vengeance is
mine & I will repay!'"

Miriam's journal is marked by a more personal sense of loss. "A young
Scotchman, who was in the Army & appeared to be quite an Invalid," she
writes on the ocean journey to Europe, "deeply interested me for the sake
of one who is never absent from my thoughts—all very young men claim
a sad interest now." Miriam is a diligent tourist, stationing herself before
all the great sights. But I can't help imagining her attention wander, to
lock eyes with the young man passing between the columns at Pompeii, or
to gaze at the boy staring at Voltaire's tomb in the Panthéon in Paris. The
change of scenery that Miriam sought couldn't distract her from her grief,
but perhaps she never expected it to.

In Paris, whose broad straight avenues Solomon prefers to the sooty
alleys of London, they meet up with Belle and Frank and "our sweet
baby" Fanny, and take in the area's sights, including "an illumination of
water-works in honour of the Sultan & the Emperor of Austria" at Ver-
sailles. From Paris this expanded group continues on together. Solomon
and Miriam have letters of introduction to people across the Continent,

among them nobles and aristocrats like "les Frères Drexel," their hosts in Frankfurt, where they tour Goethe's birthplace, and the house where Luther lived and preached from. At the Jewish cemetery there they visit the grave of Grace Aguilar, and Belle plucks a sprig of ivy, which Miriam later presses into her book.

In Venice they stand on the Bridge of Sighs, and Solomon is pleased to now be able to say, with Byron: "I stood in Venice, on the Bridge of Sighs,/ A palace and a prison on each hand." The interrogation rooms in the Doge's palace remind both Miriam and Solomon of "man's inhumanity to man." Gratz loved Byron, and Miriam finds the poet wherever she goes. "I never so fully appreciated Byron as a portrayer of Nature," she notes in Switzerland, "as well as of the passions and feelings of the human heart, as I do now, when gazing on the scenes he so perfectly as well as poetically describes."

From their hotel room on the bay in Naples, Miriam notes of Vesuvius that they "can see the smoke wreathing the mountain and hear the explosions like loud constant cannonading."

And everywhere, they visit temples and cathedrals, but not just as tourists. They attend services in synagogues as well as churches, and neither Solomon nor Miriam finds it unusual to worship at the latter. They spend the High Holidays in Frankfurt and attend services on the first day of Sukkoth.

When the Pope passes them during a procession at Christmastime in Rome, Solomon and company bow and the Pope leans out of his carriage and blesses their party.

In Cologne, Belle and Frank and Fanny leave Miriam and Solomon and Mamie to join Frank's parents in Brussels. "It was a sad day for me," Miriam writes, "for parting with my children now almost breaks my heart, each parting brings to mind that one final parting which is ever one long agony!"

Solomon never refers to Gratz's death in his travel diary. But you could see it on his face. In addition to all the written documentation, I find a picture taken of him during this period, in a photographer's studio in London. In his dark well-cut suit and shiny silk black tie, he's a prosperous-looking man of sixty-five. In the lower right-hand corner, an inch of gold watch chain passes through the bottom button of his vest. In the custom of the time, he isn't smiling. But his expression goes beyond serious; he looks haunted. His mouth is a thin downturned line separating the bushy white hair on his upper lip from the moss hanging down his chin. You could imagine those locked lips never parting or needing to, for his eyes, staring straight into the camera, appear to convey it all: an unspeakable grief. At least this is what I see in them.

Traipsing around the Continent, dutifully recording inscriptions on tombs, opining on the synagogue in Frankfurt and the salmon mayonnaise in Liverpool, cataloging every castle and sculpture and picture gallery and palace and park, quoting relevant verses of Byron, comparing Paris to London, and Berlin to Savannah, pressing a leaf from Virgil's tomb, experiencing the frisson of the most terrible and glorious moments of European history while standing among its monuments—well, I suppose it passed the time. But reading these diaries, I keep wondering how visiting cenotaphs and mausoleums and tombs, which sometimes seems the Solomon Cohens' main activity abroad, was a way to distract them from the death of their son. The irony that Gratz, a student of European history and languages, never went to Europe must have made them feel his absence even more. How often must one spouse have said to the other, "Gratz would have loved this."

But at some point I think I understand. It wasn't to escape their son's death that Miriam and Solomon went to Europe, but rather to indulge in it, glorify it the way Gratz himself did long before it happened. You couldn't do this in the United States—at least not yet—and in fact the Cohens avoided other Americans on their travels, accustomed to nothing from them but insults and hatred, as Solomon saw it. But if you could put the ravaged country behind you and immerse yourself in a place where the past has had time to gel, harden into something awesome and enduring, like the ruins of Pompeii that so impressed Solomon, then "every step you take is among memorials of the mighty dead."

More Heroism Than to Die

The city to which Solomon and Miriam returned had changed. But in many ways it was still the place whose institutions Solomon had had such a hand in shaping. The Cohens were back by the end of summer 1868, just in time for the political season. The first presidential election after the war landed the Republican candidate, Civil War hero Ulysses S. Grant, in the White House. But in Savannah, the Democrats vanquished their opponents. A poll tax and a requirement that voters prove they were paid up on taxes, among more draconian tactics, effectively blocked most Black people from voting. With 3,900 Black men registered to vote in Savannah, Grant got only 400 votes.

Perhaps none of this surprised Solomon Cohen. But what must have come as a shock was the way Mickve Israel, the synagogue just down the block, had changed. In Solomon's absence the congregation's president asked its new spiritual leader, the liberal firebrand Raphael de Castro Lewin, to form a choir. Anyone who grew up in a more traditional congregation knows how marvelously strange it feels to hear a choir in a synagogue. Sparks must have flown from Solomon's head the first time he heard it.

In February 1868, when Miriam and Solomon were still in Europe, Reverend Lewin had delivered a sermon on the differences between Reform and Orthodox Judaism. There were arcane theological distinctions, but the thrust of his address urged a spiritual renewal:

> Whatever is defective or corrupt in our present observance of religious forms, whatever abuses may exist in our worship . . . these are to be Reformed . . . Reform, my brethren, is to restore the Mosaic religion to its original beauty; Reform, my brethren, is . . . to declare . . . that God is one, and that his law is one. . . . Your first duty is to dismiss anger

and passion from your minds, so that your reason may come . . . to
your aid.

Go now to your homes, and may the spirit of truth follow you
thither, and reign triumphant in your meditations, so that peace and
harmony may prevail among you and so that our pure and lovable
faith may soon shine forth in all its pristine brilliance.

These words could have flowed from Gratz's pen, and practically did. "We
are in need of a Luther to thunder against the lifeless forms of the synagogue," he wrote Emma. "We have a spiritual want that must be satisfied
by outward rituals suited to the age in which we live."

Inspired by Lewin's words, a synagogue committee proposed a set of
reforms—not just the introduction of choral and organ music, but shorter
services as well. This group of five men was led by Octavus Cohen, who'd
sought his fortune in Savannah years before Solomon did. Octavus had
always been a man of the future, not the past, and it probably wasn't a
coincidence that he made his move to modernize the synagogue when his
older brother was away.

But eventually big brother had his say. After reassuming the presidency
of the congregation, in 1869, Solomon proposed a resolution affirming the
"fundamental principles of our ancient faith" as "eternal and unchangeable." The resolution singled out the ultimate return of the Jews to Israel
and the coming of the Messiah as examples of these principles, and recognized Judaism's dietary laws as binding, while accepting that people slip
up. It sounds innocuous enough, but this statement was a dagger pointed
squarely at Reverend Lewin, and it worked. The resolution passed and the
rabbi resigned.

Still, few practical effects ensued, and at the same meeting that the resolution was passed, an organist was hired. Solomon and Octavus battled it
out in general and special meetings, but the reforms continued. And while
Solomon was the leader of the traditionalist faction, that first resolution
showed how much he'd softened up. The resolution affirmed the principles
of Orthodoxy but took for granted that "synagogue worship involves no
moral, or religious principle, and may be altered to suit the taste of the
congregation." This wasn't the unyielding, by-the-book Solomon Cohen
from before the war, and his only son's death.

Reform Judaism was something Solomon found easier to accept than the end of slavery. On that subject he wouldn't yield. He wrote Emma, in a wistful past tense, that the "institution of slavery was refining and civilizing to the whites—giving them an elevation of sentiment and ease and dignity of manners only attainable in societies under the restraining influence of a privileged class—and at the same time the only human institution that could elevate the negro from barbarism and develop the small amount of intellect with which he is endowed." It's a well-known quotation, and mainly how Solomon Cohen is remembered today.

He died on August 14, 1875. His last words, according to his obituary in the *Savannah Morning News*, were about Miriam, who must have been the writer's source.

> For some time past Mr. Cohen had been in feeble health, but was not confined to the house. On Saturday afternoon he retired to his room after dinner to enjoy his usual nap. A short while afterwards his wife entered the room and engaged with him in conversation, during which he made the remark that if he lived until the morrow he would be seventy-three years of age, and pleasantly alluded to the happiness of their married relation. Presently he ceased speaking, and her attention was attracted to the peculiar manner in which his head was reposing, and upon approaching closer she discovered that he was unconscious, having been stricken with apoplexy.

He died that night, just before midnight. On the day of his funeral, the biggest Savannah had ever seen, the city's courtrooms were hung with black festoons.

Miriam's own, disgracefully brief yet error-riddled *Savannah Morning News* obituary, in 1891, captured almost none of her accomplishments and nothing of her personality, but managed to mention she was a Savannahian "only by adoption." While this says more about Savannahians than about Miriam—she'd lived there for fifty-three years—I wonder if she ever really stopped feeling like a stranger in a strange land.

Her own family treated her like one, especially during the war, when Northerners in Savannah fell under intense suspicion. Miriam's niece

Fanny, Octavus's daughter, had been her Hebrew pupil and like a daughter to her, and the brief journal Fanny kept during the occupation of Savannah mentions a visit to Miriam two days after Christmas, the first time the two saw each other since the city was captured. Fanny was twenty-five now, four-and-a-half years older than Gratz, and in her diary she comes off as a citified Scarlett O'Hara, pouty and petulant: "If we are conquered I see no reason why we should receive our enemies as friends and I never shall do it so long as I live." Octavus and his family lived in a since-demolished mansion with stacked columned porches on Lafayette Square, now with a Union general for a boarder, and on her walk to the house on Liberty Street, a few blocks away, Fanny observed the little wooden houses that enemy soldiers, the "wretches," had built to house themselves in the squares. Wood from the platforms on which enslaved people had been auctioned off had been reused in some of them; so had material from demolished houses of the poor, including Black homeowners. Of the visit itself Fanny writes: "This morning I went to see my Aunt Mrs. Cohen for the first time and although she is a Northern woman found her violent against the Yankees and a true sympathizer in our cause." This was remarkable enough for Fanny to report, and I can't help wondering if the real source of Miriam's sudden fury toward the Union soldiers—she'd rarely sounded principled about the South's "cause," as her husband did, or passionate about it, like Gratz—was that her only son had just left her to fight them.

The letters that I find in the Mordecai papers at Duke University chart the transformation that Fanny first noted. After Gratz's death Miriam finds it hard to perform her usual duties, including keeping up with correspondence, while Solomon, who once had a policy never to discuss his children, can't stop writing about his son. Gratz chose Aunt Emma as his last confidante and so Solomon now takes her as a sister, this Southern woman whom he'd never had to school about slavery as he had Gratz's other beloved aunt, Rebecca. Year after year, in letter after letter, Emma and Solomon summon Gratz up, extolling his virtues, analyzing his texts, finding meaning in his life, imagining what he could have been; acknowledging he never truly knew his son, Solomon now finds worth in Gratz's "natural sweetness of temper." Miriam, when she manages to write Emma, finds her own way to resurrect him. Her handwriting degrades as her outrage mounts, and it's directed at a single object, the Union army: Gratz "fell a sacrifice to the Invader!!" In a calmer moment five years after her son's death, she writes: "I like to tread Virginia's soil for I love it for the noble states men & heroes that were born & reared on it. I love it for all that it has borne & for the precious blood that has been shed on it." This woman who, when she wasn't avoiding discussing politics altogether, once wrote of her love for both North and South now sounds the way her fired-up young son did when war was something he read about in books and newspaper propaganda. Miriam's brokenness corresponds so wholly to the South's that she comes to identify, for perhaps the first time in her life, as a Southerner: "I love the South, the home of my adoption, more tenderly in its hour of humiliation than in its days of prosperity & happiness, & then it is the grave of my precious one! & must ever be held sacred for the sacrifice laid on its altar!"

Did Miriam ever direct any of that rage at her husband, for permitting their son to go to war? In letters she blames the federal government and its army, never herself or Solomon. In the European diaries the pair barely refer to each other, but perhaps this was because they both viewed their journals as impersonal travelogs. (Solomon's more so than Miriam's—he was, it turned out, taking notes for a lecture he would give at the Georgia Historical Society called "Notes on Switzerland.") And because by this point they were halves of a whole; to refer to the other half might have seemed unnecessary.

After Gratz's death, Solomon played the role of Miriam's caretaker—when, that is, he wasn't trying to reconstruct the South in his own way. Toward the end of his life, their roles were reversed. But in between, when they were alone together with the ghost of their son always between them, what did they see when they looked into each other's eyes?

The stained glass over the altar at Mickve Israel, on elegant Monterey Square, might provide a clue. The last time I went to a service there, long before I entered Solomon Cohen's world, I sat in the front row and stared up at the words OCTAVUS COHEN, illuminated from behind, and above them, on a blue field, the backs of a pair of hands with the fingers separated in a sign associated with the high priests in the days of the Temple. High priests are descendants of Moses's brother, Aaron, and *cohen* means priest in Hebrew—and as such, the men in Gratz's family would have been honored with the first blessing over the Torah at services in which it was read, at least in Mickve Israel's Orthodox days. Octavus Cohen, I figured, must have been the biggest macher of all to get such prime window real estate, the focus of the entire congregation whenever it raised its eyes toward the divine.

And when I found out who he was, I wondered why Octavus, who died a year after Solomon, was commemorated in stained glass, but not his far more illustrious brother, who served as president of the congregation from 1856 to 1866 and again from 1869 to his death, in 1875, just months before the cornerstone of the new sanctuary was laid; he was the head of the Building Committee. Henrietta Cohen, Octavus's widow, agreed to sponsor one of the three windows over the altar to honor her husband's memory. The congregation offered Miriam another of these windows, a memorial that would outlast them all, and stand for as long as the building did. Solomon had left her an estate worth $125,000, greater than $3 million in today's dollars, so whatever gift the synagogue expected of her to create the stained glass was something she could have afforded. But to the congregation's query she never replied.

After Solomon's death Miriam wasn't active in the congregation for which she'd raised funds to hire its first rabbi and whose first Hebrew school she founded. But perhaps she still showed up for Shabbat services, sat steely-eyed and expressionless, fixed as a monument, in the family's prominent pew—and avoided looking up at the stained glass behind the altar where her husband's name should have been. The Temple's historian Rabbi Saul Rubin suspects she didn't feel she should have to sponsor the window, after everything Solomon had done for the congregation. Miriam didn't refuse the honor the synagogue offered her husband, she simply ignored it. I wonder if this act of defiance, however passive, was a first and final act of revenge on a husband who should have known better than to permit their son to go to war.

Belle Cohen, the older of Gratz's sisters, apparently also maintained a connection to the synagogue in which she'd grown up; there's a program for the dedication of the neo-gothic Mickve Israel sanctuary, in 1878, with Belle's name written in her hand on the front. But to her daughter she gave a choice. When she was eleven years old, the Paris-born child of Belle Cohen and Frank O'Driscoll received a letter from her mother, though they were together in their Savannah home. "My dear Fanny," Belle wrote,

"I think you are old enough now for me to speak to you upon a subject of importance. I prefer writing to speaking because I wish you to thoroughly understand me." In a few years, Belle explained, her daughter must choose between the religion of her father or her mother. It didn't matter which religion she chose, as long as she chose one; belonging to a faith was especially important for a woman. "One religion is as good as another," Belle writes, "for although there is a difference in the belief, the great object is the same in all religions—to teach us to love God, & our fellow beings, to do no wrong to any man, & to lead good & pure lives, so that when we die we will be fitted for a life in Heaven." Belle wanted Fanny to feel free to choose for herself, without fear of displeasing her or anyone else, but this tender letter so scrupulously refrains from tilting the balance that I wonder if Belle was using the occasion simply to reaffirm her own Jewishness.

I don't know how religious Fanny ended up being, but she went on to marry a man named John Hunter. Hunter—that's a name every Savannahian knows from the huge army airfield on the southside, named after Major General Frank O'Driscoll "Monk" Hunter, Fanny and John's son. He was a World War I flying ace and commanding general of the unit providing air protection for Allied troops in World War II. Decorated to the hilt, Hunter was a "handsome, swashbuckling man," according to his *New York Times* obituary, a lifelong bachelor whose favorite hobbies were "cocktails, women and fishing." Gratz would have been his great-uncle.

Two months before Solomon's death, his son-in-law, Frank O'Driscoll, died as he'd lived, by trying to save a weaker boy. At a swimming party on what is now called Little Tybee Island, the barrier island just off Savannah's main beach where swift tides and tricky currents perennially make bad news, Frank was last seen in the ocean with teenage Charles Johnson "clinging to him. To the terrified friends on shore, it was apparent that Mr. O'Driscoll was making manful efforts to reach safe water, but it was evidently a fearful struggle, and before assistance could be rendered, they had disappeared beneath the swelling sea," according to the *Savannah Morning News*. Belle wasn't there, and when she learned of the tragedy, she was "threatened with convulsions" and had to be attended by "several physicians" into the night.

A decade later Belle married an obstetrician named Eugene Corson, almost a decade her junior, who did pioneering work with X-rays. He was originally from Washington, DC, and had worked in Vienna, Austria, after completing medical school in Philadelphia. He'd moved to Savannah for his health. Corson's first major published paper, "The Future of the Colored Race in the United States from an Ethnic and Medical Standpoint," used eugenics to conclude that Black people in fact had no future in this country, and it was presented at the Georgia Historical Society and published in the *New York Medical Times* in 1887. (Unlike other eugenicists, Corson, who wasn't Jewish, would later find evidence of "the great vitality of the Jewish race.")

In the Georgia Historical Society I find a picture of two women and a man on the landing outside the parlor door of a townhouse whose exterior is the mirror image of mine. The back of the picture identifies the building as the one next to the house where the Solomon Cohen family lived. On the left side of the photograph is a handsome bearded young man in a suit, resting his hat on the corner of the railing. This is Eugene Corson. To his left is Belle, wasp-waisted in a black high-collared dress with some big round ornament in the middle of her chest. Her black hair is up and parted in the middle, her eyes are dark, and she has the same strong chin as Gratz did. Her hands are clasped and resting on the railing. On Belle's other side is a small woman also in black, her head wrapped in a dramatic white bonnet, a tail trailing across each shoulder. This is Miriam. She's a bit stooped and her hands are closed around the railing. Each of these people is standing apart from the others and staring at the camera. Corson's look is neutral, maybe a bit imploring. Belle appears modest and serious. Miriam's gaze is intense, even ferocious. She's clutching the railing for dear life and refuses to let go.

Belle lives in this house with her children and new husband and with Miriam as well. Mamie and her family, when they aren't at Hofwyl-Broadfield, their plantation down the coast, use the big house next door, the one she and Belle and Gratz grew up in, as their city home. The year must be 1885 or 1886. Gratz has been dead for twenty years, Solomon and Frank for a decade. Miriam is around seventy-seven, Belle around forty, Corson thirty. Belle would be dead, of what I don't know, within the year, just as Corson's reputation as a medical researcher was taking off.

Miriam's mother had died when she was a girl. She'd lost her father and the aunt who raised her (Rebecca died in 1869) and now, with Belle's death, had buried two of her children, as well as the son-in-law whom she'd loved, though not quite as a son, the word *son* having "died upon my lips" when Gratz died. Miriam had six surviving grandchildren, including Belle's three daughters with Frank: Fanny, Belle, and Edith. But the joys of seeing her grandchildren grow up didn't balance Miriam's losses. "Closure" was not a concept for Miriam Cohen. You never got over a loss, you had to live with it every second of your life.

Survival was something Miriam believed in, I learn from the book she started in order to record the things she saw in Europe, then continued after she got back. Like her son she was an obsessive cataloger, of everything from the articles she'd packed in her trunks to the bill of fare for breakfast at her Paris hotel. After the Europe tour, the catalog becomes mostly an accounting and address book. Records of travel expenses sometimes give a bit of detail about her trips; there's also the occasional inspirational quotation. It's the closest thing to a diary that we have of Miriam Cohen's adult life.

Near the end of the book, there's a right-hand page dated August 16, 1876, two days after the first anniversary of Solomon's death. "Left home— took $400.00 in notes $300.00 in checks of $100.00 each—making $700.00." I don't know where she went, but she paid out a total of $130.72, including an expense of $1.00 for "Ice cream on journey," a detail that for some reason chokes me up.

And at the top of the facing page, dated 1876, these words, attributed to a woman named Leah: "Years teach us, with their repeated sorrows, that to live requires more heroism than to die."

24

Hofwyl-Broadfield and the Mysterious Painting

The fabulously named Hofwyl-Broadfield, a rice plantation an hour's drive south of Savannah, survived the Civil War but was on the verge of bankruptcy now that labor had to be paid for. Salvation came in the form of the younger of Gratz's sisters, Miriam Gratz Cohen, who in 1880 married the Hofwyl-Broadfield heir, James Troup Dent, a society Gentile and nephew of the former Georgia governor for whom Troup Square is named. Mamie's son who survived infancy, Gratz Cohen Dent, turned the plantation into a somewhat profitable dairy. His two sisters, Ophelia and Miriam, continued to run it after his death. They had social standing, these two unmarried women: their houseguests at Hofwyl-Broadfield included Margaret Mitchell, famed author of *Gone with the Wind*, and a Mr. DuPont, who gave them a chandelier that they hung only when he visited, the sisters preferring to dine by candlelight. But they earned their living by delivering milk.

The painting that hung in their parlor was a likeness of their uncle Gratz, but from what I could tell online, it didn't much look like him. Had he sat for that painting, or was it commissioned after his death? It's not that he looks so young in the Hofwyl painting; he was always young. He just looks too pretty.

And so on Father's Day my parents and I pile into my rental car and head down I-95. We turn off before Darien and point ourselves toward the coast. On the plantation we follow the narrow winding road, canopied by the branches of old live oaks, to the visitor center, then walk toward the house, four hundred yards away. I haven't been to a plantation since I was a kid, and I move with a sense of gravity. The trees end at a broad green field, at that hour bleached by a merciless sun, and on the other side is the house with the other buildings behind. Far from being Tara, it's a rather plain two-story white clapboard house with a screen front porch and various low-slung additions in back, including a kitchen. It's a farmhouse, and Hofwyl was a dairy farm into the 1940s. Now what's left of the plantation is a state park, with regular tours and events around the holidays.

Our guide is a big white fellow who calls himself Ranger Andy. Like the docent at Bentonville, he's a no-nonsense kind of guy and not at all misty-eyed about the plantation system. There are maybe ten of us seated on the front porch facing the little lawn that slopes down to the marsh. Ranger Andy begins the tour by conjuring the hellish working conditions that enslaved people endured in the rice fields, their antagonists croco-diles, mosquitoes, parasites, hurricanes, the sun—and those were just their non-human foes. "I wouldn't last a minute out there," he points out.

The marsh has long reclaimed the rice fields, and if any part of the sys-tem of gates and dikes and canals that harnessed the tides remains, it isn't visible. Signs point to the nature walk along the marsh, but my parents and I have neglected to bring water, bug spray, or a hat—we don't intend to get a closer look.

The house is full of antiques from the city house, including the tower-ing bookcases Solomon brought with him to Savannah from Georgetown and, in the dining room, a painting of Miriam Cohen's grandfather Isaac Moses, a funder of the American Revolution and founder of the coun-try's first bank. The portrait used to hang over a magnificent sideboard that made its way from Philadelphia to Liberty Street, south to Hofwyl, then north to Andy Warhol's Manhattan apartment, and now is part of the collection of Delaware's Winterthur Museum. There are also some site-specific touches, like the designs of rice plants carved into the bedposts. When Ranger Andy leads our group out of the salon, I remain. Gratz's portrait, in an oval gold frame with carved flowers, hangs above his great-aunt Rebecca's picture. He's handsome in photographs, but here he's espe-cially beautiful, the play of masculine and feminine definitively tipped toward the latter and every trace of the Semitic gone. Gratz's mustache has been bleached to near invisibility; his dark brown eyes are blue; his nostrils flare sexily; his brows appear to have been tweezed, vanishing as they rise in perfect arches; and his upper lashes, along with the inner ends of the brows, have been thickly smudged with black paint like mascara. In the painting Gratz's cherub lips are thinner than in photographs, and his brown wavy hair is completely covered by his soldier's cap. The painting's background recalls Van Gogh's self-portraits, with short Impressionistic strokes of white against blue; Gratz's head seems to be giving off sparks of divine light.

After the tour I ask Ranger Andy about Gratz. "He had so much promise!" he cries, and I realize I've happened upon perhaps the only other person in the world for whom Gratz Cohen's death more than 150 years before is as raw as if it happened yesterday. Everyone on the tour is outside, and Ranger Andy beckons me away from my folks and leads me back inside, where he shows me the gold-headed cane that Mickve Israel gave Solomon for his half-century of service to the congregation. We stand for a moment in the silence of the house, our hands gripping the cane.

I ask about the painting. Ranger Andy thinks Gratz sat for it—but I tell him I'm not convinced.

And now Ranger Andy, who knows everything, has something to ask me. He wants to know if Gratz's grave is still in ruins and I tell him that it is.

I visited it just the day before. Laurel Grove cemetery, in west Savannah, is cut in half by the connector to I-16, and Gratz is buried, along with his immediate relatives, in the northern part. The family plot is enclosed in an iron fence with the name SOLOMON COHEN scrolled atop the rusty gate askew on its hinges and a stone with the inscription PERPETUAL CARE at the bottom. Pine trees, palmettos, azaleas, and a great magnolia hanging with moss rise from the sandy soil. At the late-morning hour of my visit, Solomon's mausoleum, topped by a Doric column supporting nothing, cast a shadow on his son's. In fact it took me a while to find Gratz's tomb because I was looking for the pointed arches connected by a rib vault, a little cathedral open on both sides, that I'd seen in pictures. But the structure had been lopped off its rests, and the cathedral lay in pieces on the side of the pedestal. The roof sat upright on the ground as if sheltering a sunken chapel, and the columns lay like bones in the dead leaves and ratty grass.

"How did Gratz Cohen die?" I hear myself ask, though this wasn't the mystery I'd come to Hofwyl to solve.

"The consensus," Ranger Andy replies right away, "is friendly fire."

It's the first time I've heard this theory, so different from the published accounts, and I sit down and just stare out at the marsh for a bit. Back at the visitor center I ask Bill Giles, the site superintendent, if it's true, but he demurs. I push, but he says no one knows. Hofwyl is a charming museum, with the original furniture from the plantation and city house and other decorative objects, including a silver bowl in the shape of a heart, inscribed with the date March 19, 1865, which Gratz's parents had made to commemorate his death. But Hofwyl also safeguards letters and other written material associated with the family. That's the other reason I've come—to look for a letter I've only seen fuzzily captured on microfilm. A few days later Bill sends me images of the first two pages of another letter, one I haven't seen before. This is Margaret Mordecai's letter, which she wrote after her private interview with Frank O'Driscoll in her home, to give a fuller picture than the one her husband had already included in his own written account.

As for the painting, Bill confirms that Gratz hadn't sat for it. "The Gratz Cohen painting in the parlor was done by a family friend," he writes me, "probably sometime between 1925 and 1945 I would guess." Her name was Anne Lee Haynes, a "New York Commercial artist, who was a good friend of Miriam and Ophelia Dent," emails Ranger Andy, who has apparently dug into the provenance of the painting since I first asked about it. The portrait is another example of the mythmaking apparently so irresistible to anyone whose imagination has been captured by Gratz Cohen.

Ranger Andy and I stay in touch, and soon he's appealing to me as a "Jewish gentleman," suggesting I tap various sources of grant money to supplement funds that the Mickve Israel synagogue might be willing to provide to rebuild the grave of its esteemed past president's tragically killed son.

I'd been asked to literally build a monument to Gratz Cohen—the opposite of what I set out to do, the task already having been done, and so floridly, by others before me. These prose paeans were what I wanted to tear apart, so as to find out who Gratz Cohen really was.

"Those Jewish financial connections," I say to my uncle, himself a past president of the same congregation, shaking my head. "People think Jews can make anything happen, don't they?"

But my uncle replies, "I think it's a good idea."

Apparently Ranger Andy, eternally devoted to the family, knows how to get things done.

"But first," my uncle adds, "write the book."

Epilogue

The homeowners association had had the parapet wall that ran along the northern end of my building rebuilt and the stucco on the back wall replaced, restoring the integrity of the group of three townhouses that Solomon Cohen had developed. I wanted to show my dad, who took an interest in home repair and could do a lot of that kind of work himself. He'd already provided his services on Liberty Street, like helping me seal off the door to the little room off the landing so that we could turn it into a proper bedroom. When we did these kind of projects together, we didn't argue; for the first time since I could remember, we were in perfect agreement, even on matters beyond dummy knobs and plaster. My father had invested his time and labor in the place and no longer seemed to think it was so crazy to own a condo downtown.

The area had been my father's playground when it was a few restaurants and bars scattered across a moribund district on the verge of some great change—a demolition of the past to make way for a prosperous postwar future or, as fortune would have it, the flourishing of a spirit of preservation that brought about its own prosperity. And now historic Savannah—two square miles of bright lights, big city—belonged to tourists and bachelorettes and art students a quarter his age, with Asian places that didn't serve cashew chicken and American restaurants where you couldn't get a damn fried drumstick, and it must have been hard for him to witness his own displacement. But I would show him a good time.

Thirteen, fourteen, fifteen . . . My father's voice through the open apartment door getting louder as he ascended the stairs.

Presumably he'd started counting at one, though I only began hearing him after he'd made it more than halfway up. "Twenty-two!" he announced with amazement and mild reproach as he stepped inside. "Mazel tov!" I said against the implicit charge that I'd bought an apartment requiring exercise to reach.

He'd been here a couple times before since we'd finished work on the place, and always the same thing with the counting, as if the number of steps might have changed between visits. I tried not to take it personally, not to respond as a defensive child, which was one of the points of the flat— this wasn't my father's territory or some neutral zone, it was my own place, where I could be myself.

"Jesus, those are a lot of stairs," my father said as I directed him to a chair, one of a pair of mid-century caneback beauties with gold-striped upholstery.

"Well, you're in wonderful shape," I said, appreciating his too-big checked blazer and slacks, his slicked-back hair: for me he'd dressed up.

"I don't know about that," he shouted, for he was unable to hear himself speak. "But a person who's going to stay in a place like this is going to be an elderly type of person with a little gelt. Do they really want to climb all those stairs?"

"It's an old house," I pointed out. "If they want an elevator, they can stay at the Hilton. We tell them they have to climb stairs, don't worry."

"At least you've got a parking space," he conceded.

"Two," I pointed out.

My father knew my husband and I had had success renting the place out. I had no idea whether we attracted older guests, but I'd heard no complaints from our property management firm. On months when we did especially well—St. Patrick's Day was our bonanza holiday—I bragged to my dad and he expressed his approval. I don't know why he was still counting stairs and raising objections, but I was happy to have him there.

My mother was making herself at home—snooping around, pointing out the ways my housekeeping didn't live up to her standards. This didn't drive me crazy, as it did when I tried to be helpful under her roof. Tonight when she cried "Oh, Jason!" on seeing the faint pink splatter of spaghetti sauce in the sink, I felt her distress had more to do with her than with me. I was proud of my home, and to welcome her there as a guest.

I handed her a glass of wine and made my dad a manhattan, frothed up in a mid-century glass shaker and served in a sweet gold-patterned glass from the same era. "Jesus, I'm *shicker*," he said after three sips. It was endearing to me how poorly he held his liquor.

By the time we left to go to dinner, the sun had fallen in the interior of the country—somewhere behind the Civic Center, from our perspective—but there was still plenty of light. We stood in the lane and looked up.

Wild eyed from drink, my father said, "That stucco looks as good as new."

And then we headed down the lane and turned in the direction of the river, crossing streets and passing through squares that my parents knew from their lived experience and that I knew from mine, which now included having learned the story of a family, and the true history of my hometown, that the house had led me to. Now I had associations with the historic district other than my childhood memories of going with my grandfather to his office, high up in the Realty Building near Bay Street, or buying my bar mitzvah suit on Broughton Street. Growing up, I'd never had cause to set foot on Bay Lane, the nondescript passage that my folks and I were now crossing, dark now except for where the streetlamp cast its lurid glow on the dumpster and some piece of heavy machinery. Service entrances, backs of buildings with cracked stucco and snarls of wires, garbage bins—that's what was down there now, nothing to indicate the lane had once been at the heart of Savannah's slave trade. We stopped and I explained all this to my father, who listened and shook his head, then thanked me for teaching him something.

My father deplored the injustices of the past, those he'd never witnessed and others he could relate to me firsthand, like the segregated movie theaters in Jim Crow Savannah. Yet he lamented the disappearance of a civility he felt had given way to stridency and anger, attitudes that definitely didn't characterize the Old South of his imagination. I, meanwhile, looked toward a more equitable future. And so even as we walked on the same cobblestones and moved among the same piles of bricks, I understood that his city was not mine. This made me sad but not for long. I was a little buzzed and taking my folks out for a nice meal, in a city I realized I loved—in my own way, as they loved it in theirs.

My father had a habit of shuffling, picked up before he had his knees replaced, and in the dying light I held lightly to his elbow to steady him against eruptions of oak roots, broken old pavement, and any other hazards on our way.

Acknowledgments

Many experts have helped me, in Vaughnette Goode-Walker's words, "slather on the history" to Gratz Cohen's story. Goode-Walker has the teacher's gift of telling you what you need to know to make your own connections, and I'm indebted to her for teaching me about slavery in Savannah and shedding light on Louis's life. David Henkin kindly read early drafts of this book and taught me some of the fine points of nineteenth-century American history. With his vast knowledge of the city's built environment, Jonathan Stalcup helped me picture Savannah from its earliest days until the Civil War. Cindy Wallace got me started on the nuts and bolts of this research, in the process passing along her passion for historical detective work. Phillip Greenwalt, who wrote the book on the Battle of Bentonville, helped me imagine Gratz's final days.

My husband, Jeffrey, read version after version of this book and never once complained. He greatly improved it, as did Aurora Bell, my editor. I'm grateful to Malaga Baldi, my agent, who encouraged me over the years. Elizabeth S. Olson found and scanned Cohen documents in the Georgia Archives. Rabbi Saul Rubin took the time to talk with me about Solomon Cohen and his family. Herbert and Teresa Victor opened up Savannah's Mickve Israel archives for me. The Georgia Historical Society staff made me look forward to spending time inside the library even on the prettiest days. Nadine Epstein gave me a forum for this story in *Moment* magazine. Dale Rosengarten introduced me to the world of South Carolina Jewry. Dale Davis literally opened doors for me in Cheraw. Bill Giles and Ranger Andy brought the Cohens to life for me at Hofwyl-Broadfield and provided invaluable research assistance. I also want to thank Allen Appel, Susan Buchsbaum, Anne Cheng, Tim Dean, Julian Friedman, Dan Geller, David Groff, Donald Hershman, Ellen McGarrahan, and Sharon Wood. For those of you whose names I've inadvertently overlooked, know that I appreciate you as well.

Notes on Sources

The great thing about tackling so broad a subject was that everyone—old friends and new acquaintances, subject matter experts and folks who couldn't believe there were Jews in the South—had a book to recommend. I read, or at least skimmed, every one of those books. Rabbi Saul Rubin's *Third to None: The Saga of Savannah Jewry, 1733–1983* was an invaluable source for the history of Savannah Jews and Mickve Israel. Scholarly monographs on important nineteenth-century Jewish figures such as Rebecca Gratz, Isaac Leeser, and the Mordecais helped me understand their subjects and the worlds in which they lived. Studies of the state of the American male in the middle of the nineteenth century were useful, especially Stephen W. Berry II's highly readable *All That Makes a Man: Love and Ambition in the Civil War South*, about the personal reasons young Southern men had for going to war. I was starting from zero on how battles were fought, so books devoted to specific conflicts, such as Bentonville, helped me situate Gratz in space and time. Even the books I found more tendentious were helpful, especially Robert N. Rosen's survey *The Jewish Confederates*, product of a Herculean research effort.

Histories of Savannah during the Civil War—whether in the form of scholarly treatments, picture books, pamphlets, or online blogs and articles—helped my hometown's past come to life for me. Despite its ample illustrations and coffeetable book format, the *Civil War Savannah* series is an important work of scholarship, and its second volume, *Savannah: Brokers, Bankers, and Bay Lane—Inside the Slave Trade*, by Barry Sheehy, Cindy Wallace, and Vaughnette Goode-Walker, visually and painstakingly documents the Savannah slave economy, while providing background about its players. Richard C. Wade's classic *Slavery in the Cities: The South, 1820–1860* describes the urban form of a slave system that was more familiar to me as a plantation phenomenon, and Whittington B. Johnson's *Black Savannah, 1788–1864* explains how that system used often paradoxical means to maintain its grip in town.

I wasn't naive enough to believe that writing about a slaveholding Jewish family would be uncontroversial, but when I began telling the story of the Solomon Cohen family, I didn't know I was entering into a tradition of Jewish historiography about Jews and the Civil War. In *The Jewish Confederates*, Rosen acknowledges that Southern Jews supported slavery. But while Rosen's book is boosterish, historian Bertram W. Korn, author of the groundbreaking *American Jewry and the Civil War*, first published in 1951, is sober eyed. Rosen himself provides the supposed Talmudic justification for Solomon's defense of slavery on religious grounds. Korn concludes his 1961 essay "Jews and Negro Slavery in the Old South, 1789–1865" with a very different take on Solomon: "How ironic that the distinctions bestowed on men like Judah P. Benjamin, Major Raphael J. Moses, and the Honorable Solomon Cohen were in some measure dependent upon the sufferings of the very Negro slaves they bought and sold with such equanimity."

Korn concluded that in their participation in the slave economy, Southern Jews were just like their non-Jewish neighbors, no better or worse. This underwhelming conclusion nonetheless took a century to get to, as some Jews, understandably wary of doing anything to encourage anti-Semitism, claimed as heroes men such as Confederate secretary of state Judah Benjamin, apparently for his braininess, and indeed every Jewish Confederate, simply for showing allegiance to their host region, the faithlessness of Jews being a perennial charge. Anti-Semitism is never going away but the evils of slavery have been established, and no attempt to distinguish between good and bad enslavers is worth the effort.

With Solomon Cohen I was interested in the ways his conscience allowed him to embrace the institution, which in turn enabled him, and other well-off Jews, to assimilate into Southern society—or at least to try. Debunking the charge that Jews played an outsize role in the slave trade, Korn writes, "Slavery, therefore, played a more significant role in the development of Jewish life in the Old South, than Jews themselves played in the establishment and maintenance of the institution." Korn assumed that Jews were a priori white and therefore benefited from the South's ideology of white supremacy, whereby Black people absorbed prejudice that would otherwise be aimed at least partly at Jews. But he might have gotten this backward, according to my reading of the historian Mark I. Greenberg's essay "Becoming Southern: The Jews of Savannah, Georgia, 1830–70," which claims that "slave ownership helped solidify Jews' racial status. The South was not a region set in black and white. . . . Rather, men and women—especially Irish and Italian immigrants—had to create 'whiteness' for themselves to prevent their association with the socially degraded status of blacks. . . . Because Jews clustered in commercial ventures and purchased blacks rather than toiling as manual laborers, their 'whiteness' was rarely questioned, and they faced relatively less social ostracism than other immigrant groups." However unconsciously, Jews became white in the South simply by acting like their white neighbors.

As for Gratz Cohen, my connection with him began with artifacts including an unpublished poem, a letter soaked nearly black with ink, a few pictures, and a rotting diary, whose often eccentric punctuation I have here retained. Because his diary was so confessional, I was immediately— once I could decipher his scrawl—thrown into Gratz's consciousness. Being dropped into the head of a seventeen-year-old at the University of Virginia in 1862 isn't the most disorienting experience possible; but I needed bearings. I went to Chapel Hill to read Gratz's letters in UNC's Southern Historical Collection, then Charlottesville to see what his room might have looked like. I traced Gratz's route through the Carolinas. An element of obsession, I admit, entered in. But by reading everything that I could find that Gratz had written—for public, family, and private view—and following in his footsteps, all the way to his very last ones, I came to know him as a man rather than as a Lost Cause legend. This is not to deny his bravery; it's to admit his humanness.

I wish I knew as much about Louis. United States Census slave schedules don't name enslaved individuals; nor do Solomon's tax records. If Louis knew how to write, there's no trace of it. Nor could I find a likely candidate for Louis in postwar census records, city directories, or cemetery records. Louis's story is partial and told mostly by Gratz, who felt the need to set to paper his feelings for his valet but little about what Louis was like as a person. In the end he seems to have emancipated himself, possibly finding his way to freedom at Fort Pulaski, and the National Park Service's *African Americans at Fort Pulaski National Historic Site, 1733–1900: A Special History Study*, by Julie de Chantal, Heidi Moye, and Anastatia Sims, helped me understand the role the fort played as "a sanctuary for men, women, and children eager to cast off the bonds of slavery."

I am at heart a storyteller, and I see the world of the story through the eyes of its characters. I didn't want to report on the things that Louis or the Cohen family members did or that happened to them. I wanted instead to understand these people and their world well enough for these actions and events to emerge inevitably and naturally in a narrative. I also permitted myself to take imaginative leaps where the historical record was silent, while signaling in the text whenever I set foot on such uncharted terrain. This kind of speculation was an important aspect of my own story, a way to connect this strange world to the one in which I lived.

Finally, there's F. D. Lee and J. L. Agnew's *Historical Record of the City of Savannah*, the little black book that my father kept in an airtight bag and gave me the moment I told him of this project. It appears to be a first edition and its binding has held up, though the frontispiece map has been cut out and many of the pages are stained and lined with pencil. The book contains primary sources, engravings of long-gone buildings, figures showing exports of commodities from the port from 1749 through 1868, and delightful anecdotes such as the one about emboldened alligators strolling the streets of the new settlement. While Lee strives for objectivity and, forward-looking, shows an interest in the history of the common person, the book comes straight out of the psyche of a vanquished people and projects a pride in a city whose commercial culture, as noted in its dedication, has survived "WAR, FIRES, GALES, AND PESTILENCE." The lives of the enslaved are not among the disparate subjects this book treats ("Laws and Customs," "Shipment of the First Bale of Cotton," "Placing Obstructions in the River"), and the very institution of slavery has been expunged from the historical record it purports to give. These omissions were as revealing to me as what the author chose to include.

Selected Bibliography

MANUSCRIPT COLLECTIONS

Cohen/Gratz/Moses Family Papers. Georgia Archives, Morrow.

Cohen-Hunter Papers. Georgia Historical Society, Savannah.

Cohen, Miriam Gratz Moses. Papers. Southern Historical Collection, University of North Carolina at Chapel Hill.

Cohen and Phillips Family Papers. Georgia Historical Society, Savannah.

Cohen, Solomon. Papers. Georgia Historical Society, Savannah.

DeJarnette, Elliott. Autograph Album. 1863–1868. 1901. RG-30/17/1.0713. Special Collections, University of Virginia Library, Charlottesville.

Dixon, Harry St. John. Papers. Southern Historical Collection, University of North Carolina at Chapel Hill.

Gratz Family Papers. American Philosophical Society Library, Philadelphia.

Mordecai Family Papers. Southern Historical Collection, University of North Carolina at Chapel Hill.

Mordecai, Jacob. Papers. Duke University Libraries, Durham.

Staley Autograph Albums. 1863–1872. RG-30/17/1.074. Special Collections, University of Virginia Library, Charlottesville.

PUBLISHED PRIMARY SOURCES

American Jewess (Emma Mordecai). "The Duty of Israel." *The Occident and American Jewish Advocate* 2, no. 10 (January 1845). http://www.jewish -history.com/Occident/volume2/jan1845/duty.html.

Beveridge, Charles E., and Charles Capen McLaughlin, eds. *Papers of Frederick Law Olmsted*. Vol. 2, *Slavery and the South, 1852–1857*. Baltimore: Johns Hopkins University Press, 1981.

Einhorn, David. Response to "A Biblical View of Slavery." Jewish-American History Foundation, 1861. http://www.theoccident.com/civilwar/einhorn.html.

Jefferson, Thomas. *Notes on the State of Virginia*. Edited and with an introduction by Robert Pierce Forbes. New Haven, CT: Yale University Press, 2022.

Jones, Charles C., Jr. *The Siege and Evacuation of Savannah, Georgia in December 1864*. Augusta, GA: Chronicle Publishing, 1890.

Kemble, Frances Anne. *Journal of a Residence on a Georgian Plantation in 1838-1839*. Edited and with an introduction by John A. Scott. Athens: University of Georgia Press, 1984.

McLaws, Lafayette. *A Soldier's General: The Civil War Letters of Major General Lafayette McLaws*. Edited by John C. Oeffinger. Chapel Hill and London: University of North Carolina Press, 2002.

Official Proceedings of the Democratic National Convention, Held in 1860, at Charleston and Baltimore. Ann Arbor: University of Michigan Library, 2005.

Proceedings of the Democratic National Convention, Held at Baltimore, June 1–5, 1852, for the Nomination of Candidates for President and Vice President of the United States. Whitefish, MT: Kessinger, 2010.

Raphall, M. J. *The Bible View of Slavery.* Jewish American History Foundation, 1861. http://www.theoccident.com/civilwar/raphall.html.

Russell, William Howard. *My Diary North and South.* Baton Rouge: Louisiana State University Press, 2001.

Sheftall, Mordecai. "The Jews in Savannah." *The Occident and American Jewish Advocate* 1, no. 8 (November 1843). http://www.theoccident.com/Occident /volume1/nov1843/savannah2.html.

Sherman, William Tecumseh. *Memoirs of General William Tecumseh Sherman.* New York: Penguin, 2000.

Smith, D. E. Huger. *A Charlestonian's Recollections, 1846–1913.* Charleston, SC: Carolina Art Association, 1950.

A Southern Jew (probably Solomon Cohen). "Jews in Savannah." *The Occident and American Jewish Advocate* 1, no. 5 (August 1843). http://www.theoccident .com/occident/volume1/aug1843/savannah.html.

Taylor, Susie King. *Reminiscences of My Life in Camp with the 33d United States Colored Troops, Late 1st S.C. Volunteers.* Self-published, 1902.

The War of the Rebellion: A Compilation of the Official Records of the Union and Confederate Armies. Washington: Government Printing Office, 1880–1901.

SELECTED SECONDARY SOURCES

Ashton, Dianne. *Rebecca Gratz: Women and Judaism in Antebellum America.* Detroit, MI: Wayne State University Press, 1997.

Augst, Thomas. *The Clerk's Tale: Young Men and Moral Life in Nineteenth-Century America.* Chicago: University of Chicago Press, 2003.

Berry, Stephen W., II. *All That Makes a Man: Love and Ambition in the Civil War South.* New York: Oxford University Press, 2003.

Bingham, Emily. *Mordecai: An Early American Family.* New York: Farrar, Straus and Giroux, 2003.

Davis, David T., and Phillip S. Greenwalt. *Calamity in Carolina: The Battles of Averasboro and Bentonville, March 1865.* Emerging Civil War Series. El Dorado Hills, CA: Savas Beatie, 2015.

De Chantal, Julie, Heidi Moye, and Anastatia Sims. "African Americans at Fort Pulaski National Historic Site, 1733–1900: A Special History Study." Organization of American Historians and National Park Service, 2022.

Dundas, Deborah. "The Cohen Family and the Jewish Community in Coastal South Carolina and Georgia: 1669–1915." Master's thesis, California State University, Dominguez Hills, 2012.

Ely, Carol, Jeffrey Hantman, and Phyllis Leffler. *To Seek the Peace of the City: Jewish Life in Charlottesville.* Charlottesville: Hillel Jewish Center of the University of Virginia, 1994. Exhibition catalog.

Elzas, Barnett A. *The Jews of South Carolina: From the Earliest Times to the Present Day.* Philadelphia: J. B. Lippincott, 1905.

Faber, Eli. *A Time for Planting: The First Migration, 1654–1820.* Vol. 1 of *The Jewish People in America.* Baltimore: Johns Hopkins University Press, 1992.

Ferris, Marcie Cohen, and Mark I. Greenberg, eds. *Jewish Roots in Southern Soil: A New History.* Hanover, NH, and London: University Press of New England, 2006.

Foster, Thomas A. *Rethinking Rufus: Sexual Violations of Enslaved Men.* Athens: University of Georgia Press, 2019.

Fraser, Walter J., Jr. *Savannah in the Old South.* Athens: University of Georgia Press, 2005.

Freeman, Michael. *Native American History of Savannah.* Charleston, SC: History Press, 2018.

Greenberg, Mark I. "Becoming Southern: The Jews of Savannah, Georgia, 1830–70." *American Jewish History* 86, no. 1 (March 1998): 55–75.

———. "Creating Ethnic, Class, and Southern Identity in Nineteenth-Century America: The Jews of Savannah, Georgia, 1830–1880." PhD diss., University of Florida, 1997.

Harris, Leslie M., and Diana Ramey Berry, eds. *Slavery and Freedom in Savannah.* Athens: University of Georgia Press, 2014.

Haunton, Richard H. "Law and Order in Savannah, 1850–60." *Georgia Historical Quarterly* 56, no. 1 (Spring 1972): 1024.

———. "Savannah in the 1850's." PhD diss., Emory University, 1968.

Hughes, Nathaniel Cheairs, Jr. *Bentonville: The Final Battle of Sherman and Johnston.* Chapel Hill and London: University of North Carolina Press, 1996.

Johnson, John Lipscomb. *The University Memorial: Biographical Sketches of Alumni of the University of Virginia Who Fell in the Confederate War.* Baltimore: Turnbull, 1871.

Johnson, Whittington B. *Black Savannah, 1788–1864.* Fayetteville: University of Arkansas Press, 1996.

Jones, Jacqueline. *Saving Savannah: The City and the Civil War.* New York: Vintage, 2008.

Jordan, Ervin L., Jr. *Charlottesville and the University of Virginia in the Civil War.* Lynchburg, VA: H. E. Howard, 1998.

Jordan, Michael L. *Hidden History of Civil War Savannah.* Charleston: History Press, 2017.

Joyner, Charles. *Shared Traditions: Southern History and Folk Culture.* Champaign: University of Illinois Press, 1999.

Korn, Bertram W. *American Jewry and the Civil War.* Philadelphia: Jewish Publication Society, 2001.

Lee, F. D., and J. L. Agnew. *Historical Record of the City of Savannah.* Savannah, GA: J. H. Estill, 1869.

Moore, Mark A. *Moore's Historical Guide to the Battle of Bentonville.* Boston: Da Capo Press, 2001.

Osborne, Haley E. "Shackles and Servitude: Jails and the Enslaved in Antebellum Savannah." Honors thesis, Georgia Southern University, 2020.

Rosen, Robert N. *The Jewish Confederates.* Columbia: University of South Carolina Press, 2000.

Rubin, Saul Jacob. *Third to None: The Saga of Savannah Jewry, 1733–1983.* Savannah, GA: Congregation Mickve Israel, 1983.

Sarna, Jonathan D., and Adam D. Mendelsohn, eds. *Jews and the Civil War: A Reader.* New York: New York University Press, 2011.

Sheehy, Barry, Cindy Wallace, with Vaughnette Goode-Walker. *Savannah, Immortal City.* Vol. 1 of *Civil War Savannah.* Austin, TX: Emerald Book, 2011.

———. *Savannah: Brokers, Bankers, and Bay Lane—Inside the Slave Trade.* Vol. 2 of *Civil War Savannah.* Austin, TX: Emerald Book, 2012.

Shenk, Joshua Wolf. *Lincoln's Melancholy: How Depression Challenged a President and Fueled His Greatness.* Boston and New York: Houghton Mifflin, 2006.

Sussman, Lance J. *Isaac Leeser and the Making of American Judaism.* Detroit, MI: Wayne State University Press, 1995.

Wade, Richard C. *Slavery in the Cities: The South 1820–1860.* New York: Oxford University Press, 1964.

Wall, Charles Coleman. "Students and Student Life at the University of Virginia, 1825 to 1861." PhD diss., University of Virginia, 1978.

Wilson, Thomas D. *The Oglethorpe Plan: Enlightenment Design in Savannah and Beyond.* Charlottesville and London: University of Virginia Press, 2012.

Woodard, Vincent. *The Delectable Negro: Human Consumption and Homoeroticism within US Slave Culture*, edited by Justin A. Joyce and Dwight A. McBride. New York and London: New York University Press, 2014.